knitting
Stitches and patterns

Over 80 designs to make.   70 colour photographs

by Diana Biggs

Octopus Books

First published 1972 by
Octopus Books Limited
59 Grosvenor Street, London W 1

ISBN 0 7064 0077 1

© Octopus Books Limited

Produced by Mandarin Publishers Limited
77a Marble Road, North Point, Hong Kong
and printed in Hong Kong

Contents

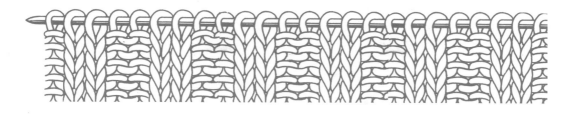

Introduction

For those who want to learn and those who already can knit, this book has been planned with care, for knitting is a loving craft.

Such an ancient craft which has remained popular through the years, must have great satisfaction to offer. It has, it satisfies the creative urge and is very soothing too. For those who have to keep a close and careful hand on the purse strings, it is an economical craft as well. As for the loving, well, when you make a sweater for one of your family, you do demonstrate your love for them, don't you?

For all this, no expensive equipment is needed, just two knitting needles and some yarn, with a little of your spare time.

So, for the beginners, we would like to show you how to knit. Soon you will be able to do the two basic stitches, plain and purl. Then, with casting on and off, you can start to make something useful.

Step by step we will take you through the first stages then we shall add simple stitches, husky cables and dainty lace. All the time your mastery of the craft will grow. All the time, we shall be showing you how to make beautiful things you will want to knit again and again.

For those who can already knit, we know our patterns will appeal to everyone. We want to show you how to make the most of your craft, some of the tricks of the trade. We want to help to give your work that original and professional touch. Can you take that favourite pattern and make it look quite different? We will show you how. There will be some stitches you may never have seen before and some old favourites you have forgotten how to do. There is something for every member of your family plus the toys and gifts you will want to make for birthdays and bazaars. Nice things to make for your home and for that final touch, all the trimmings.

We hope you will all find the book helpful and if the pages become well thumbed, we shall know we have helped you to make the most of the wonderful craft of knitting.

page 1, Rainbow Shawl

page 2, Check coat (pattern, page 122)

opposite, Tools of the Trade

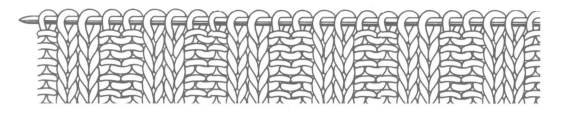

Golden Rules of Knitting

Before you begin to knit, there are a few good points which beginner, and expert alike, need to remember. They are so important, that the best of knitting will not prove to be quite satisfactory if they are ignored.

First and perhaps the most important of all is the tension.

Tension: Every knitting pattern will give the tension at which the garment should be knitted. This will be stated as so many stitches and rows to one inch.

The size of the garment is regulated by the tension at which you knit. If the pattern states a tension of five stitches to one inch and you are told to cast on 100 stitches for the back of a garment, you can see that, at the correct tension, the measurement across the back would be twenty inches.

If you arre knitting too tightly and are getting six stitches to one inch, the work will be smaller than you expected.

His and Her Aran Sweaters
Instructions for these sweaters begin on page 70

So, the first rule is to make a **Tension Square:** Make it a habit, to knit a four inch square, everytime, before you start on a garment. You will then have no trouble and you will get the measurement you expect.

Your time will not be wasted. The squares can be made up into a shawl or blanket.

To measure tension see Sketches Nos. 2 and 2a. If your tension is too tight, then you must use a thicker needle, and if too loose, change to finer needles.

Generally, you will find that you knit to a certain tension on given needles, but this can change. Under stress and strain, tension can become tighter, quite naturally. If you are tired or very relaxed, your tension can slacken, so please, do knit a square and test for sure. It is too heartbreaking to finish a garment and then find it is either too small or too large.

For extra encouragement, see our shawl on page 1. This was just a number of tension squares. They were sorted into shading colours and sewn together, then fringed, with very pretty results. Even the kitten basket has a little rug made in the same way. No doubt a small girl would like a doll's pram rug. So you can put your squares to very good use.

Sketch No. 2a   Sketch No. 2

The second rule is to buy the yarn the pattern states. This will be the yarn in which the original garment was knitted. This is important, because even the same ply yarn in a different brand may vary. Some are spun either tighter or looser than others. The result is a different number of yards of yarn in a ball, even though the weight of yarn is the same. This can cause great trouble, the less yards to the ball, the less times round the knitting needle. It means you can need more or less yarn, if you change from the original. This can make a garment more expensive, or you may be unable to match the dye lot. Even left over yarn can be annoying. So if you do have to change a yarn, take this into consideration and make certain extra is available, just in case you need it.

If you can buy all the yarn required at a time, it is wise to do so. You may buy the same colour, later on, but by then the shade could vary. It will perhaps be unnoticeable in the ball, but can make an obvious line in your knitting, so check the dye lot on every ball band as well.

Always read the instructions through before starting. In this way you will be able to check up on anything you do not quite understand. Many patterns are found difficult because they are misread in a hurry or an essential point has been overlooked.

Do keep your knitting clean. Keep it wrapped when you are not working on it and keep a clean cloth on your lap while knitting.

Begin at the beginning of a pattern and work through to the end. If you start with the sleeves, which may appear half way through, the instructions may refer back to a part already worked, and you won't understand easily.

Finally, do take time and care in making-up. You will have spent hours making your own fabric, don't spoil your work at this point.

Follow our simple instructions, given in the special section and it will be time well spent. The final finish is just as important as the actual knitting and you will get even more pleasure in wearing a garment which has been done well in every way.

Instructions for making-up are not repeated after every set of instructions in this book. Refer, if in doubt, to the special section

Starting to Knit

CASTING ON

Make a slip knot and place it on one needle. (sketch No. 3) Holding this needle in your left hand, take the second needle and insert the point in the loop on the left-hand needle.

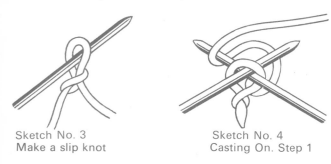

Sketch No. 3
Make a slip knot

Sketch No. 4
Casting On. Step 1

Pass the yarn round the point of the right-hand needle, (sketch No. 4) draw a loop through. (sketch No. 5) Place this loop on left-hand needle. (sketch No. 6) Continue to make loops and place on left-hand needle until the required number of stitches have been cast on.

For a firmer edge, for thicker yarns, begin in the same way, but for the third stitch, insert the right-hand needle between the first and second loops on left-hand needle. (sketch No. 7) Draw a loop through as before and place on left-hand needle. Continue in this way until the required number of stitches are on left-hand needle, placing the point of right-hand needle, behind the last loop cast on.

KNIT OR PLAIN STITCH

Hold the needle with your cast on stitches in your left hand and the second in your right hand. Insert the point of right-hand needle into the first loop from front to back. (sketch No. 8) Keeping the yarn at the back of the work when each stitch is finished, pass the yarn round the point of right-hand needle and draw a loop through. Keep this loop on right-hand needle and allow the used loop to drop from left-hand needle.

Continue in this way along all stitches on left-hand needle, to the end of the row of cast on stitches. Now turn the work and taking the empty needle in the right hand again, work another row. If you continue in this way you will be knitting garter stitch. (sketch No. 9) In a pattern it would be written as every row K. and the stitch is abbreviated to g. st., for garter stitch.

Sketch No. 5
Casting On. Step 2.

Sketch No. 6
Casting On. Step 3.

Sketch No. 7
Casting on tor a firmer edge.

PURL STITCH

Start as before with the needle holding the cast on stitches in the left hand and the empty needle in the right hand. This time, keep the yarn at the front of the work when the stitch is finished. Insert right-hand needle into first loop from back to front of work. (sketch No. 10) Pass the yarn round the point of right-hand needle and draw a loop through. Keep this loop on right-hand needle and allow the used loop to drop from left-hand needle. Continue in this way and you are knitting the purl stitch.

STOCKING STITCH

This makes a smooth fabric and is the basic stitch in knitting. It is the most economical to use and is worked by knitting the first row in knit or plain stitch and the second row in purl stitch. (See sketch No. 11) When these two rows are repeated in turn, the result should look like the sketch.

CASTING OFF

Be careful, don't cast off too tightly. The tension of the work should be maintained at this point, to avoid making the edge of the fabric tighter than it should be. If you find this difficult at first, then use a size larger needle, just for casting off.

To cast off, work in this way. (sketch No. 12) Knit the first two stitches from left-hand needle, slip the first over the second and off right-hand needle. Now knit the next stitch from left-hand needle and repeat the action, until only one stitch is left, knitted on to right-hand needle. Break the yarn and draw it through the last loop. Pull close and fasten off.

When casting off in rib, knit and purl the stitches as usual, to make a more elastic edge.

When casting off in stocking stitch it is best to cast off on a right side (smooth) row. This will avoid a ridge on the smooth side of the fabric.

Sometimes it is a good idea to cast off two sets of stitches together, for example, on the shoulders of a sweater in stocking stitch, to make a smooth join. To do this, place the two sets of stitches together, with right sides facing each other. Knit together the first stitch from each needle, then the second two. You wil! now have two stitches on right-hand needle. Pass the first over the second in the usual way and continue to end of row.

Most garments have a ribbed welt and cuffs

Sketch No. 8
Purl Stitch

Sketch No. 9
Garter stitch

Sketch No. 10
Knit or Plain Stitch

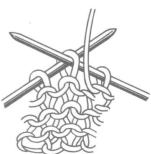

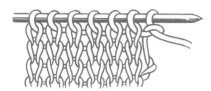

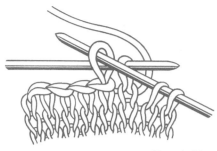

to make a snug fit. This part can be knitted in a variety of different ribbed patterns but the most usual are single and double rib.

SINGLE RIB (sketch No. 13)

This is worked on an even number of stitches in this way.

1st row: — *Knit one, purl one, repeat from the * to end of the row. Repeat this row for the required length. If this row was repeated on an uneven number of stitches it would give you moss stitch.

DOUBLE RIB (sketch No. 14)

This is worked over a multiple of four stitches and gives a wider rib.

1st row: — *Knit two, purl two, repeat from the * to end of the row. Repeat this row for length required.

If this row is repeated twice, then two rows starting, purl two, knit two are worked, and these four rows are repeated, you will be knitting a small block pattern, or double moss stitch.

TO JOIN YARN

Never do this in the middle of a row. Make a knot at the end of a row and when the work is finished, undo the knot and darn the ends into the knitting.

Some yarns can be spliced in this way. Unravel the ends and break off two inches from half the threads from each piece to be joined. Lay the remaining halves together, end to end on the palm of your hand, the short ends meeting and long ends overlapping. Rub together to twist threads.

Double Rib

Single Rib

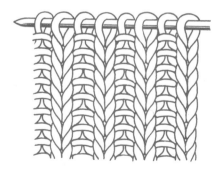

Making Up and Shaping

BLOCKING AND PRESSING

Having made the pieces of a garment, the next step is to block them all out to the correct size and shape.

If they are slightly larger or smaller than they should be, it is possible to ease them to the

First, on an ironing blanket on a table, pin out a piece at the widest point, then pin to the correct length. See sketches Nos. 15 and 16. Now pin all round the edges, placing pins about half an inch apart. If the welts and cuffs are ribbed, place the pins inside ribbed

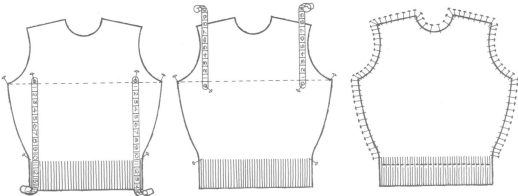

Sketches 15, 16 & 17
The diagrams show you how to pin out the pieces of a garment ready for pressing

correct size at this point. Uneven knitting will be improved and Fair Isle work, which may have been a little uneven when knitted, can become neater with correct pressing.

edges. See sketch No. 17. Ribbing should not be blocked and pressed unless the garment is worked entirely in ribbing.

When the piece is pinned out completely, with

the wrong side uppermost, press lightly with a warm iron over a damp cloth. Leave the piece to dry before unpinning. Deal with each piece in turn in the same way.

When all pieces have been blocked and pressed, tack them together with care, matching row by row and taking care to match any shapings. The garment is now ready for seaming.

SEAMS AND JOINS

There are four methods by which seams can be made in knitted garments. Each is suitable for a particular purpose.

The Back stitch seam (See sketch No. 18)
This seam gives a very clean line. Place the two pieces of knitting together with right sides facing and wrong sides outside. With matching yarn, thread a large eyed needle. Make a small stitch at end of seam and secure firmly. Bring the point of needle out of work about $\frac{1}{4}$ inch along seam and insert it again into the end of last stitch made. Continue in this way along whole seam.

Sketch No. 18
Back stitch seam

The Flat seam (See sketch No. 19)
This is a simple over-sewn seam which, when pressed is flat. It is suitable for joining ribbing and stitching the front bands to cardigans and jackets. Hold the pieces together with right sides facing each other. Taking care to match stitch for stitch, neatly oversew.

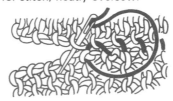

Sketch No. 19
The Flat Seam

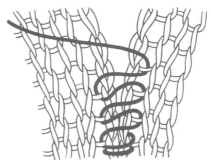

Sketch No. 20
The Invisible Seam

The Invisible seam (See sketch No. 20)
This is ideal for smooth classic garments in stocking stitch where there are no shapings at the edge of the fabric. Lay the pieces, edge to edge with right sides uppermost. Draw yarn through the lower edge of one side and secure firmly. The needle must be on the right side of the work before starting the seam.

Take the needle over the second edge and insert it under the thread lying between the first and second stitch from bottom to top. Draw the yarn through and repeat on the other edge, matching stitch for stitch. Continue up the work in this way, and work into every stitch.

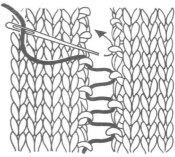

Sketch No. 21
The Lace-up Seam

The Lace-up seam (See sketch No. 21)
This is very suitable for fine work and baby garments. In fact anywhere a very comfortable seam is essential .

Place the two pieces together with right sides facing and edge to edge. With yarn secured at lower edge of one side, lace edges together by inserting needle from bottom to top of each ridge stitch, taking one from each edge in turn.

14

Two sets of stitches can also be joined by knitting together and casting off at the same time.

Place the two needles with the stitches on them with right sides together, needle points at right hand side and yarn also at right. Knit together one stitch from front and back needle. Repeat this and then pull the first stitch on right hand needle over the second. Continue until all stitches are worked off.

GRAFTING

Grafting is the method used for joining two sets of stitches without a ridge. When finished the line joined appears as knit stitches. This is useful for the toes of socks and can be employed for the shoulders of sweaters. To Graft, for a toe, divide the number of stitches equally between two needles. For shoulders of sweaters, place the back and front together with wrong sides together. The points of needles to right hand side and the end of yarn on the back needle at the right. Thread yarn into a large eyed needle.

Insert needle purlwise through loop of first stitch on front needle but do not slip stitch off, then insert needle knitwise through first stitch on back needle but do not slip off.

* Insert needle knitwise through first stitch on front needle and slip off, purlwise through second stitch on front needle, but do not slip off. Now insert yarn needle purlwise through first stitch on back needle and slip off needle, then through second stitch on back needle knitwise and do not slip off. Repeat from * until all stitches are worked off.

Grafting in k. l, p. l, rib (See sketches Nos. 23 and 23a)

This will be needed if an unbroken line of stitches is to remain in ribbing joined by this method.

You will need a set of four needles with points at both ends.

Take the first piece of ribbing and slip all the knit stitches on to one needle and hold at front of work. Slip the purl stitches on to a second needle and hold at back of work. See sketch No. 23 Arrange the stitches from second piece of ribbing in the same way.

Graft the two sets of knit stitches as given for

Sketch No. 23
Knit stitches on one needle and purl stitches on the second to prepare a piece of ribbing for grafting

ordinary grafting. See sketch 23a. Turn work to other side and the purl stitches on right side will have become knit stitches. Deal with them as before.

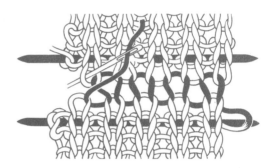

Sketch No. 23a
Two sets of ribbed stitches placed together and the grafting of the knit stitches on one side

BUTTONHOLES

You will need to make buttonholes for a number of your knitted garments. Here is the way to make them, from the smallest ones up to the larger bound variety used for heavier coats.

Small Buttonholes (see sketches Nos. 24 and 24a) for baby garments or those needing a tiny button, simply make them by working a, yarn forward, knit 2 together on the row where the buttonhole is required. When the next row is worked a small hole will be in the correct position for your buttonhole.

Horizontal Buttonholes (see sketch No. 25) can be made on two rows and can be as large as needed. On the first row, cast off the number of stitches required to make the size of the buttonhole. On the next row cast on the same

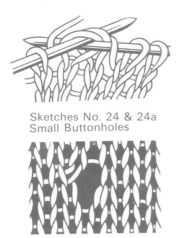

Sketches No. 24 & 24a
Small Buttonholes

number of stitches. The best way to cast on for buttonholes is to make a loop on the thumb and slip the loop on to the needle. Continue until the correct number of stitches have been replaced. (see sketch No. 26) To avoid a loose stitch on the second row of the buttonhole, as some knitters find, try casting on one stitch less on the second row but knitting twice into the stitch before the cast off stitches.

Sketch No. 25
Horizontal Buttonholes

These buttonholes can be made larger by knitting up the work between the cast off and the cast on rows, thus making a larger buttonhole. On a coat this would be best worked dou-

Sketch No. 26
Replacing the stitches
cast off in previous row

ble. The coat fronts should have facings and the buttonhole procedure should be worked twice on the same rows. When the facing is folded back and the buttonholes are placed face to face, they can be sewn together or bound.

To bind a buttonhole cast on a number of stitches about twice the width your finished binding should be. Work in stocking stitch, knitting 2 together at the beginning of knit rows and increasing 1 at the end. The next row, purl. Continue in this way until the bias binding is the required length.

Set it to the buttonhole, starting half way along a straight edge, not at the corner, joining the bias edges with a neat flat seam and folding the binding in half to the wrong side, and catching firmly down.

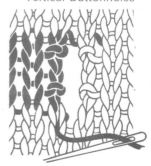

Sketches No. 27 & 27a
Vertical Buttonholes

Vertical Buttonholes (see sketch Nos. 27 and 27a) are made by simply dividing the work where the buttonhole is required. At this point, use two balls of yarn, one for each piece as you work up both sides of the buttonhole. When the vertical slit is the size you wish, simply break off the second ball and work

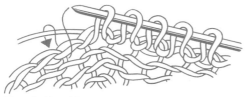

Sketch No. 22
Picking up stitches along an edge.

across all stitches and the buttonhole is complete. Remember to slip the first stitch at the beginning of every row at the edge of the buttonhole to keep a neat edge.

PICKING UP STITCHES.
(See sketch No. 22)

Stitches are picked up round necklines and armholes and on any edge where this is required, by holding one needle in the right hand with right side of garment facing. Join the yarn into the first stitch to be picked up, insert the needle through both loops of the first edge stitch, draw a loop of yarn through. Continue along the edge picking up the number of stitches stated in the pattern you are following. When the required number of stitches are on the needle, take the second needle and knit in the usual way.

A dropped stitch is easily picked up. If the work is in stocking stitch, hold the work with right side facing you, insert the point of needle into dropped loop, push the point of the needle under the strand of yarn across the gap left by the dropped stitch and pull the loop over. Continue until all strands have been taken up, then place loop back on needle, ready to continue knitting. If the work is in garter stitch, the same method is used but it is necessary to take a thread up, working from alternate sides, to retain the garter stitch.

SHAPING

Decreasing. This reduces the number of stitches on the needle during the course of the work, in order to shape the pieces of the garment you are making. Decreases should be made on alternate rows or at regular intervals during the work. This makes certain that the shaping is even. There are several ways to decrease and the method given in a pattern should be followed carefully. It will be so stated for a particular reason. For instance,

Knit 2 stitches together through the front of the loops and the decrease will slant to the right.

Knit 2 stitches together through the back of the loops and the decrease will slant to the left.

Correctly worked these decreases can make all the difference to the appearance of a raglan sleeve.

Slip 1 stitch, knit 1 stitch and pass the slipped stitch over the knit stitch. Again, the decrease will slant to the left.

Sometimes it is necessary to reduce two stitches at the same time and this can be done by slip 1, knit 2 together and passing the slip stitch over the 2 knitted together.

Decreases can be made in the same way on the wrong side of the work or the purl side by purling the stitches instead of knitting.

Increasing. To add to the number of stitches on the needle in order to shape the work there are three ways to increase.

1. Pick up the thread lying between the stitch last knitted and the next on the left hand needle and knit into this thread. This is almost invisible.

2. Knit first into the front and then into the back of next stitch.

3. Pick up the loop in the previous row below the next stitch to be knitted. Knit into this and then knit the next stitch in the usual way.

Making stitches in lace patterns.

When working lace patterns, stitches are made by what is known as the 'Over' principle. These made stitches are usually counteracted by decreases in the same row and a static number of stitches are maintained in the row. In more complicated lace patterns, stitches are made in one row and counteracted by decreases in another row.

Stitches made or increased in this way are made by passing the yarn over the needle.

a. *Between Knit stitches*. Knit a stitch, bring the yarn forward as if to purl a stitch then take it over the right hand needle to the back of the work, ready to knit the next stitch. This is, yarn over needle and is shortened in patterns to y.o.n. In some patterns this is referred to as wool over needle and is abbreviated to w.o.n.

b. *Making a stitch between a knit and a purl stitch*. Knit a stitch, take the yarn forward between the needles and right round the right hand needle to the front of the work again, ready for the purl stitch. Yarn round needle, shortened to y.r.n.

c. *Making a stitch between purl stitches*. This is done in the same way as when making a stitch between a knit and a purl stitch.

d. *Making a stitch between purl and knit stitches*. Purl a stitch and without moving the yarn to the back of the work, knit a stitch. The yarn will automatically have made a stitch. y.o.n.

POCKETS

Pockets are easily added to knitted garments, from the simple patch pocket, which is just a rectangle of knitting to the required size. Care should be seen that this is applied evenly and sewn neatly to the finished garment.

Slit Pocket

First knit the pocket lining, casting on the number of stitches for the size required, and knitting to the correct length.

When the position of pocket top is reached on front of garment, work along row to beginning of pocket top, cast off the same number of stitches as those used for lining and work to end. On the return row, when pocket position is reached, place lining stitches in place of those cast off and work across them. When the pieces of the garment are finished and pressed, the lining is slip-stitched down on the inside.

Pocket with flap

The same procedure as above is followed, but the flap is also knitted. When the pocket position is reached, after the cast off row, place flap stitches in position and knit across them, then work to end. The lining is stitched into position separately, on wrong side.

Average Tensions and Comparative Needle Sizes

No. of Needle:	3-Ply Sts.	3-Ply Rows	4-Ply Sts.	4-Ply Rows	Double Knitting Sts.	Double Knitting Rows
6 [7]	5½	7½	5	7	5	6½
7 [6]	6	8	5½	7½	5¼	7
8 [5]	6½	8½	6	8	5½	7½
9 [4]	7	9	6½	8½	5¾	7¾
10 [3]	7½	9½	7	9	6	8
11 [2]	8	10	7½	9½	6¾	9
12 [1]	8½	10½	8	10	7¼	10
13 [0]	9	11	8½	10½	—	—
14 [00]	9½	11½	9	11	—	—

The above chart gives what were considered to be the average tension at which most knitters will work in the given thickness of yarn and needle size. The average is taken in stocking stitch and if you work to this tension you will find your work correct in shape and size. If you find it impossible, and some of us do, change your needles to a size which will give the correct tension.

COMPARATIVE KNITTING NEEDLE SIZES

ENGLISH	000	00	0	1	2		3	4	5	6	7	8	9	10	11	12	13	14
AMERICAN		15	13	12	11	10½	10	9	8	7	6	5	4	3	2	1	0	00

Knitting needle sizes are not yet uniform in all countries and it is not always easy to decide which size is required. The above chart tells you how American and English sizes compare. The tension chart will also help you to decide, if you are using a pattern which does not state a needle size you can readily understand.

COMPARATIVE WOOL AND YARN CHART (see page 168)

Note: American needle sizes are in [ ] in all patterns in this book.
Note: Figures in ( ) refer to the larger sizes.

Abbreviations

Abbreviations are used in knitting patterns to save space and to make instructions easier and less tedious to follow. Most are easily recognisable to most knitters, but it is wise to read through those which appear at the beginning of each set of instructions you choose. Make sure you understand them all before you begin to knit the pattern. This will save you time and trouble later.

The following abbreviations are those appearing in the patterns in this book.

Abbreviations

K., knit.
P., purl.
M. st., moss stitch.
G. st., garter stitch.
Rep., repeat.
St. st., stocking stitch.
St(s)., stitch(es).
Inc., increase.
Dec., decrease.

Alt., alternate.
Foll., following.
Folls., follows.
Beg., beginning.
Cont., continue.
Patt., pattern.
Tog., together.
M. 1., make one.
Sl., slip.

P.s.s.o., pass slipped stitch over.
S. k. p. o., slip 1, knit 1, pass slipped stitch over.
T. b. l., through back of loop(s).
Y. f., yarn at front.
Y. b., yarn at back.
Y. r. n., yarn round needle.
Y. o. n., yarn over needle.
Y. fwd., yarn forward.
C. n., cable needle.
RS., rice stitch.
C. 4 *B.*, cable 4 back thus: (sl. next 2 sts., on to c. n. and leave at back of work, k. 2, then k. 2 from c. n.).
C. 4 F., cable 4 front thus: (As C. 4 b., but holding the 2 sts. on c. n. at *front* of work).
C. 6 B., cable 6 back thus: (sl. next 3 sts. on to c. n. and leave at back of work, k. 3, then k. 3 from c. n.).
C. 6 F., cable 6 front. (As cable 6 back, but

holding the 3 sts. on c. n. at *front* of work).
M. B., make bobble thus: Into next stitch, y. fwd., (k. 1, y. fwd., k. 1) twice, turn and p. these sts., turn, k. 5, turn, p. 5.
Now pass 2nd, 3rd and 4th sts. over 1 st., k. tog. last 2 sts.
K. 2 in., knit twice into next st.
M. I. make one by passing y. o. n.
CS., cross stitch thus: (sl. 1, k. 1, y. o. n., p. s. s. o.).
C. P7., Claw pattern 7 thus: (S1. next 2 sts. on to c. n. and leave at back of work, k. 1, then k. 2 from c. n., k. next st., sl. next st. on to c. n., leave at front, k. 2, then k. 1 from c. n.)
C. 2 R., cross 2 right thus: (sl. next st. on to c. n., leave at back, k. 2, then p. 1 from c. n.)
C. 2. L., cross 2 left thus: (sl. next 2 sts. on to c. n., leave at front, p. 1, then k. 2 from c. n.)
P. u. k., pick up loop lying before the next st. and k. into it.
In(s)., inch(es).
Rem., remain(ing).
K. B. 1, Knit 1 into row below.
P. B. 1., Purl 1 into row below.
K. 1. R B., Knit 1 into row below.
M., main colour.   **B.,** black.
C., contrast colour.   **R.,** red.
D., dark.   **W.,** white.
L., light.   **G.,** gold.

Patterns and Trimmings

TASSELS

Take a piece of cardboard the length you wish the finished tassel to be. Wind yarn round the cardboard as many times as you need for your tassel. Thread a large eyed needle with a length of matching yarn. Pass it through the loops at the top of your cardboard several times and secure it but do not cut yarn.

Cut end of wound yarn at bottom of cardboard. Pass the needle through the top to about an inch below the cut ends. Take another length of matching yarn and wind it round the top of tassel, about $\frac{1}{4}$ of total length from top. Tie firmly and with the needle, pass the ends through to join the cut ends. Trim ends.

A golliwog can be made from a large tassel. Bind the top of the tassel twice, once for hairline and once for neck. Then divide the ends into four equal sections. Keep one each side for arms and bind the remainder again for waist. Divide remainder equally for legs. Bind ends of arms and legs. Trim ends of hair, arms and legs. Add eyes, nose and mouth with embroidery. (See picture on page 159).

POMPONS

Cut two circles of firm cardboard. The diameter should be that required for the finished pompon. Cut a circle out of the centre of each piece. Place the circles together. Wind yarn through the centre hole and round both pieces of cardboard until the centre hole is completely filled up.

Thread matching yarn through a large eyed needle. Cut the loops of yarn between the two circles. Bind yarn in needle tightly between the circles, round the centre of the cut lengths of yarn. Tie very firmly. Remove the cardboard circles and trim the pompon evenly. A large ball can be made as a toy for a small child.

TWISTED CORDS

Cords will make belts or ties to thread through bags. Really thick ones with tassels will make smart ties for curtains. To make a cord, take several lengths of yarn. They should be about three times the length required for the finished cord and about half as thick. Secure one end firmly and taking the other end, twist until it forms a firm, tight cord. Fold in half and allow the two sides to twist together from the centre. Tie a knot in each end and trim with a tassel. A two coloured cord can be made in the same way. It looks neatest if the original strands are half one colour and half the other, the two colours being tied in the middle. When the twisted strands are

The diagram shows you how to make a simple fringe.
Step 1 begins at left hand side, followed by step 2 and then the finished fringe is shown

allowed to run together, the colours will appear to be striped neatly.

FRINGES

The most simple form of fringe is easily made and can add a touch of colour to many items. It can be thick or not, depending on the number of lengths of yarn used for the fringe.

Cut lengths of yarn a little more than twice the length of the required fringe. Take two or more strands, according to the thickness of fringe you want to make. Fold in half and with a crochet hook, draw the fold through the edge which is to be decorated. (See sketch No. 30)

Draw the ends through the loop of the fold and pull tight.

For a fancier fringe use longer strands. Divide each individual tassel into two equal parts. Start from one end of fringe and knot together the second half of first tassel and first half of second together, about 1 inch below tassel loops. Continue to end, keeping row of knots level. On next row, one inch below knots, take all the alternate halves of tassels and knot in the same way. This forms a net with fringed ends hanging below.

CAPS AND SCARVES

Simple to make and smart to wear, cosy caps and scarves to knit for cold days
Materials: —*Pompon scarf and cap.* —16 ozs. of Robin Vogue 4-ply for scarf and cap (or 14 ozs. for scarf and 4 ozs. for the cap); a pair of No. 12 [1] knitting needles. *Fringed scarf and cap*: —16 ozs. of Robin Vogue 4-ply for scarf and cap (or 14 ozs. for scarf and 4 ozs. for cap); a pair of No. 12 [1] knitting needles; oddments of yarn in black and white for the embroidery. *Striped scarf and cap*: —10 ozs. of Robin Vogue 4-ply in white and 4 ozs. each in red and emerald for the scarf and cap (or 8 ozs. white, 3 ozs. each of red and emerald for the scarf and 2 ozs. white and one oz. each in red and emerald for the cap); a pair of No. 12 [1] knitting needles.

Measurements: —*Scarves.* —92 ins. long (excluding the fringe or pompon); 6 ins. wide when made up. *Caps*: —To fit an average head.

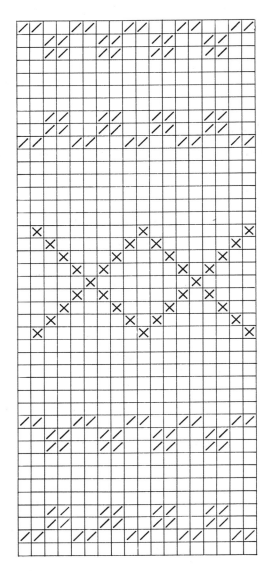

◢ WHITE

☒ BLACK

Chart No. 4
Follow the chart to add the pattern to the Fringed cap and scarf. Turn to page 57 for the instructions on Swiss darning and see sketch No. 33

Tension: —8 sts. to one in.

Abbreviations: —See page 20.

POMPON SCARF AND CAP

Scarf: —With Red, cast on 100 sts. Work in st.st. for 92 ins. Cast off.

Cap: —With Red, cast on 124 sts. Work 2 ins. in k. l, p. 1 rib, then work 7 ins. in st. st. Cast off.

FRINGED SCARF AND CAP

Scarf: —With Emerald, work as given for pompon scarf.

Cap: —With Emerald cast on 124 sts. Work 2 ins. in k. l, p. 1 rib. Now work in st. st. for 2 ins., then dec. 1 st. at both ends of every alt. row until 6 sts. rem. Cast off. Add pattern to cap and scarf in Swiss darning, following chart No. 4. Turn to page 57 for instructions on Swiss darning.

STRIPED SCARF AND CAP

Scarf: With Red, cast on 100 sts. and proceed in st.st., working in stripes as follows: 6 rows Red, 6 rows White, 14 rows Emerald, 6 rows White, 6 rows Red and 24 rows White. Rep. the last 62 rows until work measures 92 ins. Cast off.

Cap: —With White cast on 124 sts. Work 2 ins. k. l, p. l rib, then proceed in st.st., working in stripes as follows: 4 rows White, 6 rows Red, 6 rows White, 14 rows Emerald, 6 rows White, 6 rows Red and 24 rows White, at the same time dec. 1 st. at both ends of the 13th of these rows and every foll. alt. row until 6 sts. rem. Cast off.

Press work on wrong side with a warm iron over a damp cloth. Fold scarf in half lengthwise, right side inside. Join the long seam and the seam at one end. Turn scarf to right side. At open end, turn in the edges to meet and slip stitch them together. Press seamed edge. Join the seam of cap neatly.

Pompon scarf and cap: —With Red make 3 pompons, using two circles of cardboard about 5 ins. in diameter with hole at centre 1 in. in diameter. Gather each end of scarf and sew on pompons. Gather cast off edge of cap and sew on pompon.

Fringed scarf and cap: —Cut 16 in. lengths of yarn in Emerald and place 9 strands together and fold them double. Insert crochet hook at one end of scarf and draw the looped end through; pass the ends through the loops and pull knot tightly. Knot fringe evenly along both ends of scarf. Cut 30 lengths of Emerald, place them together and fold double. Sew folded end to point of cap and bind strands about 2 ins. below to form tassel.

Striped scarf and cap: —As fringed scarf and cap, but use all the colours in rotation for fringes.

STRIPED CUSHION

Just two squares to make a super cushion

Materials: —4 ozs. of Lister Lavenda Double Knitting Wool in Coffee Tan and 2 ozs. each in Golden Sand and Cream Parchment; a pair of No. 10 [3] knitting needles; a cushion 15 ins. square.

Measurements: —15 ins. square.

Tension: —6 sts., and 8 rows to one in.

Abbreviations: —See page 20.

To work:

Plain side: —With No. 10 [3] needles and Tan cast on 90 sts. Work in st. st. until work measures 15 ins. Cast off.

Striped side: —With No. 10 [3] needles and Tan cast on 90 sts. Work in st. st. in stripes of (12 rows Tan, 12 rows coffee, 12 rows Sand) 3 times, then work 12 rows Tan. Cast off.

To make up:

Press work lightly on wrong side. Join the two pieces together, leaving one end open. Insert cushion and join remaining seam. Using the 3 colours make a twisted cord and sew all round outer edge of cushion as shown in photograph on page 26. Make 3 colour tassels and sew one to each corner.

SLEEVELESS PULLOVER

The plain classic pullover most men like to have and a beginner could knit it for him

Materials: —11 (12, 13, 14) balls of Lee Target Motoravia Double Knitting Wool; a pair each of Nos. 9 [4] and 10 [3] knitting needles.

Measurements: —Chest: —36(38, 40, 42) ins.;

Length: —24(24½, 25, 25½) ins.

Tension: —6 sts. and 8 rows to 1 inch on No. 9 [4] needles.

Abbreviations: —See page 20.

BACK

With No. 10 [3] needles, cast on 109(115, 121, 127) sts. and work in k. I, p. I rib for 22 rows. Change to No. 9 [4] needles and st.st. and cont. until Back measures 15(15, 15½, 15½) ins. from beg., ending with a wrong-side row.

To Shape Armholes: —Cast off 6(8, 8, 10) sts. at beg. of next 2 rows. Cont. thus: — *1st row:* —K. 1, sl. I, k. I, p. s. s. o., k. to last 3 sts., k. 2 tog., k. I. *2nd row:* —Sl. 1, p. 2 tog., p. to last 3 sts., p. 2 tog. t. b. I., k. I. Rep. 1st and 2nd rows 3 times, then 1st row once. *Next row:* —Sl. 1, p. to last st., k. I. Cont. in st. st. and dec. 1 st. as before at each end of next and foll. 2 alt. rows. Then cont. straight until Back measures 24(24½, 25, 25½) ins. from beg., ending with a wrong-side row.

To Shape Shoulders: —Cast off 7 (7, 8, 8) sts. at beg. of next 6 rows. Cast off.

FRONT

Work as for Back until armhole shaping is reached.

To Shape Armhole and Neck: —Cast off 6 (8, 8, 10) sts. at beg. of next 2 rows. *Next row:* —K. 1, sl. I, k. I, p. s. s. o., k. 45 (46, 49, 50) sts., sl. next st. on to a safety-pin for centre front and rem. sts. on to a spare needle.

Working on first set of sts. work thus: — *1st row:* —Sl. 1, p. to last 3 sts., p. 2 tog. t. b. I., k. I. *2nd row:* —K. 1, sl. 1, k. I, p. s. s. o., k. to end. *3rd row:* —As 1st row. *4th row:* — K. 1, sl. I, k. I, p. s. s. o., k. to last 3 sts., k. 2 tog., k. I. Cont. in st.st. and dec. 1 st. at armhole edge on every row and *at the same time* dec. 1 st. at neck edge on every foll. 4th row until 37 (38, 41, 42) sts. rem. *Next row:* —Sl. 1, p. to last st., k. I. Cont. in st.st. and dec. at neck edge only on every foll. 4th row until 21 (21, 24, 24) sts. rem.

To Shape Shoulder: —Cast off 7 (7, 8, 8) sts. at beg. of next and foll. 2 alt. rows.

With right side facing, rejoin yarn to remaining sts. leaving the single centre st. on safety-pin. Work to match first side.

NECKBAND

With No. 10 [3] needles and with right side facing, pick up and k. 53 (55, 57, 59) sts. evenly down left side of neck, one st. from safety-pin and 54 (56, 58, 60) sts. up right side of neck and 31 (33, 33, 35) sts. across back of neck. *1st row:* —Sl. 1, * p. 1, k. I. rep. from * 41 (43, 44, 46) times, p. 2 tog., p. 1, p. 2 tog. t. b. I., work in k. I, p. I. rib to last st., k. 1. *2nd row:* —Sl. 1, k. 1, * p. 1, k. I, rep. from * 24 (25, 26, 27) times, p. 2 tog. t. b. I., k. 1, p. 2 tog., work in k. I, p. 1 rib to last 2 sts., k. 2. Cont. in rib thus and dec. at each side of centre st. on every row until 123 (129, 133, 139) sts. rem. Cast off loosely in rib.

ARMBANDS

With No. 10 [3] needles and with right side of work facing, pick up and k. 115 (119, 127, 133) sts. evenly round armhole. Work 9 rows in k. 1, p. 1 rib. Cast off loosely in rib.

To make up

Join shoulder seams, and side and armband seams. Press seams.

PINK SLEEVELESS CARDIGAN
A useful extra to add to your wardrobe. Team it with shirt and trousers or wear it for that extra warmth over a dress

Materials: —11 (12, 12, 13) ozs. Lister Lavenda Double Knitting Wool; a pair each of Nos. 9 [4] and 11 [2] knitting needles; 5 buttons.

Measurements: —To fit Bust 32 (34, 36, 38) ins. Length from shoulder; 23 ins.

Tension: —6 sts. and 8 rows to 1 inch over stocking stitch on No. 9 [4] needles.

Abbreviations: —See page 20.

BACK
With No. 11 [2] needles, cast on 98 (104, 110, 116) sts. and work in k. 1, p. 1 rib for 12 rows. Change to No. 9 [4] needles and st. st. and work until Back measures 16 ins. from lower edge, ending with wrong-side row.
To Shape Armholes: —Cast off 6 (7, 8, 9) sts. at beg. of next 2 rows, then dec. 1 st. at each end of next and every foll. alt. row until 78 (80, 82, 84) sts. rem. Cont. without further shaping until Back measures 23 ins. from lower edge.
To Shape Shoulders: —Cast off 11 (12, 12, 13) sts. at beg. of next 2 rows and 11 (11, 12, 12) sts. at beg. of foll. 2 rows. Cast off.

RIGHT FRONT
With No. 11 [2] needles cast on 48 (52, 54, 58) sts. and work in k. l, p. 1 rib for 12 rows. Inc. 1 st. at beg. of last row of 1st and 3rd sizes only: 49 (52, 55, 58) sts. Change to No. 9 [4] needles and st. st. until Front measures 15 ins. from beg., ending wrong side.
To Shape Front: Next row: —K. 1, s. k. p. o., k. to end. *Next row:* —P. *Next row:* —K. *Next row:* —P. Rep. last 4 rows once more. *Next row:* —K. 1, s. k. p. o., k. to end.
To Shape Armhole: —With wrong side facing, cast off 6 (7, 8, 9) sts., p. to end. *Next row:* —K. to last 2 sts., k. 2 tog. *Next and alt. rows:* —P. Next row: K. 1, s. k. p. o., k. to last 2 sts., k. 2 tog. Rep. last 4 rows until 34 (35, 35, 36) sts. rem. Keeping armhole straight, cont. to shape front edge as before until 22

(23, 24, 25) sts. rem.
To Shape Shoulder: —With wrong side facing, cast off 11 (12, 12, 13) sts., p. to end. *Next row:* —K. Cast off.

LEFT FRONT
Work to match Right Front, reversing all shapings.

FRONT BANDS
With No. 11 [2] needles cast on 8 sts. and work in k. 1, p. 1 rib for 3 ins. *Buttonhole row:* —Rib 3, cast off 2 sts., rib to end. *Next row:* —Rib 3, cast on 2 sts., rib to end. Cont. in rib making 4 more buttonholes at intervals of 2¾ ins. Cont. in rib until band slightly stretched reaches up Right Front, round back of neck and down Left Front. Cast off in rib.

ARMBANDS
Join shoulder seams. With right side of work facing and starting at side seam, rejoin yarn and with No. 11 [2] needles, pick up and k. 56 (57, 58, 59) sts. up to shoulder seam and 56 (57, 58, 59) sts. down other side to side seam. Work in k. 1, p. 1 rib for 6 rows. Cast off loosly in rib.

To make up
Press pieces on wrong side with warm iron over a damp cloth, avoiding ribbing. Join seams. Sew Front bands into position. Add buttons to match buttonholes. Press all seams.

BABY COAT, CAP AND MITTS
Neat coat is suitable for boy or girl. It has a centre zip fastener and can be left perfectly plain. Decoration can be added in Swiss darning, animal motifs could be sewn on or the edges could be trimmed with braid

Materials: —11 (12, 14) balls of Robin Vogue Double Knitting Wool in White; oddments of contrast for embroidery; a pair each of Nos. 8 [5] and 10 [3] knitting needles; a 12 (14, 16) inch open-ended zip fastener; 1 button; binding for lower edge of coat.

Measurements: —Chest: 20 (22, 24) ins.; Length: 14½ (16½, 18½) ins.; Sleeve: 7 (9, 10½) ins.

Tension: —6 sts. and 8 rows to 1 inch over st.st. on No. 8 [5] needles.

Abbreviations: —See page 20.

COAT-BACK

With No. 8 [5] needles, cast on 78 (84, 90) sts. and work in st. st. Dec. 1 st. at each end of 13th and every foll. 10th row until 66 (72, 78) sts. are on needle. Cont. without further shaping until Back measures 11 (12½, 14) ins. from beg., ending with a p. row.

To Shape Armholes: —Cast off 4 sts. at beg. of next 2 rows. Then dec. 1 st. at each end of every row until 44 (48, 52) sts. rem. Work straight until armhole measures 2½ (3, 3½) ins. from beg., ending with a p. row. Work 2 rows p., 3 rows k., 3 rows p.

To Shape Shoulders: —Cast off 5 sts. at beg. of next 2 rows, then 6 sts. at beg. of foll. 2 rows. Cast off rem. sts.

LEFT FRONT

With No. 8 [5] needles, cast on 39 (42, 45) sts. and work in st. st. dec. 1 st. at beg. of right side edge on the 13th and then every 10th row until 33 (36, 39) sts. rem. Work to same length as Back, ending p. row.

To Shape Armhole: —Cast off 4 sts. at beg. of next row. Work 1 row. Now dec. 1 st. at armhole edge on every row until 22 (24, 26) sts. rem. Work straight until armhole measures 2 (2½, 2½) ins. from beg., ending at front edge.

To Shape Neck: —Cast off 4 (5, 5) sts. at beg. of next row, then dec. 1 st. at neck edge on next 2 (2, 4) rows. Cont. to dec. on every row at neck edge and *at the same time*, when armhole measures 2½ (3, 3½) ins. from beg., ending on a p. row. Work 2 rows p., 3 rows k., 3 rows p. as for Back. Cont. to dec. at neck edge until 11 sts. rem. Cast off.

RIGHT FRONT

Work as for Left Front, reversing all shapings.

SLEEVES

With No. 8 [5] needles, cast on 34 (36, 38) sts. and knit 1 row. Work 3 rows p., 3 rows k., 3 rows p. Cont. in st.st. and inc. 1 st. at each end of next and foll. 8th rows until there are 44 (48, 54) sts. on needle. Work without further shaping until sleeve measures 7 (9, 10½) ins. from beg.

To Shape Top: —Cast off 4 sts. at beg. of next

2 rows. Now dec. 1 st. at each end of every row until 26 (30, 32) sts. rem. Then dec. 1 st. at each end of every right side row until 18 (22, 22) sts. rem. Then at each end of every row until 12 sts. rem., ending with a wrong-side row. Cast off.

COLLAR

With No. 8 [5] needles, cast on 14 (20, 20) sts. and work in st.st. Cast on 10 sts. at beg. of 3rd and foll. 5 rows. Work 2 rows without further shaping. *Next row:* —K. 1, p. u. k., k. to last st., p. u. k., k. 1. *Next row:* —P. Rep. last 4 rows 3 times more. Next row K. Knit next row to mark hemline. Work 2 rows st.st. *Next row:* —K. 1, k. 2 tog., k. to last 3 sts., k. 2 tog., k. 1. *Next row:* —P. Rep. last 4 rows 3 times more. Now cast off 10 sts. at beg. of next 6 rows, Work 2 rows straight. Cast off.

CAP

With No. 10 [3] needles cast on 109 (115, 123) sts. and work 3 rows g. st. *Next row:* —(Buttonhole). K. 4, cast off 2, k. to end. *Next row:* —K. to end, casting on 2 over those cast off in previous row. Work 2 more rows g. st. *Next row:* —Cast off 17 (17, 18) sts. k. to end. *Next row:* —Cast off 17 (17, 18) sts. Change to No. 8 [5] needles and k. to end. Cont. in st. st. until work measures 6 (6¼, 6½) ins. from beg., ending with a p. row.

To Shape Top: —3rd size : Next row: —*K. 2 tog., k. 7, k. 3 tog., k. 8, k. 2 tog., k. 7, rep. from * to end. *Next row:* —P. *2nd size:* Next row: K. 2 tog., k. 7, k. 3 tog., k. to last 19 sts., k. 3 tog., k. 7, k. 2 tog., k. 7 *Next row:* —P. Cont. for all sizes. *1st row:* —* K. 2 tog., k. 6, k. 3 tog., k. 6, k. 2 tog., k. 6, rep. from * to end. *2nd and every alt. row:* —P. *3rd row:* —* K. 2 tog., k. 5, rep. from * to end. *5th row:* —* K. 2 tog., k. 4, rep. from * to end. Cont. to work in this way working 1 st. less between decs. until 18 sts. rem., ending with a p. row. *Next row:* —* K. 2 tog., rep. from * to end. Break yarn, thread through rem. sts., draw up and fasten off securely. Join Back seam for 2½ (2½, 3) ins. With No. 10 [3] needles and right side of work facing, knit up 62 (66, 70) sts. from lower edge. Work ½ inch g. st. Cast off.

MITTS

With No. 10 [3] needles, cast on 32 (34, 36) sts. and work 6 rows g. st. Change to No. 8

[5] needles and st.st. and work 11 (13, 15) rows. *Next row*: —P. 12 (13, 14) sts., slip next 8 sts. on to a safety-pin, cast on 8 sts., p. to end. Work 12 (14, 16) rows st.st.

To Shape Top: —*1st row*: —K. 2 (4, 1), * k. 2 tog., k. 3, rep. from * to end. *2nd and alt. rows*: P. *3rd row*: —K. 2 (4, 1), * k. 2 tog., k. 2, rep. from * to end. *5th row*: —K. 2 (4, 1), * k. 2 tog., k. 1, rep. from * to end. *7th row*: —K. 2 tog. to end. Break yarn, thread through rem. sts., draw up and fasten off securely. Join side seam.

Thumb: —Slip 8 sts. from safety-pin on to No. 8 [5] needle and cast on 3 sts. k. to end, turn and cast on 3 sts., p. to end. Work 4 (6, 6) rows st. st. *Next row*: —K. 2 tog., to end. *Next row*: —P. *Next row*: —K. 1, * k. 2 tog., rep. from * to end. *Next row*: —P. Break yarn, draw through rem. sts., draw up and fasten off securely. Join seam and base of thumb.

To make up

Press pieces. Join shoulder, side and sleeve seams of coat and set in sleeves. Fold collar at hemline with right sides together, join seam and turn to right side. Set to neckline. Face lower edge with binding and set zip into centre front. Add button to cap. Embroider in Swiss darning as shown in picture on page 31 or follow any suitable chart to decorate the set. Give final press.

HIS AND HER STRIPED SWEATERS

Materials: Of Patons Limelight Double Crêpe 2 (3, 3, 3) (50 gram) balls in dark colour, 3 (3, 4, 4) (50 gram) balls in medium colour; 3 (4, 5, 5) (50 gram) balls in light colour; a pair each of Nos. 8 [5] and 10 [3] knitting needles; a set of four No. 10 [3] double-pointed needles.

Measurements: To fit Bust/chest: 34 (36, 38, 40) ins. Length: 23½ (24, 26½, 27) ins. Sleeve seam: 16½ (17, 18, 18½) ins.

Tension: 11 sts. and 15 rows to 2 ins. over stocking stitch on No. 8 [5] needles.

Abbreviations: See page 20.

FRONT
With No. 10 [3] needles and Dark, cast on 94 (100, 106, 110) sts. and work in rib as follows:

1st, 3rd and 4th sizes only: *1st row*: —* P. 2, k. 2, rep. from * to last 2 sts., p. 2. *2nd row*: * K. 2, p. 2, rep. from * to last 2 sts., k. 2. *2nd size only*: *1st row*: —P. 1, * k. 2, p. 2, rep. from * to last 3 sts., k. 2, p. 1. *2nd row*: —K. 1, * p. 2, k. 2, rep. from * to last 3 sts., p. 2, k. 1. *All sizes*: Work 18 (18, 22, 22) rows more in rib. Change to No. 8 [5] needles and breaking off and join on colours as required, cont. in rib, working stripes thus: 10 (10, 12, 12) rows Light, 6 rows Dark, 14 (14, 16, 16) rows Medium, 6 rows Dark, 20 (20, 22, 22) rows Light, 20 (20, 22, 22) rows Medium, (6 rows Dark, 6 rows Light) twice, 6 rows Dark Cont. in Medium, working as follows:

To Shape Armholes: —Cast off 4 (5, 5, 5) sts. at beg. of next 2 rows, then dec. 1 st. at each end of next 3 rows. Now dec. 1 st. at each end of every foll. alt. row until 74 (78, 82, 86) sts. rem. Work 1 row. **

With Light, cont. straight until work measures 4½ (5, 6, 5½) ins. from beg. of armhole shaping, ending with right side facing.

To Shape Neck: —*Next row*: —Work a-cross 28 (29, 31, 32) sts., turn and slip rem. sts. on a spare needle. Cont. on these sts. for first side as follows: Dec. 1 st. at neck edge on next 4 rows, then on foll. alt. row: 23 (24, 26, 27) sts. Cont. straight until work measures 7 (7½, 8½, 9) ins. from beg. of armhole shaping, ending with right side facing.

To Shape Shoulder: —Cast off 8 (8, 9, 9) sts. at beg. of next and foll. alt. row. Work 1 row. Cast off rem. sts. With right side facing slip centre 18 (20, 20, 22) sts. on to a length of yarn. Rejoin Light to rem. sts. and work to end.

Complete to match first side, reversing the shaping.

BACK
Work as for Front to **, then cont. in Light until Back matches Front at armhole shaping edge, ending with right side facing.

To Shape Shoulders: —Cast off 8 (8, 9, 9) sts. at beg. of next 4 rows and 7 (8, 8, 9) sts. at beg. of foll. 2 rows. Slip rem. 28 (30, 30, 32) sts. on a length of yarn.

SLEEVES

With No. 10 [3] needles and Dark, cast on 44 (48, 56, 60) sts. and work 20 (20, 24, 24) rows in rib as for 2nd size of Front. Change to No. 8 [5] needles and work 36 rows in rib and stripes as follows: (6 rows Light, 6 rows Dark) 3 times, *and at the same time* inc. 1 st. at each of 3rd and every foll. 6th row until there are 56 (60, 68, 72) sts., working extra sts. into rib. Cont. in Medium, inc. as before but on every foll. 7th row from previous inc. until there are 70 (74, 84, 90) sts. Now work straight until sleeve seam measures 16½ (17, 18, 18½) ins., ending with right side facing.

To Shape Top: —With Light, cast off 4 (5, 5, 6) sts. at beg. of next 2 rows. Dec. 1 st. at each end of next and every foll. alt. row until 42 (40, 50, 52) sts. rem., then at each end of every row until 24 (26, 28, 30) sts. rem. Cast off rem. sts.

To make up and neckband

Do not press. Using a fine back-stitch seam, join shoulders.

With right side facing, using the set of No. 10 [3] needles and Light, starting at left shoulder k. up 88 (96, 96, 100) sts. all round neck, including sts. at centre front and back.

Work 6 rounds in k. 1, p. 1 rib. Cast off loosely in rib.

Using a fine back-stitch seam, join side and sleeve seams. Insert sleeves. Using a *cool* iron and *dry* cloth, press seams lightly.

TURQUOISE COAT

Materials: 31 (32, 33) ozs. Lee Target Leemont Double Crêpe; a pair each of Nos. 11 [2] and 9 [4] knitting needles; a set of 4 double-pointed needles No. 11 [2]; 6 buttons.

Measurements: —Bust: 38 (40, 42) ins.; Length: 33 ins.; Sleeve: 17 ins.

Tension: —6 sts. and 10 rows to 1 inch over pattern on No. 9 [4] needles.

Abbreviations: —See page 20.

BACK

With No. 9 [4] needles cast on 134 (138,

His and her striped sweaters, see his in colour on page 49

142) sts. and work in patt. as follows: *1st row*: —K. 2, p. 2, k. 2, rep. from to end. *2nd row*: —P. 2, k. 2, p. 2 rep. from to end. *3rd row*: —As 2nd row. *4th row*: As 1st row. These four rows form the patt. Cont. in patt. until work measures 11 ins. Dec. 1 st. at each end of next and every foll. 13th row until 114 (118, 122) sts. rem. Cont. without further shaping until Back measures 25 ins. from beg., measuring at centre Back.

To Shape Armholes: —Cast off 6 sts. at beg. of next 2 rows, then dec. 1 st. at each end of next 8 rows. Work without further shaping until armhole measures 8 ins. from beg. of shaping.

To Shape Shoulders: —Cast off 5 sts. at beg. of next 8 rows and 5 (6, 7) sts. at beg. of foll. 2 rows. Cast off.

POCKET LININGS: —(Make 2)

With No. 9 [4] needles cast on 34 sts. and work in st. st. for 4½ ins., ending with a p. row. Slip sts. on to a spare needle.

LEFT FRONT

With No. 9 [4] needles cast on 74 (78, 78) sts. and work in patt. for 11 ins. Dec. 1 st. at side edge on next and every foll. 13th row until 69 (73, 73) sts. rem. *At the same time*, when Front measures 13¼ ins. from beg., ending at side edge.

Place pocket. *Next row*: Patt. 4 sts. Slip next 34 sts. on to a thread of yarn for pocket top, patt. across 34 sts. of pocket lining, patt. to end. Cont. on these sts. until Front has 69 (73, 73) sts. on needle. Work without further shaping until Front measures 25 ins.

To Shape Armhole and Front edge: — Cast off 6 sts. at side edge, then dec. 1 st. at this edge on next 8 rows. *At the same time* dec. 1 st. at Front edge on next and foll. alt. row until 10 (14, 14) sts. have been decreased at this edge, then dec. 1 st. at front edge on every 3rd row until 30 (33, 32) sts. *in all* have been decreased at this edge. When these decreases are all completed, work without further shaping until armhole measures 8 ins. from beg. of shaping.

To Shape Shoulder: —Cast off at armhole edge on alt. tows, 5 sts. 4 times and 5 (6, 7) sts. once.

RIGHT FRONT

Mark 4 button positions on Left Front. The bottom one in line with pocket placing, the top one at beg. of front edge shaping, and the remaining two evenly spaced between. Now work Right Front as for Left Front, reversing the shapings. Make 4 buttonholes to correspond with markers thus: — From centre front edge, patt. 3, cast off 4 sts., patt. to end. Cast on 4 sts. on foll. row, to complete buttonhole.

POCKET FLAPS

Slip 34 sts. of pocket top on to No. 9 [4] needle and patt. 1½ ins. Change to set of No. 11 [2] needles and pick up and k. 11 sts. from side edge of flap. (Right side is on top when flap is turned down). Work in k. 1, p. 1 rib across all sts. and pick up and k. 11 sts. from other side of flap. Work 4 rows k. 1, p. 1 rib across all sts. Cast off.

SLEEVES

With No. 9 [4] needles, cast on 58 (62, 66) sts. and work in patt. for 2½ ins. Inc. 1 st. at each end of next and every foll. 8th row until there are 86 (90, 94) sts. on needle. Work without further shaping until sleeve measures 17 ins. from cast on edge.

To Shape Top: —Cast off 6 sts. at beg. of next 2 rows. Then dec. 1 st. at each end of next and every foll. alt. row until 38 (42, 46) sts. rem. Cast off 2 (3, 4) sts. at beg. of next 4 rows and 2 sts. at beg. of next 6 rows. Cast off rem. sts.

THE BRAID

With No. 11 [2] needles, cast on 7 sts. *1st row*: — (Wrong side) K. 1, p. 2, k. 1, p. 2, k. 1. *2nd row*: —P. 1, (k. 2 tog. but do not slip sts. off needle, k. into first st. then slip both sts. from needle, p. 1) twice. These 2 rows form the patt. Rep. them until braid fits from centre front hem, up front, round neck and down front and round hem to meet at front edge again. Cast off. Make two strips to fit sleeve edges.

To make up

Press pieces on wrong side with a warm iron over a damp cloth. Join shoulder and side seams. Join sleeve seams and set in sleeves.

Hem down pocket linings and press down pocket flaps. Sew edgings to sleeves and edges of coat. Press all seams. Add 4 buttons to coat and one to each pocket flap.

BLUE BELTED SWEATER

Materials: —15 (16, 17) ozs. Lister Lavenda Crisp Crêpe 4-ply Wool in main colour; 3 (4, 4) ozs. contrast; a pair each of Nos. 11 [2] and 12 [1] knitting needles; a 2 inch buckle; 1¼ yds. petersham 2 in. wide.

Measurements: —Bust: 34 (36, 38) ins.; Length: 24½ (24¾, 25) ins.; Sleeve: 16½ ins.

Tension: —7½ sts. and 10 rows to 1 inch over st. st. on No. 11 [2] needles.

Abbreviations: —See page 20.

BACK

With main colour and No. 12 [1] needles, cast on 126 (134, 142) sts. and work in st.st. for 11 rows, ending with a k. row. K. next row to mark hemline. Beg. with a k. row, work in st. st. for 2 ins. Change to No. 11 [2] needles and cont. in st.st., inc. 1 st. at each end of every 25th row until there are 136 (144, 152) sts. on needle. Work straight until Back measures 17½ ins. from hemline, ending with a p. row.

To Shape Armholes: —Cast off 8 (9, 10) sts. at beg. of next 2 rows, then dec. 1 st. at each end of next and every foll. k. row until 106 (110, 114) sts. rem. Cont. until armhole measures 7 (7¼, 7½) ins. from beg.

To Shape Shoulders: —Cast off 7 sts. at beg. of next 8 rows and 8 (9, 10) sts. at foll. 2 rows. Cast off rem. sts. for back of neck.

FRONT

Work as for Back until Front measures 1 inch less than Back to armhole shaping. (136, 144, 152) sts.

Divide for neck opening: —*Next row*: — Work across 61 (65, 69) sts., cast off centre 14 sts., work to end. Cont. on last set of sts., slipping other sts. on to a spare needle.

**Work until Front is same length as Back to armhole.

To Shape Armhole: —Cast off 8 (9, 10) sts. at side edge, then dec. 1 st. at same edge on every right side row until 46 (48, 50) sts. rem. Work until armhole measures 5 (5¼, 5½) ins. from beg.

To Shape Neck: —Dec. 1 st. at neck edge on next 10 (11, 12) alt. rows. *At the same time* when armhole measures the same as Back to shoulder.

To Shape Shoulder: —Cast off 7 sts. at armhole edge on alt. rows 4 times. Cast off rem. ** Rejoin yarn to inner edge and work from ** to **, reversing shapings.

NECK INSET

Join shoulder seams. With right side of work facing, with No. 12 [1] needles, and main colour, pick up and k. 50 (51, 52) sts. from left front neck opening. Drop main and join in contrast. Work in st.st. in stripes and inc . 1 st. at neck edge on every right side row. 4 rows contrast, 2 rows main, rep. last 6 rows twice, 3 rows contrast. P. 1 row in contrast to mark hemline. Now work stripe sequence again, and dec. 1 st. at neck edge on every k. row. Cast off with main. Work other side to match.

COLLAR

With No. 12 [1] needles and main, and with right side of work facing, pick up and k. 104 (106, 108) sts. all round neck. Join in contrast and inc. 1 st. at each end of every k. row, and working in stripe sequence to match neck inset. Then dec. 1 st. at each end of every k. row and rep. stripes. Cast off with main.

BELT.

With No. 12 [1] needles and contrast, cast on 270 (284, 298) sts. and work in st.st. for 9 rows, ending with a k. row. K. next row to mark hemline. Beg. with a k. row, work stripe sequence as for Neck Inset, ending with 4 rows contrast, P. 1 row contrast for hemline. Beg. with a p. row, work 9 rows contrast. Cast off.

SLEEVES

With No. 12 [1] needles and contrast, cast on 70 (72, 74) sts. and work in st. st. in stripe sequence as for Neck Inset. K. 1 row contrast for hemline. Rep. stripe sequence once more. Cont. in main and change to No. 11 [2] needles. Inc. 1 st. at each end of every 6th row until there are 104 (108, 112) sts. on needle. Cont. straight until sleeve measures 16½ ins. from hemline.

To Shape Top : — Cast off 8 (9, 10) sts. at beg. of next 2 rows and dec. 1 st. at each end of every alt. row until 40 sts. rem. Now cast off 3 sts. at beg. of next 6 rows. Cast off.

To make up

Press pieces. Join side and sleeve seams and turn hems to wrong side and catch down. Join collar and neck inset and fold hem to wrong side and hem down. Wrap right side of inset over left and sew down at centre front. Turn belt over petersham lining and hem. Add buckle and finish off. Press belt and seams.

Variety is the Spice

Plain and well made classics are always favourites. They find a well earned place in the wardrobe of all the members of any family.

We all enjoy a change now and then and it is a very easy matter to add a little variety to the simplest of knitting. Ringing the changes can be done in many ways.

Simple stripes and bands of a contrasting colour can be worked into the cuffs and welts, or you may like to make the whole garment in stripes.

Simple stitches will change the appearance of a garment completely. Try bands of stocking stitch and moss stitch in the same colour, for a change. Choose an easy fancy rib instead of plain double ribbing and see the difference it will make.

There are many two-colour stitches which involve no more effort than a slip stitch at regular intervals along the row. You don't have to twist two different coloured yarns. Each colour is used in turn and the slipped stitches make the effective pattern.

If you see a stitch you like and want to try out, don't forget to make a square of four to six inches each time. Collect squares in the same weight yarns and eventually you will be able to make that rug or shawl we mentioned.

You will need to know how many stitches you must cast on to get an even pattern repeat. Some instructions will give the repeat in brackets. In this book the pattern repeats are set between stars. Count the number of actual stitches to be knitted, this means ignoring a yarn round needle, for instance. Count only the loops on the needle you will need. If the repeat required six stitches, and you cast on 24 stitches, at a tension of six stitches to one inch, this would give you a piece 4 inches wide, and four pattern repeats. Knit for four inches and you will have a four inch square.

CHILD'S RED SWEATER

Simple moss stitch bands add interest to a holiday sweater for a little girl. It would even suit her brother

Materials : —7 (8, 9) ozs., Sirdar Talisman 4-ply ; a pair each of Nos. 11 [2] and 10 [3] knitting needles ; a set of four double-pointed needles No. 11 [2].

Measurements : —Chest : 24 (26, 28) ins. ; Length 15 (15½, 16) ins. ; Sleeve : 10 (10½, 11) ins.

Tension : —7 sts. and 9 rows to 1 inch over st.st. on No. 10 [3] needles.

Abbreviations : —See page 20.

BACK
With No. 11 [2] needles, cast on 86 (92, 100) sts. and work 12 rows k. 1, p. 1 rib.
* Change to No. 10 [3] needles and patt. Work 6 rows st.st., then 5 rows m.st. Rep. these rows until Back measures 10 (10½, 11) ins. from beg., ending with a right-side row. *
To Shape Raglan : —Cast off 6 (7, 8) sts. at beg. of next 2 rows. *Next row :* —Work without shaping. *Next row :* —P. 1, k. 1, s. k. p. o., work to last 4 sts., k. 1, k. 2 tog., p. 1. Keeping patt. correct cont. to dec. on alt. rows in this way until 30 (32, 34) sts. rem. Work 1 row and slip rem. sts. on to a spare needle.

FRONT
Work as for Back from * to *. Now cast off for raglan in the same way and dec. 1 st. on alt. rows until 50 (50, 50) sts. rem.
To Divide for Neck : —Work 10 (10, 10) sts., turn and complete this side of neck first. Cont. to dec. 1 st. at raglan edge on alt. rows and *at the same time*, dec. 1 st. at neck edge on the same row until all sts. are worked off. Fasten off.
Return to rem. sts. and slip centre 30 sts. on to a spare needle. Join yarn to neck edge and work to match first side of neck.

SLEEVES
With No. 11 [2] needles cast on 50 (52, 56) sts. and work as for Back in patt. Inc. 1 st. at each end of 17th and every foll. 5th row until there are 70 (72, 76) sts. on needle. Cont. until sleeve measures 10 (10½, 11) ins. from beg., ending on same patt. row as Back and Front.
To Shape Raglan : —Cast off 6 (7, 8) sts. at beg. of next 2 rows and then dec. 1 st. at each end of alt. rows as for Back until 12 (12, 14) sts. rem. Place remaining sts. on a safety-pin.

COLLAR
Join raglan seams. With the set of four No. 11 [2] double-pointed needles, and with right side of work facing, k. across 30 (32, 34) sts. from back of neck 12 (12, 14) sts. from left sleeve, pick up and k. 10 sts. down left side of

neck, k. 30 sts. from centre neck, pick up and k. 10 sts. up to right sleeve and 12 (12, 14) sts. from right sleeve. Work in k. 1, p. 1 rib for 3½ ins. Cast off in rib.

To make up
Press pieces, omitting ribbing. Join side and sleeve seams. Press seams.

MAN'S FANCY RIB SWEATER

Materials : —20 (22, 24) ozs. of Robin Vogue Double Knitting Wool; a pair each of Nos. 10 [3] and 8 [5] knitting needles.

Measurements : —Chest : 40 (42, 44) ins. ; length : 25 (25½, 26) ins. ; sleeve seam : 18½ (19½, 20) ins.

Tension : 11 sts. and 14 rows to 2 ins.

Abbreviations : —See page 20.

BACK
* Cast on 116 (124, 128) sts. with No. 10 [3] needles. Work 3 ins. k. 1, p. 1 rib.
Change to No. 8 [5] needles and work in patt. as follows : —
1st row : —* K. 3, p. 1 ; rep. from * to end.
2nd row : —* K. 2, p. 1, k. 1 ; rep. from * to end.
These 2 rows form the patt., so rep. then until work measures 16 ins. from cast-on edge, ending with a 2nd row.
To Shape Armholes : —Cast off 6 (7, 7) sts. at beg. of next 2 rows, then dec. 1 st. at both ends of next row and every foll. alt. row until 88 (92, 94) rem.*
Work straight until armhole is 9 (9½, 10) ins. from beg. of shaping, ending with a 2nd patt. row.
To Shape Shoulders : —Cast off 9 sts. at beg. of next 4 rows and 8 (9, 10) sts. at beg. of foll. 2 rows. Leave sts. on a stitch-holder.

FRONT :
—Work as given for the Back from * to *. Cont. straight until armhole measures 6¼ (6½, 6¾) ins. from beg. of shaping, ending with a 2nd patt. row.
To Divide for Neck : —*Next row :* —Patt. 34 (35, 36) sts., turn leaving the remaining sts. on a spare needle.

Work on first set of sts. as follows : —
** Dec. 1 st. at neck edge on every row until
26 (27, 28) sts. rem. Work straight until armhole is same depth as back armholes to beg.
of shoulder shaping, ending at armhole edge.
To Shape Shoulder: — Cast off 9 sts. at beg.
of next row and foll. alt. row. Work one row,
then cast off. **
Return to the sts. left on spare needle and with
right side of work facing, slip next 20 (22, 22)
sts. on to a stitch-holder. Join yarn to next st.
and patt. to end of row.
Now work as for first side from ** to **.

SLEEVES : —
Cast on 56 (60, 64) sts. with No. 10 [3] needles and work 3½ ins. in k. 1, p. 1 rib.
Change to No. 8 [5] needles and work 8
rows in patt. as given for the Back, then inc.
1 st. at both ends of the next row and every foll.
6th row, until there are 86 (92, 96) sts. Work
straight until sleeve measures 18½ (19½, 20)
ins. from cast-on edge, ending with a 2nd.
patt. row.
To Shape Top: — Cast off 5 sts. at beg. of
next 2 rows. Dec. 1 st. at both ends of next row
and every foll. alt. row until 44 (48, 50) sts.
rem. then dec. 1 st. at both ends of every row
until 40 (42, 44) sts. rem. Cast off 2 sts. at beg.
of next 4 rows. Cast off.

NECKBAND : —
Join right shoulder seam. With right side of
work facing join yarn to neck at left front shoulder, then with No. 10 [3] needles pick up and
k. 34, (35, 37) sts. from left neck edge, k. the
sts. from holder, pick up and k. 34 (35, 37) sts.
from right neck edge, then k. the back neck
sts. from holder: 124 (130, 134) sts.
Work 24 rows k. 1, p. 1 rib. Cast off loosely in
rib.
To make up
Join left shoulder seam, set in sleeves, then
join side and sleeve seams. Double neckband
to wrong side and hem neatly into position.
Press all seams.

SLIP STITCH SWEATER

Materials : —13 (14, 15) ozs. Sirdar Double Crêpe in Ivory ; 6 ozs. Green ; 4 ozs. Brown ;
a pair each of Nos. 9 [4] and 11 [2] knitting
needles.

Measurements : —Bust : 34 (36, 38) ins. ;
Length : 24 (24½, 25) ins. ; Sleeve : 17 ins.

Tension : —6½ sts. and 10 rows to 1 inch over
pattern. 6 sts. and 8 rows over st.st.

Abbreviations : —See page 20.

BACK
With No. 11 [2] needles and Ivory, cast on
116 (124, 132) sts. Work in k. 2, p. 2 rib for
23 rows. On next row inc. 3 sts. evenly across
row. (119, 127, 135) sts. Change to No. 9 [4]
needles and work in tri-colour patt. thus :
1st row : —With Ivory, K.
2nd row : —With Ivory, K. 3, insert needle into
next st. as if to knit, wrap yarn 3 times round
needle, then k. the st. keeping extra loops on
needle. (this will now be called K. 1-3 wraps).
* k. 7, k. 1-3 wraps, rep. from * to last 3 sts.,
k. 3.
3rd row : —With Green, K. 3, sl. 1 purlwise,
with yarn at back of work, drop extra loops
off needle, * K. 7, sl. 1, dropping extra loops,
rep. from * to last 3 sts., k. 3.
4th row : —With Green, P. 3, sl. 1 purlwise
with yarn at front, * p. 7, sl. 1 with yarn at front,
rep. from * to last 3 sts., p. 3.
5th row : —With Brown, K. 3, sl. 1 with yarn
at back, * K. 7, sl. 1 with yarn at back, rep. from
* to last 3 sts., k. 3.
6th row : —With Brown, * K. 3, sl. 1 y. f., k. 3,
k. 1-3 wraps, rep. from * ending k. 3, sl. 1, k. 3.
7th row : —With Green, * K. 3, sl. 1, y. b., k. 3,
sl. 1, drop extra loops, rep. from * ending k. 3,
sl. 1, k. 3.
8th row : —With Green, P. 3, * sl. 1, y. f., p. 3,
rep. from * to end.
9th row : —With Ivory, K. 7, * sl. 1, y. b., k. 7,
rep. from * to end.
10th row : —With Ivory, * K. 3, k. 1-3 wraps,
k. 3, sl. 1, y. f., rep. from * ending k. 3, k. 1-3
wraps, k. 3.
11th row : —With Green, * K. 3, sl. 1, y. b., drop
extra loops, k. 3, sl. 1, y. b., rep. from * ending
k. 3, sl. 1 drop extra loops, k. 3.
12th row : —With Green, P. 3, * sl. 1, y. f.,
p. 3, rep. from * to end. Rep. 5th to 12th rows
of patt. Cont. until Back measures 16½ ins.
from beg., ending with a wrong-side row.

To Shape Armholes: —Cast off 12 sts. at beg. of next 2 rows. Cont. without further shaping until armhole measures 7½ (8, 8½) ins., ending with a wrong-side row.

To Shape Shoulders: —Cast off 9 (10, 11) sts. at beg. of next 4 rows and 10 (11, 12) sts. at beg. of foll. 2 rows. Leave rem. sts. on a spare needle.

FRONT

Work as for Back until armholes measure 5¼ (5¾, 6¼) ins., ending with a wrong-side row.

To Shape Neck: —*Next row:* —Work 37 (40, 43) sts. and leave them on a spare needle, work the next 21 (23, 25) sts. and leave on a stitch-holder, work to end, turn. Cont. on the first set of sts. Dec. 1 st. at neck edge on next 9 rows. Now cont. straight until armhole measures same as back armhole, ending at armhole edge.

To Shape Shoulders: —Cast off 9 (10, 11) sts. at beg. of next 2 wrong-side rows, and cast off rem. 10 (11, 12) sts. on next wrong-side row. Rejoin yarn to sts. on spare needle at neck edge and work this side to match, reversing shapings.

SLEEVES

With No. 11 [2] needles and Ivory cast on 64 (68, 72) sts., Work in k. 2, p. 2 rib for 24 rows. Change to No. 9 [4] needles and work another 4 rows rib. Cont. in rib and inc. 1 st. at each end of next and every foll. 6th row 17 times in all. Cont. straight until sleeve measures 19 ins. from beg.

To Shape Top: Cast off 6 sts. at beg. of next 12 rows. Cast off rem. sts.

COLLAR

Join right shoulder seam. With right side facing, and with No. 11 [2] needles, and Ivory, pick up and k. 26 (25, 24) sts. down left side of front neck, 21 (23, 25) sts. from stitch holder, 26 (25, 24) sts. up right side of front neck and 39 (41, 43) sts. from spare needle at back of neck. Work in k. 2, p. 2 rib for 2 ins. Change to No. 9 [4] needles and cont. in rib until collar measures 5 ins. Cast off in rib.

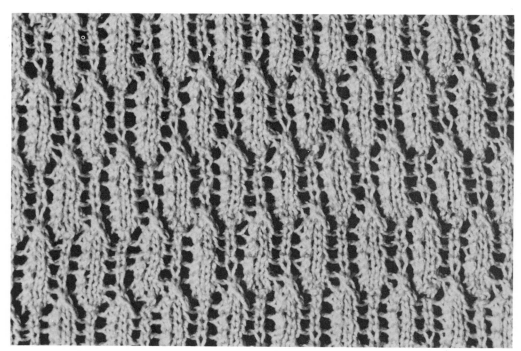

Detail of the lace stitch
for lacy cotton jumper

To make up

Press pieces on wrong side with a warm iron over a damp cloth, omitting ribbing. Join left shoulder seam. Join edges of collar. Set in sleeves, setting last 2 ins. into cast off sts. at underarm. Join side and sleeve seams. Press seams.

LACY COTTON JUMPER

Materials: — 11 (12, 13) balls of Coats Chain Mercer Crochet cotton No. 20.; a pair of No. 14 [00] knitting needles.

Measurements: — Bust: 34 (36, 38) ins.; Length: 21 (21½, 22) ins.; Sleeve: 17 ins.

Tension: — 11 sts. and 12 rows to 1 inch measured over pattern.

Abbreviations: — See page 20.

BACK

Cast on 175 (187, 199) sts. and work 10 rows in g.st. Inc. 24 sts. evenly on last row: 199 (211, 223) sts. Now work in patt. thus: *1st row*: —K. 1, * k. 2 tog., y.fwd., k. 1, y.fwd., sl. 1, k. 1, p. s. s. o., k. 1, rep. from * to end of row. *2nd row*: —P. Rep. 1st and 2nd rows 3 times. *9th row*: —K. 2 tog., * y.fwd., k. 3, y.fwd., sl. 1, k. 2 tog., p. s. s. o., rep. from * to last 5 sts., y.fwd., k. 3, y.fwd., k. 2 tog. *10th row*: —P. *11th row*: —K. 1, * y.fwd., sl. 1, k. 1, p. s. s. o., k. 1, k. 2 tog., y. fwd., k. 1, rep. from * to end. *12th row*: —P. Rep. 11th and 12th rows 3 times. *19th row*: —K. 2, * y.fwd., sl. 1, k. 2 tog., p. s. s. o., y. fwd., k. 3, rep. from * ending last rep. k. 2. *20th row*: —P. These 20 rows form the patt. Cont. in patt. until Back measures 14 ins.

To Shape Armholes: —Keeping patt. correct cast off 12 sts. at beg. of next 2 rows. Now dec. 1 st. at the beg. of every row until 151 (163, 175) sts. rem. Work without further shaping until armhole measures 7 (7½, 8) ins. from beg.
To Shape Shoulders: —Cast off 12 sts. at beg. of next 4 rows. Cast off.

FRONT

Work as Back until armhole measures 5½ (6, 6½) ins. from beg., ending with a wrong-side row.

To Shape Neck: —Patt. 24 sts., cast off 103 (115, 127) sts., patt. to end. Cont. on the last set of sts. until armhole measures the same as Back to beg. of shoulder shaping.
To Shape Shoulder: —Cast off 12 sts. at beg. of next and foll. alt. row. With wrong side facing, rejoin yarn to remaining sts. and work to match first side, reversing shapings.

SLEEVES

Cast on 67 (73, 79) sts. and work 10 rows in g.st. Inc. 12 sts. evenly across last row. Work in patt. as for Back and inc. 1 st. at each end of 3rd and every foll. 6th row until there are 139 (145, 151) sts. on needle. Work without further shaping until sleeve measures 17 ins. from beg., ending with same patt. row as Back to armhole shaping.
To Shape Top: —Cast off 12 sts. at beg. of next 2 rows. Now dec. 1 st. at each end of foll. 12 rows. Then dec. 1 st. at each end of every foll. alt. row until 67 (73, 79) sts. rem. Cast off 3 sts. at beg. of every row until 19 sts. rem. Cast off.

NECKBAND

Join left shoulder seam. With right side facing, pick up and k. 92 (100, 108) sts. along back of neck, 18 sts. down left neck edge, 92 (100, 108) sts., along front of neck and 18 sts. up right neck edge. *1st row*: —K. 16, k. 2 tog., twice, k. 88 (96, 104), k. 2 tog. twice, k. 108 (116, 124) sts. *2nd row*: —K. 107 (115, 123) sts., k. 2 tog. twice, k. 86 (94, 102), k. 2 tog. twice, k. 15. *3rd row*: —K. 14, k. 2 tog. twice, k. 84 (92, 100), k. 2 tog. twice, k. 106 (114, 122). *4th row*: —K. 105 (113, 121), k. 2 tog. twice, k. 82 (90, 98), k. 2 tog. twice, k. 13. Cast off loosely.

To make up

Press pieces. Join side and sleeve seams. Join right shoulder and set in sleeves.

STRIPED SHORTIE

Materials: — 7 (8, 8) ozs. of Lister Lavenda Double Knitting Wool in Purple; 2 (2, 3) ozs. each in tan, blue and pink; a pair each of Nos. 9 [4] and 10 [3] knitting needles; 2 buttons; a press fastener.

Measurements: —Bust: 34 (36, 38) ins.; Length: 18 (18½, 18½) ins.; Sleeve: 6 ins.

Tension: —6 sts. and 8 rows to 1 inch on No. 9 [4] needles.

Abbreviations: —See page 20.

BACK

With No. 10 [3] needles and purple, cast on 91 (97, 103) sts. and work in rib. 1st row: — K. 2, *p. 1, k. 1, rep. from * to last st., k. 1. *2nd row:* —K. 1, *p. 1, k. 1, rep. from * to end. Rep. these 2 rows, 4 times more. Change to No. 9 [4] needles and tan. Beg. with a k. row, work in st.st. in stripes of 8 rows tan, 8 rows blue, 8 rows pink and 8 rows purple throughout. When 12 rows of first stripe have been worked, inc. 1 st. at each end of next and every foll. 8th row until there are 107 (113, 119) sts. on needle. Work without further shaping until Back measures 11 ins. from beg., ending with a p. row.

To Shape Armholes: —Cast off 4 (5, 6) sts. at beg. of next 2 rows and 5 sts. at beg. of next 4 rows. Now work straight until work measures 18 (18½, 18½) ins. from beg.

To Shape Shoulders: —Cast off 7 (8, 9) sts. at beg. of next 4 rows and 8 sts. at beg. of foll. 2 rows. Cast off rem. sts. for back of neck.

LEFT FRONT

With No. 10 [3] needles cast on with purple, 83 (87, 91) sts. and work 9 rows in rib, as for Back. *10th row:* — Rib 8 and slip these sts. on to a safety-pin and leave for front border. Cont. along row, increasing into next st. and ribbing to end.

** Change to No. 9 [4] needles and tan. Work in striped pattern as before but when 4th row has been worked, begin front edge shaping. Dec. 1 st. at end of next row and every alt. row 34 (35, 36) times. Then dec. 1 st. at same edge on every foll. 4th row 14 times. *At the same time*, inc. 1 st. at beg. of 13th row and at same edge (side edge) on every foll. 8th row until 8 increases have been worked at this edge. Cont. to dec. at front edge and keep side edge straight until work measures 11 ins. from beg. and stripes match those of back, ending at side edge.

To Shape Armhole: —Cast off 4 (5, 6) sts.

at beg. of next row and 5 sts. at same edge on next 2 alt. rows. Keeping this edge straight, cont. with front edge decreasing until they are completed. Cont. straight on the rem. 22 (24, 26) sts. until work measures 18 (18½, 18½) ins. from beg. and stripes match those of back, ending at side edge.

To Shape Shoulder: —Cast off 7 (8, 9) sts. at beg. of next row and foll. alt. row. Work 1 row and cast off rem. sts. Slip the 8 sts. for front border on to No, 10 [3] needles and join in purple. Work in rib until strip fits, slightly stretched, along front edge to shoulder. Work a further 2¾ ins. Cast off in rib.**

RIGHT FRONT

Work as for Left Front for 9 rows. *10th row:* —Rib 74 (78, 82) sts., inc. in next st., turn and slip remaining 8 sts. on to a safety-pin for border. Cont. on remaining 76 (80, 84) sts. of main part as given for left front from ** to **, reversing shapings.

SLEEVES

With No. 10 [3] needles and purple, cast on 69 (73, 77) sts. and work in rib as for Back for 10 rows. Change to No. 9 [4] needles and still with purple, cont. in rib but inc. 1 st. at each end of every foll. 4th row until there are 85 (89, 93) sts. Now cont. without further shaping until sleeve measures 6 ins. from beg. Place marker loops of contrast colour on needle at each end of last row. Now work 20 (22, 24) rows straight.

To Shape Top: —Cast off 4 sts. in rib at beg. of next 16 rows. Cast off rem. sts.

To make up

Press pieces, avoiding ribbing. Join shoulder seams. Sew in sleeves, matching markers to beg. of armhole casting off, so that the cast off sts. are joined to straight rows of sleeves above markers. Remove markers from sleeve tops. Join side seams, matching stripes. Join sleeve seams. Join front border strips at back of neck and sew borders carefully to front edges. Lay garment flat, with seams level and wrap right front over left. Sew a button to point on left front and make a button loop on right front. Sew a button to matching point on right front and the press fastener to hold underwrap. Press seams.

Boy's Roll Neck Sweater

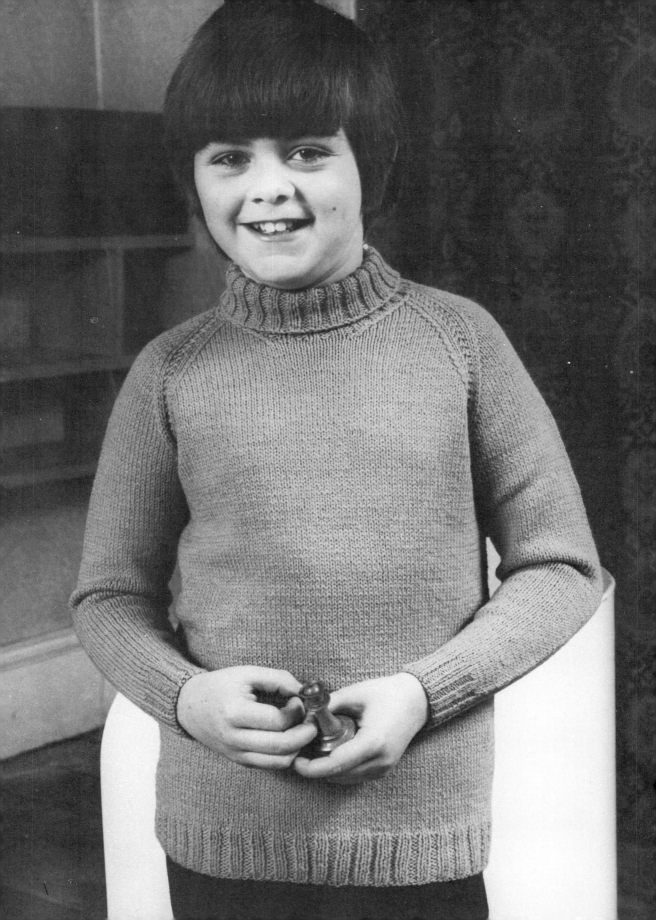

BOY'S ROLL NECK SWEATER

Materials: —13 (14, 15) ozs. Lister Lavenda Double Knitting Wool; a pair each of Nos. 9 [4] and 11 [2] knitting needles.

Measurements: —Chest: 30 (32, 34) ins.; Length: 22 (23, 24) ins.; Sleeve: 14 (15, 16) ins.

Tension: —6 sts. and 8 rows to 1 inch on No. 9 [4] needles.

Abbreviations: —See page 20.

BACK
With No. 9 [4] needles, cast on 92 (100, 108) sts. and work as follows: *1st row*: —* K. 1, p. 2, k. 1, rep. from * to end. *2nd row*: —* P. 1, k. 2, p. 1, rep. from * to end. Rep. last 2 rows until work measures 2 ins. Change to st. st. and cont. until Back measures 14 (14½, 15) ins. from beg.
To Shape Raglan: —With right side facing, cast off 5 (6, 7) sts. at beg. of next 2 rows. *Next row*: —K. 2, s. k. p. o., k. to last 4 sts., k. 2 tog., k. 2. *Next row*: —K. 1, p. to last st., k. 1.
** Rep. the last 2 rows until 30 (32, 34) sts. rem. Leave these sts. on spare needle.

FRONT
Work as Back as far as ** Rep. last 2 rows until 50 (52, 54) sts. rem.
To Shape Neck: —With right side facing, *1st row*: —K. 2, s. k. p. o., k. 16, turn. *2nd row*: —P. to last st., k. 1. *3rd row*: —K. 2, s. k. p. o., k. to last 3 sts., k. 2 tog., k. 1. *4th*

row: —As 2nd row. Rep. last 2 rows until all sts. are worked off. Return to remaining sts. Slip first 10 (12, 14) sts. on to a safety-pin, rejoin yarn and work to match first side, working s. k. p. o. in place of k. 2 tog., and k. 2 tog., in place of s. k. p. o.

SLEEVES
With No. 11 [2] needles, cast on 40 (44, 48) sts. and work as follows:
Work 2 ins. rib as for Back. Change to No. 9 [4] needles and st. st. Inc. 1 st. at each end of 5th and every foll. 6th row until there are 70 (76, 82) sts. on needle. Cont. straight until sleeve measures 14 (15, 16) ins. from beg.
To Shape Raglan: —With right side facing, cast off 5 (6, 7) sts. at beg. of next 2 rows. Then dec. as for Back raglan until 8 sts. rem. Leave these sts. on a safety-pin.

COLLAR
Join raglan seams, leaving back seam open. With right side facing, rejoin yarn and with No. 11 [2] needles, k. across 8 sts. at top of first sleeve, pick up and k. 18 sts. down to safety-pin, k. across 10 (12, 14) sts. on safety-pin and pick up and k. 18 sts. up right front, k. across 8 sts. at top of second sleeve and k. across 30 (32, 34) sts. at back of neck. Work in rib until collar measures 4 ins. Cast off in rib.

To make up
Press pieces, avoiding ribbing. Join remaining raglan seam. Join side and sleeve seams. Press seams.

Simple Additions

SIMPLE ADDITIONS

If you are just learning to knit, you may find you can manage a good garment, but in plain stocking stitch. Beginner and expert alike can add something to the plainest piece of work with very little effort.

Saddle stitching can outline a collar or the edges of a jacket. In the case of the little dress for a small girl on page 59 it definitely adds to the attraction.

The Emerald cap and scarf on page 22 is quite simple and absolutely straight knitting, so is easy enough for a beginner and smart enough for anyone to wear. The pattern was added in Swiss darning and it makes the set look quite a complicated piece of Fair Isle knitting.

To add the pattern to this cap and scarf follow chart No. 4. Sketch No. 33 will show you the method.

If you thought that beads needed to be sewn on after a garment was finished, take heart. It is easy to knit them in as you go. The design you use can be as simple or as complicated as you feel inclined to tackle. In any case, beads can add sparkle to your knitting with very little trouble.

BEADED KNITTING

Plain evening garments can be given that added touch of sparkle with bead knitting.

Knitting beads are available and have extra large holes. They are threaded on to each ounce of yarn, before starting to work.

For a solid band of beads on the reverse side of stocking stitch, work as follows. Purl a stitch in usual way, push a bead into position, purl next stitch. Continue in this way to the end of the row. Knit the next row without beads. Continue until band is required width. (sketch No. 34) To place beads on smooth side of stocking stitch, work in this way. On a purl row, purl to bead position, yarn to back of work, push bead into position, k. 1, yarn to front of work, purl to next bead position. Simple charts may be followed, using beads instead of coloured stitches.

SWISS DARNING

If you find Fair Isle and coloured knitting difficult, you may find it easier to add colour in this way.

Any chart may be followed and any number of colours used.

The garment is knitted in plain stocking stitch and the pattern added afterwards in Swiss darning, so that it looks like a knitted pattern. The darning stitch follows the path of the knitted stitch. Thread a large eyed, blunt pointed needle with the required colour. Insert needle into base of stitch, from the back of work, pass needle behind the two threads forming the stitch and down again into base from front. Continue in this way until required stitches are covered. (sketch No. 33) The blue sweater on page 59 was worked in this way for the vertical stripes and the pattern of the Emerald cap and scarf added in the same way.

Sketch No. 33

Insert needle through bottom of stitch to be worked, then behind the two threads forming the stitch and then down into base of stitch again (sketch No. 33)

Sketch No. 34

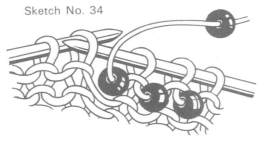

Adding beads as you knit a purl row

BEADED EVENING SWEATER

Materials: —17 ozs., Wendy 4-ply Nylonised a pair each Nos. 11 [2] and 12 [1] knitting needles; Approx. 1200 pearl beads.

Measurements: — Bust: 34-36 inch; Length from shoulder: 25 ins.; Sleeve: 18 ins.

Tension: —7 sts. and 10 rows to 1 inch on No. 11 [2] needles.

Abbreviations: —See page 20.

BACK AND FRONT ALIKE

Thread approx 300 beads on to each of 4 ozs. Yarn.

With No. 12 [1] needles, cast on 145 sts. and beg. with a k. row, work 9 rows st.st. K. next row for hemline. Join in beaded yarn. Change to No. 11 [2] needles. *1st row:* —K. 1, * Bead 1, k. 11, rep. from * to end. *2nd and alt. rows:* — P. *3rd row:* —K. 2, *bead 1, k. 9, bead 1, k. 1, rep. from * to last 11 sts. bead 1, k. 10. *5th row:* —*K. 3, bead 1, k. 7, bead 1, rep. from * to last 13 sts., k. 3, bead 1, k. 9. *7th row:* —K. 4, * bead 1, k. 5, rep. from * to last 3 sts., bead 1, k. 2. *9th row:* —K. 5, *bead 1, k. 3, bead 1, k. 7, rep. from * to last 8 sts., bead 1, k. 3, bead 1, k. 3. *11th row:* —K. 6, * bead 1, k. 1, bead 1, k. 9, rep. from * to last 7 sts., bead 1, k. 1, bead 1, k. 4. *13th row:* —K. 7, * bead 1, k. 11, rep. from * to last 6 sts., bead 1, k. 5. *15th row:* —As 11th. *17th row:* —As 9th *19th row:* —As 7th. *21st row:* —As 5th. *23rd row:* —As 3rd. *25th row:* —As 1st. Join in an unbeaded ball of yarn and break off the beaded yarn. Cont. in st. st. Beg. with a p. row and work until piece measures 17½ ins. from hemline. *To Shape Armholes:* —Cast off 4 sts. at beg. of next 2 rows and dec. 1 st. at each end of every row until 101 sts. rem. Cont. without further shaping until work measures 25 ins. from hemline.

To Shape For Shoulders: —Cast off 9 sts. at beg. of next 2 rows, then cast off 10 sts. at beg. of foll. 2 rows. Purl next row to mark hemline of neck. Change to No. 12 [1] needles and work 7 rows st.st., beg. with a p. row. Cast off. Work another piece to match.

SLEEVES

With No. 12 [1] needles, cast on 125 sts. and work hem as for back and front. Change to No. 11 [2] needles and beaded yarn. Work in beaded patt. as for Back for 26 rows. 1st row will read: —K. 2 * bead 1, k. 11, rep. from * to last 3 sts., bead 1, k. 2. *2nd and all alt. rows:* P. *3rd row:* —K. 1, bead 1, k. 1, * bead 1, k. 9, bead 1, k. 1, rep. from * to last 2 sts., bead 1, k. 1. *5th row:* —K. 4, * bead 1, k. 7, bead 1, k. 3, rep. from * to last st. k. 1. Cont. with beaded patt. as now set until 26 rows have been worked. Break off beaded yarn and join in unbeaded yarn. *Next row:* —K. 1, *k. 2 tog., p. u. k., k. 10, rep. from * to last 4 sts., k. 2 tog., p. u. k. k. 2. *Next row:* —P. Now work lace patt. *1st row:* —* K. 2 tog., y. fwd., k. 1, y. fwd., k. 2 tog. t.b.l., k. 7, rep. from * to last 5 sts., k. 2 tog., y. fwd., k. 1, y. fwd., k. 2 tog. t. b. l. *2nd and alt. rows:* —P. *3rd row:* —K. 4, * y.fwd., k. 2 tog. t. b. l., k. 5, k. 2 tog., y.fwd., k. 3, rep. from * to last st., k. 1. *5th row:* —K. 2 tog., k. 3, * y.fwd., k. 2 tog., t. b. l., k. 3, k. 2 tog., y.fwd., k. 5, rep. from * to last 12 sts., y.fwd., k. 2 tog. t. b. l., k. 3, k. 2 tog., y.fwd., k. 3, k. 2 tog. (123 sts.) *7th row:* —K. 5, * y.fwd., k. 2 tog. t. b. l., k. 1, k. 2 tog., y.fwd., k. 7, rep. from * to last 10 sts. y.fwd., k. 2 tog. t. b. l., k. 1, k. 2 tog., y.fwd., k. 5. *9th row:* —K. 6, * y.fwd., k. 3 tog., y.fwd., k. 9, rep. from * to last 9 sts., y.fwd., k. 3 tog., y.fwd., k. 6. *11th row:* —K. 5, * k. 2 tog., y. fwd., k. 1, y. fwd., k. 2 tog. t. b. l., k. 7, rep. from * to last 10 sts., k. 2 tog., y. fwd., k. 1, y. fwd., k. 2 tog. t. b. l., k. 5. *13th row:* —K. 4, * k. 2 tog., y. fwd., k. 3, y. fwd., k. 2 tog. t. b. l., k. 5, rep. from * to last 11 sts., k. 2 tog., y. fwd., k. 3, y. fwd., k. 2 tog. t. b. l., k. 4. *15th row:* —K. 2 tog., k. 1, * k. 2 tog., y. fwd., k. 5, y. fwd., k. 2 tog. t. b. l., k. 3, rep. from * to last 12 sts., k. 2 tog., y.fwd., k. 5, y. fwd., k. 2 tog. t. b. l., k. l. k. 2 tog. (121 sts.) *17th row:* —K. 1, * k. 2 tog., y. fwd., k. 7, y. fwd., k. 2 tog. t. b. l., k. 1. rep. from * to end. *19th row:* —K. 2 tog., y. fwd., * k. 9, y. fwd., k. 3 tog., y. fwd., rep. from * to last 2 sts. k. 2 tog. t. b. l. *20th row:* —P. Cont. to keep patt. correct and dec. 1 st. at each end of every 10th row until 93 sts. rem. and work measures 18 ins. from hemline.

To Shape Top: —Cast off 4 sts. at beg. of next 2 rows. Now dec. 1 st. at each end of next and every alt. row until 49 sts. rem. Purl 1 row. Now dec. 1 st. at each end of every row until 29 sts. rem. Cast off.

To make up

Press pieces, avoiding beaded parts. Join shoulder, side and sleeve seams. Set in sleeves. Turn hems to wrong side and catch down. Press seams.

BLUE SWEATER WITH SWISS DARNING

Mainly in stocking stitch, the horizontal stripes are knitted as you go along. The vertical stripes are worked in Swiss Darning, or you could use chain stitch embroidery. It is an easy way to work checked fabric

Materials: —18 (20, 22) ozs. of Sirdar Double Knitting Wool in Blue and 1 oz. each in Black and White; a pair each of Nos. 9 [4] and 11 [2] knitting needles.

Measurements: —Bust: 34 (36, 38) ins.; Length: 21½ (22, 22½) ins.; Sleeve: 18 ins.

Tension: —6 sts. and 8 rows to 1 inch over st.st.

Abbreviations: —See page 20.

BACK AND FRONT ALIKE

With No. 11 [2] needles and Blue, cast on 114 (118, 122) sts. Work in k. 2, p. 2 rib. *1st row*: —K. 2, * p. 2, k. 2, rep. from * to end. *2nd row*: —P. 2, *k. 2, p. 2 rep. from * to end. Rep. these 2 rows for 2 ins. Change to No. 9 [4] needles and st.st. Work 18 rows. Cont. in st.st. and work in stripes as folls. * 1 row White, 3 rows Blue, 1 row Black, 3 rows Blue, 1 row white, 3 rows Blue, 1 row Black, 3 rows Blue, 1 row White. * Now work 35 (37, 39) rows Blue, then rep. from * to * once. Purl 1 row Blue.
To Shape Armholes: —With Blue, cast off 9 sts. at beg. of next 2 rows. Work 32 (34, 36) rows straight, then rep. from * to * once again. With Blue, work 12 rows straight.
To Divide for Neck: —Next row: —P. 35 (37, 39), cast off next 26 sts., p. to end. Work on last set of sts.
** *Next row:* —Work to last 2 sts., k. 2 tog. *Next row:* —Cast off 8 sts., work to end. Rep. last 2 rows once.

To Shape Shoulder: —Next row: —Cast off 4 (5, 6) sts., work to last 2 sts., work 2 tog. *Next row:* —Cast off 8 sts., work to end. Cast off. ** Rejoin yarn to inner end of remaining sts. and k. 1 row. Now work as first side from ** to **.

NECKBAND

With right side facing, join Blue and with No 11 [2] needle, pick up and k. 122 sts. across neck edge. Work rib as for Back, starting with 2nd row. Dec. 1 st. at each end of every row until 84 sts. rem. Cast off in rib.

SLEEVES

With No. 11 [2] needles and Blue, cast on 58 (62, 66) sts. and work in rib as for Back for 3½ ins. Change to No. 9 [4] needles and keeping rib correct, inc. 1 st. at each end of next and every foll. 6th row until there are 94 (98, 102) sts. Cont. without further shaping until sleeve measures 17½ ins. from beg. Now inc. 1 st. at each end of next 4 rows. Mark each end of last row with contrasting thread for top of sleeve seam.
Work another 1½ ins. straight. Cast off.

To make up

Press pieces. Work vertical lines in Swiss darning to complete plaid pattern. Use black and white in turn as shown in the colour picture on page 73. Begin at the top of the welt and work to top of sweater, spacing the lines evenly. Follow instructions for Swiss darning on page 57.
Join shoulder seams, including shaped edges of neckband. Set in sleeves, placing straight sleeve edges above the markers to the cast-off edge of armholes. Join side and sleeve seams.

LITTLE GIRL'S PLEATED DRESS

Materials: —7 (7, 8) 1 oz. balls of Sirdar Talisman 4-ply in main colour and 1 oz. in White; a pair of No. 10 [3] knitting needles; 4 small buttons; press fasteners.

Measurements: —Chest: 20 (22, 24) ins.; Length: 13 (15, 17) ins.; Sleeve: 8 (9, 10) ins.

Tension: —14 sts., and 19 rows to 1 inch.

Abbreviations : —See page 20.

FRONT

With No. 10 [3] needles and main colour, cast on 142 (150, 158) sts. *1st Row:* —K. *2nd row:* —P. *3rd row:* —K. 29 (31, 33), p. u. k., k. 2 tog. t. b. l., K. 4, p. u. k., k. 2 tog. t. b. l., k. 8, k. 2 tog., p. u. k., k. 4, k. 2 tog., p. u. k., * k. 36, (40, 44), rep. from * to * k. 29 (31, 33). *4th row:* —P. Rep. last 2 rows twice, then 3rd row once. *Next row:* —K. for hemline. Keeping panel as set, dec. 1 st. at each end of 13th and every 10th (12th, 14th) row foll. until 130 (136, 142) sts. rem. Cont. until work measures 9 (10½, 12) ins. from hem, ending on a wrong-side row.

To Shape Armholes: —Cast off 4 sts. at beg. of next 2 rows, then dec. 1 st. at each end of next and foll. 2 (3, 4) alt. rows. *Next row:* —P. *Now work thus:* —Work 40 sts., turn, p. 24, turn, k. 24, turn, p. 24, turn and cast off 24. With right side facing, rejoin yarn and work 60 (64, 68) sts., turn, p. 24, turn, k. 24, turn, p. 24, turn, cast off 24. With right side facing, rejoin yarn and work 16 sts. *Next 3 rows:* —K. ** Cont. in st. st., beg. with a k. row, for 2 (2¼, 2¼) ins., ending with a p. row.

To Shape Neck: —K. 26 (28, 30) sts., turn and p. to end. Dec. 1 st. at neck edge on next and every alt. row until 22 (24, 26) sts. rem., ending with a p. row.

To Shape Shoulder: —Cast off 11 (12, 13) sts. at beg. of 1st and 3rd rows. Slip next 16 sts. at centre neck, on to a safety-pin. Rejoin yarn to rem. sts. and work to match left side of neck.

BACK

Work as for Front as far as **.
Divide for Back opening.

Next row: —K. 36 (38, 40) sts., turn. k. 4, p. to end. Working on these sts. only, rep. last 2 rows until armhole measures the same as Front armhole, ending at armhole edge.

To Shape Shoulder: —Cast off 11 (12, 13) sts. at beg. of 1st and 3rd rows. *Next Row:* —Cast off 2, k. 2, p. to end. Leave these sts. on a spare needle.

Rejoin yarn to remaining sts. at centre back. Cast on 4, k. to end. *Next row:* —P. to last 4 sts., k. 4. Rep. last 2 rows until armhole matches other side, ending at armhole edge.

SLEEVES

Cast on 38 (42, 46) sts. and work in st. st., increasing 1 st. at each end of 7th and every 8th row until there are 54 (60, 66) sts. on needle. Cont. until sleeve measures 8 (9, 10) ins. from beg.

To Shape Top: —Cast off 4 sts. at beg. of next 2 rows. Then dec. 1 st. at each end of next and foll. 2 (3, 4) alt. rows.

Next row: —P. Now cast off 5 sts. at beg. of next 6 rows. Cast off rem. sts.

COLLAR

Join shoulder seams. With white, and with right side of work facing, k. across 12 sts. at back of left side, pick up and k. 13 (14, 15) sts. down left side of neck, across 16 sts. at centre, pick up and k. 13 (14, 15) sts. up right side of neck and k. across 12 sts. at back of neck. *Next row:* —K. *Next row:* —K., inc. 1 st. at each end. Rep. last 2 rows 3 times. K. 6 rows. Cast off.

LEFT CUFF

With white, cast on 40 (44, 48) sts., and k. 4 rows. *Next row:* —Inc. 1 st. at beg., k. to end. *Next row:* —K. to last st., k. twice into last st. Rep. last 2 rows twice. *Next row:* —Dec. 1 st. at beg. of row, k. to end. *Next row:* —K. to last 2 sts., k. 2 tog. Rep. last 2 rows twice. Cast off. Make right cuff to match, reversing shaping.

To make up

Press pieces. Sew top of pleats at back of yoke. Sew in sleeves, join side and sleeve seams. Turn up hem. Sew down bottom of button flap.

Add press fasteners and buttons.

Using 2 strands of white yarn, embroider a row of saddle stitching down each side of pleats and across yoke. Add cuffs to sleeves and sew a button to each cuff. Press seams.

Traditional Knitting

TRADITIONAL PATTERNS

Many countries have their own particular patterns for which they have become well known throughout the world.

Perhaps the most sought after are those from Fair Isle and the island of Aran. Both are quite distinctive and quite different.

The true Fair Isle sweater will be in many colours and each band of pattern will be different. The knitter used her own taste and imagination to make her unique garment. It might start with seed stitch, and be followed by water stitch, to water the seed of life. This, in the natural course of events would be followed by the flower. One needs help and guidance through life, so an anchor motif might be used, or a star, to guide, perhaps a heart or a cross as a reminder of one's faith. Finally, if the life is well lived, the reward would be the crown of glory and this would decorate the shoulder of the sweater.

The dyes for the soft colours would be made from the natural materials at hand on the island. Shell fish would provide the pinks, seaweed, mosses and lychens make the browns and greens and yellows. So the whole product was of the island.

A Shetland sweater differed in that it was an all over pattern. The same band might be repeated in different shades of the natural wool. Since the sheep of the island came in all the shades, from cream and brown, right through to black, these were the shades used. With modern methods now, the wool is dyed and a Shetland sweater may be in any colour.

Shetland lace was different again, the patterns never written down but handed from mother to daughter and worked into the garment as taste or fancy dictated. The softest wool comes from the neck of the Shetland sheep. It is plucked and not sheared and is used for the finest ring shawls. These are made of finely spun wool in a combination of beautiful lace stitches and a 72 inch square shawl is so fine it will pass through a wedding ring.

Aran sweaters were thick and husky to keep out the weather when worn by the fishermen. It is said that it was possible to tell from which village a man came and to which family he belonged and which son he was, just from his sweater.

The true Aran sweater has different bands of pattern on back, front and sleeves and all the stitches used are evocative of the surrounding country and the fisherman's life.

The cables were the ropes and chains of his boat and the lobster claw cable speaks for itself. Zig-zag lines were the twisting rocky paths and the sand and shingle of the beach was represented by moss stitch or block stitches. The stout stone walls which protect the little homesteads from the fierce gales, the rocks, the fisherman's nets are all present in an Aran pattern.

In the following pages there are patterns in the Aran and Fair Isle tradition.

Around the English shores there are many coastal towns which have their own traditional stitches too.

We all have heard of the jersey, originally the traditional garb for the fishermen of the island of the same name. Guernsey also had its sweater and in these traditional pages you will find two sweaters, one for a boy and one for a girl. These are typical of the type of knitting done on the island.

GUERNSEY FOR A GIRL

Materials : 11 (13, 15, 17) balls of Twilley's Cortina ; a pair each of Nos. 11 [2] and 8 [5] knitting needles and a set of 4 double-pointed No. 11 [2] knitting needles.

Measurements : Chest/Bust : 28 (30, 32, 34) ins. ; Length : 19 (20, 21, 22) ins. ; Sleeve : 16 (17, 18, 19) ins.

Tension : 6 sts. and 9 rows to 1 inch on No. 8 [5] needles.

Abbreviations : See page 20.

FRONT

With No. 11 [2] needles and using yarn double cast on 93 (99, 105, 111) sts. Change to single yarn and work in k. 1, p. 1 rib for 3 ins. Change to No. 8 [5] needles and knit 1 row.

2nd row : —For size 28 only : (Right side) K. 5, * k. 1 into row below, k. 1, k. 1 into row below, k. 7, rep. from * ending k. 1 into row below, k. 1, k. 1 into row below, k. 5. *3rd row : —*k. 6, * k. 1 row below, k. 9, rep. from * ending k. 1 row below, k. 6.

2nd row : —Size 30 only. (Right side) K. 1, * k. 7, k. 1 row below, k. 1, k. 1, row below, rep. from * ending k. 8. *3rd row : —* * K. 9, k. 1 row below, rep. from * ending k. 9. *2nd row : —Size 32 only :* (Right side) k. 1, * k. 1 row below, k. 1, k. 1 row below, k. 7, rep. from * ending k. 1 row below, k. 1, k. 1 row below, k. 1. *3rd row : —*K. 2 * k. 1 row below, k. 9, rep. from * ending k. 1 row below, k. 2.

2nd row : —Size 34 only : (Right side) K. 4, * k. 1 row below, k. 1, k. 1 row below, k. 7, rep. from * ending k. 1 row below, k. 1, k. 1 row below, k. 4. *3rd row : —*K. 5 * k. 1 row below, k. 9, rep. from * ending k. 1 row below, k. 5.

Rep. 2nd and 3rd rows of patt. until work measures 15¾ (16½, 17¼, 18) ins.

*To Shape Neck : —*Work 44 (46, 48, 50) sts. in patt. cast off 5 (7, 9, 11) sts., work to end, and complete this side first.

*2nd row : —*Work to neck edge, turn. *3rd row : —*Cast off 4 sts., work to end. *4th row : —*As 2nd. *5th row : —*Cast off 2 sts. work to end. Rep. last 2 rows twice. *10th row : —*Cast off 1 st., work to end. *11th row : —*As 2nd. Rep. last 2 rows twice. When work measures 19 (20, 21, 22) ins. Cast off rem. sts. Rejoin yarn to other side of neck and complete to match first side.

BACK

Work as for Front until Back measures 16¾ (17½, 18, 18½) ins.

*To Shape Neck : —*In patt., work 38 (40, 42, 44) sts., cast off 17 (19, 21, 23) sts., work to end and complete this side first. *2nd row : —*Work to neck edge, turn. *3rd row : —*Cast off 3 sts., work to end. *4th row : —*As 2nd. *5th row : —*Cast off 2 sts., work to end. *6th row : —*As 2nd. When work measures 18 (19, 20, 21) ins. cast off rem. sts. Rejoin yarn to other side of neck and finish to match other side.

SLEEVES

With No. 11 [2] needles and using yarn double, cast on 54 (58, 62, 66) sts. Work 4 ins. k. 1, p. 1 rib. Inc. 1 st. at end of last row. Change to No. 8 [5] needles and knit 1 row. *2nd row : —Size 28 only.* K. 6, * k. 1 row below, k. 1, k. 1 row below, k. 7, rep. from * ending k. 1 row below, k. 1, k. 1 row below, k. 6. *3rd row : —*K. 7, * k. 1 row below, k. 9, rep. from * ending k. 1 row below, k. 7.

2nd and 3rd rows : —Size 30 only. As for Front.

2nd row : —Size 32 only. K. 2, k. 1 row below,

* k. 7, k. 1 row below, k. 1, k. 1 row below, rep. from * ending k. 7, k. 1 row below, k. 2. *3rd row:* — K. 11, * k. 1 row below, k. 9, rep. from * ending k. 1 row below, k. 11.

2nd Row: — *Size 34 only.* K. 4, k. 1 row below, * k. 7, k. 1 row below, k. 1, k. 1 row below, rep. from * ending k. 7, k. 1 row below, k. 4. *3rd row:* — K. 3, * k. 1 row below, k. 9, rep. from * ending k. 1 row below, k. 3.

Cont. in patt. and inc. 1 st. at each end of every 18th row 5 (6, 7, 7) times. When work measures 16 (17, 18, 19) ins., cast off, using yarn double.

COLLAR

Join shoulder seams. With set of No. 11 [2] needles pick up and k. 110 (114, 120, 126) sts. evenly round neck edge. Work in k. 1, p. 1 rib for 7¾ (8, 8¼, 8½) ins. Cast off in rib loosely using yarn double.

To make up

Press pieces with a warm iron over a damp cloth. Join side seams leaving 6½ (7, 7½, 8) ins. for armholes, Join sleeve seams and set in sleeves. Turn hem at lower edge and cuff to wrong side and slip stitch to first row of pattern.

GUERNSEY FOR A BOY

Materials : 10 (12, 14, 16, 17) balls of Twilley's Cortina ; a pair each of Nos. 10 [3] and 12 [1] knitting needles and a set of 4 double-pointed knitting needles No. 12 [1].

Measurements : — Chest: 30 (32, 34, 36, 38) ins. ; Length: 22 (23, 24, 24¾, 25½) ins. ; Sleeve seam: 15 (16, 17, 18, 19) ins.

Tension : — 7 sts. and 8 rows to 1 inch on No. 10 [3] needles.

Abbreviations : — See page 20.

FRONT AND BACK ALIKE

With No. 12 [1] needles and using yarn double, cast on 104 (112, 120, 128, 136) sts. Change to single yarn and work 2 (2, 2¼, 2¼, 2½) ins. k. 2, p. 2 rib. Change to No. 10 [3] needles and stitch No. 1 thus : *1st row:* — K.

2nd row: — P. *3rd and 4th rows:* — K. *5th row:* — P. *6th row:* — K. Rep. these 6 rows twice, then work 3 rows st.st. Change to Stitch No. 2 thus : *1st row:* — K. 2, p. 2 to end of row. *2nd row:* — K. *3rd row:* — P. 2, k. 2 to end of row. *4th row:* — K. Cont. in this stitch until 32 rows of stitch No. 2 have been completed. Now rep. Stitch No. 1 again. Change to Stitch No. 3 thus : *1st row:* — K. 2, p. 2 to end of row. *2nd row:* — P. 1, * k. 2, p. 2, rep. from * to last 3 sts. k. 2, p. 1. *3rd row:* — P. 2, k. 2, to end of row. *4th row:* — K. 1, * p. 2, k. 2, rep. from * to last 3 sts. p. 2, k. 1. Rep. these 4 rows until 16 rows have been completed in all, then reverse the pattern for 16 rows, thus : 3rd row, 2nd row, 1st row, 4th row and repeating the rows in that order.

The stitches are repeated in this order throughout. When work measures 9 (9¼, 9½, 10, 10¼) ins. from beg., start the gusset at each side edge. Inc. 1 st. at each end of every 6th row until 5 (6, 8, 9, 10) sts. have been increased at each side, keeping the increased sts. in st.st. When work measures 15 (15½, 16, 16½, 17) ins. cast off gusset sts. at beg. of next 2 rows. Cont. without further shaping until armhole measures 6¼ (6½, 7, 7¼, 7½) ins.

To Shape Neck: — *1st row:* — Work in patt. for 39 (42, 45, 48, 51) sts., cast off 26 (28, 30, 32, 34) sts., work to end in patt. and complete this side first.

2nd row: — Work to neck edge. *3rd row:* — Cast off 5 sts., work to end. *4th row:* — As 2nd. *5th row:* — Cast off 4 sts. work to end. Work 1 (2, 3, 4, 4) rows more then cast off. Rejoin yarn to other side and complete to match first side.

SLEEVES

Sew shoulder seams and with a No. 10 [3] needle, pick up and k. 90 (100, 110, 120, 130) sts. evenly round the armhole. Work in stitch No. 1, stitch No. 2, stitch No. 1, stitch No. 3, and stitch No. 1. Then cont. in st.st. *At the same time,* dec. 1 st. at each end of every 6th and 4th rows alternately until 58 (70, 80, 86, 92) sts. rem. Cont. until sleeve measures 12 (13, 14, 15, 16) ins. or length required. Change to No. 12 [1] needles and work 3 ins. k. 2, p. 2 rib. Cast off in rib using yarn double.

NECK

With the set of No. 12 [1] needles, pick up

and k. 90 (96, 104, 116, 128) sts. evenly round neck edge. Work 1 (1¼, 1½, 1¾, 2) ins. k. 2, p. 2 rib. Cast off in rib loosely and using yarn double.

To make up
Press pieces with a warm iron over a damp cloth. Join side and sleeve seams. Press seams.

CHILD'S CAP & MITTS

Materials : —2 balls of Lister Lavenda Double Knitting Wool in Pink (main colour); 1 (1, 2) balls white and 1 ball black; a pair each of Nos. 11 [2] and 9 [4] knitting needles.

Measurements : —Cap: (Unstretched) 15 (16, 17) ins. ; Mitts : Top of wrist to finger tip : 4½ (5, 5½) ins.

Tension : —6 sts. and 8 rows to 1 inch on No. 9 [4] needles.

Abbreviations : —See page 20.

CAP
With W. and No. 11 [2] needles, cast on 88 (96, 104) sts. and work 2 rows k. 1, p. 1 rib. Change to No. 9 [4] needles and purl 1 row. Inc. 1 st. at end of row. Now begin patt.
1st row : —(right side) K. 1 B., * K. 2 W., k. 3 M., k. 2 W., k. 1 B., rep. from * to end.
2nd row : —P. 1 W., * p. 1 B., p. 2 W., p. 1 M., p. 2 W., p. 1 B., p. 1 W., rep. from * to end.
3rd row : —K. 1 W., * k. 1 W., k. 1 B., k. 3 W., k. 1 B., k. 2 W., rep. from * to end.
4th row : —P. 1 M., * p. 2 W., (p. 1 B., p. 1 W) twice, p. 1 W., p. 1 M., rep. from * to end.
5th row : —K. 1 M., * K. 1 M., p. 2 W., k. 1 B., k. 2 W., K. 2 M., rep. from * to end.
With W. purl 2 rows to mark ridge for turn-up. Change to No. 11 [2] needles and p. 1 row. Change to M. and work 8 rows in k. 1, p. 1 rib. Change to No. 9 [4] needles and beg. with a p. row, cont. in M. and st. st. and work until 4 (4½, 5) ins. have been completed from turn-up ridge, ending with a p. row. Dec. 1 st. at end of last row.
To Shape Crown : —1st row : —* K. 2 tog., k. 7 (8, 9), s. k. p. o., rep. from * 8 times. P. 1 row, k. 1 row, p. 1 row.

5th row : —* K. 2 tog., k. 5 (6, 7), s. k. p. o., rep. from * 8 times. Cont. to dec. by 16 sts. in same way on every right side row until 24 (16, 24) sts. rem., ending after a p. row. *Next row :* k. 2 tog., to end. Draw yarn through rem. sts. and fasten off securely.

MITTS
With M. and No. 11 [2] needles and cast on 32 (34, 36) sts. and work 15 rows in k. 1, p. 1 rib. *Next row :* P. Change to W. and No. 9 [4] needles. Inc. 1 st. at beg. of next row and work 4 rows st.st., beg. with a k. row.
To Shape Thumb : —and to work colour patt. for right-hand mitt : —*1st row :* —K. 4 (4, 5) W., k. 1 B., k. 2 W., k. 3 M., k. 2 W., k. 1 B., K. 3 (4, 4) W., with W., p. u. k., k. 1, p. u. k., k. 16 (17, 18). *2nd row :* —P. 23 (25, 26) W., p. 1 B., p. 2 W., p. 1 M., p. 2 W., p. 1 B., p. 5 (5, 6) W. *3rd row :* —K. 6 (6, 7) W., k. 1 B., k. 3 W., k. 1 B., k. 5 (6, 6) W., with W., p. u. k., K. 3, p. u. k., k. 16 (17, 18) *4th row :* —P. 27 (29, 30) W., p. 1 B., p. 1 W., p. 1 B., p. 7 (7, 8) W. *5th row :* —K. 5 (5, 6) W., k. 1 M., p. 2 W., k. 1 B., k. 2 W., k. 1 M., k. 4 (5, 5) W., with W., p. u. k., k. 5, p. u. k., k. 16 (17, 18) (39, 41, 43) sts. *6th row :* —In W. purl. Cont. in W. and work another 2 (2, 4) rows st.st. making 2 sts. in same way on k. rows.
To Work thumb : Next row : —k. 25 (26, 29) turn.
Next row : —P. 9 (9, 11) cast on 2, turn. Work another 12 (14, 16) rows in st.st. on these 11 (11, 13) sts. Draw yarn through rem. sts. and fasten off securely.
Hand : —With right side facing join in W. and k. 16 (17, 18) sts. on left hand needle, turn.
Next row : P. 16 (17, 18), pick up and p. 2 sts. from base of thumb, p. remaining 16 (17, 18) sts. *Next row :* —K. 4 (4, 5) W., k. 1 B., k. 2 W., k. 3 M., k. 2 W., k. 1 B., k. 21 (23, 24) W. Complete the 5-row colour patt. on sts. as set. *For 2nd and 3rd sizes :* With W. and beg. with p. row, work 5 (7) rows st. st., and then work 5 patt. rows again. *For all sizes :* —With W. and beg. p. row, cont. in st.st. until work measures 3½ (4, 4½) ins. from top of wrist ribbing, ending with p. row.
Top of hand : —1st row : —* k. 1, k. 2 tog., k. 11 (12, 13), s. k. p. o., k. 1, rep. from * twice.
2nd and alt. rows : P.
3rd row : —* K. 1, k. 2 tog., k. 9 (10, 11),

s. k. p. o., k. 1, rep. from * twice. Now dec. 4 sts. on 5th and 7th rows in same way. Cast off on 9th row.

For Left Hand Mitt: Work as for Right hand, but reading instructions for colour patt. rows from end of row to beg.

To make up

Press pieces. Sew seam at back of head of cap. Sew thumb seam and seam round hand of each mitt. Press seams. Trim cap with a pom-pon.

SHETLAND SWEATER

Materials: —6 (7, 7, 8, 9, 9. 10, 11. 12, 13) ozs. of Templeton's H. & O Shetland Fleece in main shade; 4 (4, 4, 4, 5, 5, 6, 6, 7, 7) ozs. in contrast; a pair each of Nos. 11 [2] and 9 [4] knitting needles.

Measurements: —Chest: 24 (26, 28, 30, 32, 34, 36, 38, 40, 42) ins.; Length: 16 (18, 20, 21½, 22½, 23½. 24½, 25, 26, 26½) ins.; Sleeve: 11½ (12½, 14, 16, 16½, 18, 18, 18½, 19, 19½) ins.

Tension: —7½ sts. and 7 rows to 1 inch over pattern.

Abbreviations: —See page 20.

BACK

With No. 11 [2] needles and main shade, cast on 104 (116, 122, 128, 140, 146, 152, 164, 170, 176) sts. Work in k. 1, p. 1 rib for 1½ (1½, 1½, 2, 2, 2, 2, 2, 2½, 2½) ins. Change to No. 9 [4] needles and work Fair Isle pattern from chart No. 3. Beg. and end each row with 1 st. in main shade for seam allowance and starting chart on 7th st. for 1st, 2nd, 4th, 5th, 7th, 8th and 10th sizes.

When work measures 10 (11½, 13, 14, 14½, 15, 15½, 15½, 16, 16) ins. from beg.

To Shape Armholes: —Keeping pattern correct, cast off 6 (7, 7, 7, 8, 8, 8, 9, 9, 9) sts. at beg. of next 2 rows. Then dec. 1 st. at each end of foll. 6 (7, 7, 7, 8, 8, 8, 9, 9, 9) alt. rows. Work without further shaping until armhole measures 5½ (6, 6½, 7, 7½, 8, 8½, 9, 9½, 10) ins. from beg.

To Shape Shoulders: —Cast off 6 (6, 7, 7, 8, 8, 9, 9, 10, 10) sts. at beg. of next 4 rows and 7 (8, 8, 9, 9, 9, 9, 10, 10, 11) sts. at beg. of next 4 rows. Leave rem. sts. on a spare needle.

FRONT

Work as for Back until armhole measures 4¼ (4½, 5, 5½, 6, 6½, 6¾, 7, 7½, 7¾) ins. from beg.

To Shape Neck: —*Next row:* —Patt. 34 (38, 40, 42, 44, 46, 48, 52, 54, 56) sts., turn and leave rem. sts. on a spare needle. * Cast off 2 sts. at beg. of next and foll. 3 (4, 4, 4, 4, 5, 5, 6, 6, 6) alt. rows. Work without further shaping until armhole measures the same as Back, ending at shoulder edge.

To Shape Shoulder: —Cast off 6 (6, 7, 7, 8, 8, 9, 9, 10, 10) sts. at beg. of next and next alt. row and 7 (8, 8, 9, 9, 9, 9, 10, 10, 11) at beg. of the foll. 2 alt. rows. Keeping centre 12 (12, 14, 16, 20, 22, 24, 24, 26, 28) sts. on spare needle, rejoin yarn to rem. sts. and complete to match first side from *.

SLEEVES

With No. 11 [2] needles and main shade, cast on 50 (54, 58, 62, 66, 70, 74, 78, 82, 86) sts. and work in k. 1, p. 1 rib for 1½ (1½, 1½, 2, 2, 2, 2, 2, 2, 2½, 2½) ins. Change to No. 9 [4] needles and work in Fair Isle from chart No. 3, beg. with 12th (10th, 8th, 6th, 4th, 8th, 6th, 4th, 8th, 6th) st. and ending repeats with 1st (3rd, 5th, 7th, 9th, 5th, 7th, 9th, 5th, 7th) st. Cont. to work inc. 1 st. at each end of every 5th row until there are 76 (82, 90, 98, 104, 112, 116, 120, 126, 130) sts. on needle. Work without further shaping until sleeve measures 11½ (12½, 14, 16, 16½, 18, 18, 18½, 19, 19½) ins. from beg.

To Shape Top: —Cast off 6 (7, 7, 7, 8, 8, 8, 9, 9, 9) sts. at beg. of next 2 rows, then 1 st. at each end of next and every foll. alt. row until 46 (48, 56, 64, 76, 80, 84, 86, 92, 96) sts. rem. Dec. 1 st. at each end of every row until 26 (26, 26, 30, 30, 34, 34, 34, 38, 38) sts. rem. Cast off.

NECKBAND

Join right shoulder seam. With No. 11 [2] needles and main shade, and with right side of work facing, pick up and k. 15 (16, 17, 18, 18, 19, 19, 20, 21, 22) sts. down left front of neck, across 12 (12, 14, 16, 20, 22, 24, 24,

65

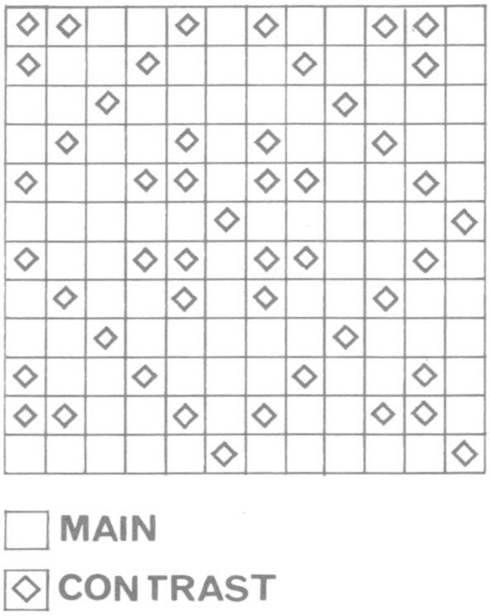

☐ **MAIN**

◇ **CONTRAST**

Chart No. 3

26, 28) sts. on spare needle, stitches up right front neck and across 28 (32, 34, 36, 40, 46, 48, 52, 54, 56) sts. on other spare needle. Work in k. 1, p. 1 rib for 12 (12, 12, 12, 12, 14, 14, 14, 14, 14) rows. Cast off in rib.

To make up

Press pieces. Join left shoulder, side and sleeve seams. Set in sleeves. Fold neckband to wrong side and catch down neatly and loosely, to allow for stretching over head. Press seams.

CARDIGAN WITH FAIR ISLE YOKE

Materials: —9 (10, 11, 12) ozs. natural; 1 oz. each of Scarlet, Lerwick, Green, Black, Honeygold, Fiord Blue and White Templeton's H. & O. Shetland Fleece; a pair each of Nos. 12 [1] and 10 [3] knitting needles; a No. 10 [3] circular needle; 10 buttons; 5 stitch holders and a medium crochet hook.

Measurements: —Bust: —34 (36, 38, 40) ins.; Length: —20 (21, 22, 23) ins.; Sleeve seam: 17 (18, 19, 20) ins.

Tension: —6½ sts. and 8½ rows to 1 inch on No. 10 [3] needles over stocking stitch.

Abbreviations: —See page 20.

BACK

Cast on 109 (113, 117, 121) sts. with No. 12 [1] needles and natural yarn and work 32 rows in k. 1, p. 1 rib. Change to No. 10 [3] needles and st. st. Inc. 1 st. at each end of 7th and every foll. 8th row until there are 115 (121, 127, 133) sts. on needle. Cont. without further shaping until work measures 13½ (14, 14½, 15) ins., ending with a p. row.

To Shape Armholes: Cast off 6 sts. at beg. of next 2 rows. Then dec. 1 st. at each end of every alt. row until there are 103 sts. on needle. P. 1 row. *Next row*: K. 2 tog., k. 33, k. 2 tog., leaving rem. sts. on a stitch-holder. Cont. on sts. on needle, dec. 1 st. at each end of every k. row until 3 sts. rem. *Next row*: —K. 2 tog., k. 1, turn, p. 2, turn, k. 2 tog. Fasten off.

Return to the sts. on holder. Put the first 29 on to a holder for the yoke. Join yarn to next 37 sts. K. 2 tog., k. 33, k. 2 tog., Cont. on these sts. to match other side.

LEFT FRONT

Cast on 50 (52, 54, 56) sts. with natural yarn and No. 12 [1] needles and work 32 rows k. 1, p. 1 rib. Change to st.st. and No. 10 [3] needles. Inc. 1 st. at beg. of 7th and every foll. 8th row until there are 57 (60, 63, 66) sts. on needle. Work without further shaping until Front measures 13½ (14, 14½, 15) ins., ending with a p. row.

To Shape Armhole: —Cast off 6 sts. at beg. of next row and dec. 1 st. at beg. of every k. row until 51 sts. rem. *Next row*: —P. 14 sts. and place on holder. Return to sts. on needle and dec. 1 st. at each end of every k. row until 3 sts. rem. Finish as for Back.

RIGHT FRONT

Work as for Left Front reversing all shapings

SLEEVES

Cast on 58 (60, 62, 64) sts. with natural yarn and No. 12 [1] needles, Work 38 rows k. 1, p. 1 rib. Change to st. st. and No. 10 [3] needles. Inc. 1 st. at each end of 5th and every foll. 6th row until there are 84 (90, 96, 102) sts. on needle. Work without further shaping until sleeve measures 17 (18, 19, 20) ins. from beg.

To Shape Top: Cast off 6 sts. at beg. of next 2 rows. Now dec. 1 st. at each end of every k. row until 36 sts. rem. Place these

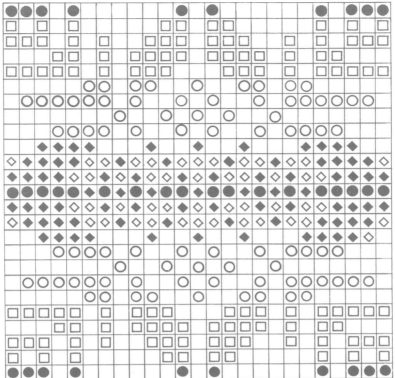

Chart No. 1

Chart No. 2

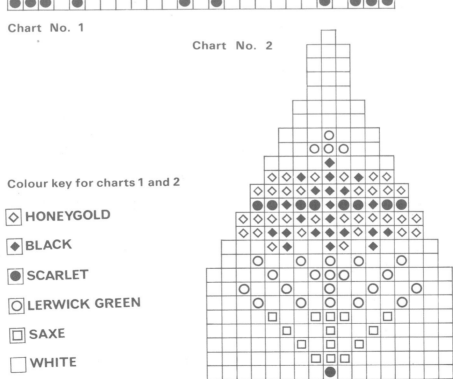

Colour key for charts 1 and 2

◇ HONEYGOLD

◆ BLACK

● SCARLET

○ LERWICK GREEN

▫ SAXE

▫ WHITE

67

sts. on a holder for yoke. Join raglan seams of sleeves, back and front. With right side of work facing, and with No. 10 [3] circular needle pick up and k. 14 sts. on holder from right front, 28 (31, 34, 37) sts. from raglan side, 36 sts. from sleeve holder, 28 (31, 34, 37) sts. from back raglan, 29 sts. from centre back, 28 (31, 34, 37) sts. from back raglan, 36 sts. from next sleeve, 28 (31, 34, 37) sts. from left front raglan and 14 sts. from left front. 241 (253, 265, 277) sts. on needle.

YOKE

With natural, p. 1 row. Break off and join in Fiord Blue and white. *Next row*: — K. 2 White, 3 Fiord Blue, 3 white, rep. from to last 5 sts. 3 Fiord Blue, 2 White. Break off Fiord Blue, join in Green. *Next row*: — Purl, 1 White, 1 green, 3 white, 1 green, rep. from * to last st. 1 white. *Next row*: — Knit 1 green, 5 white, rep. from * to last st. 1 green. Break off green. With white, and beg. with a p. row, work 3 rows st. st. Now work from charts. *First, 2nd and 3rd sizes*: — Omit 1st and last 18 (12, 6) sts. of chart 1 thus starting on 19th (13th, 7th) st. of chart 1. Knit remaining 7 (13, 19) sts. of chart 1, knit full patterns (42 sts.) of charts 2 and 1 five times, then the 17 sts. of chart 2 once and end the round with the first 7 (13, 19) sts. of chart 1. Cont. with the remaining 24 rows of the charts, taking care to start knit rows on stitch 19 (13, 7) and all purl rows on st. 7 (13, 19) at front edge of garment. *Fourth Size*: — Work from charts. Knit from 1st row of chart 1 followed by 1st row of chart 2 across the work, ending with 25 sts of chart . *For all sizes* Dec. 1 st. at each end of 9th and alt. rows, on chart 2. When 25 rows of chart have been knitted, break off all colours except white and green. Purl 1 row white. *Next row*: — K. 10 (7, 4, 1) * k. 2 tog., k. 1, rep. from * to last 9 (6, 3, 0) sts., k. 9, (6, 3, 0): 103 (109, 115, 121) sts. P. 1 row White Join green. *Next row*: — * K. 1 green, 5 White, rep. from * to last st. 1 Green. *Next row*: — * P. 1 White, 1 Green, 3 White, 1 Green, rep. from * to last st. 1 White. Break off green Join in Fiord Blue. *Next row*: — K.

2 white, * 3 Fiord Blue. 3 white, rep. from * to last 5 sts. 3 Fiord Blue, 2 W. Break off Fiord Blue and white. Join in natural and p. one row. *Next row*: — K. 2 (3, 1, 2) * k. 2 tog., k. 3, rep. from * to last 1 (1, 4, 4) sts., k. 1 (K. 1, k. 2, k. 2 tog., k. 2, k. 2 tog.) Change to No. 12 [1] needles and work in k. 1, p. 1 rib for 20 rows. Cast off in rib. Fold ribbing in half to wrong side and catch down neatly.

FRONT BANDS

With No. 12 [1] needles, cast on 11 sts. and natural yarn and work in m. st. for 204 (214, 223, 232) rows. Cast off. Make buttonhole band in same way, working buttonholes on 9th and 10th rows thus. *1st row*: — M. st. 4, cast off 3, m. st. 4. On next row, cast on sts. over those cast off in previous row. Cont. to make buttonholes on every 20 (21, 22, 23) row until 10 have been made. Work a further 6 rows. Cast off.

To make up

Press pieces carefully with a hot iron over a damp cloth, omitting ribbing. Join side and sleeve seams. Sew bands to fronts and add buttons to left band to correspond with buttonholes. Press seams.

JUMPER WITH FAIR ISLE YOKE

Materials: As for Cardigan omitting buttons.

Measurements: Bust: 34 (36, 38, 40) ins. Length: 20 (21, 22, 23) ins. Sleeve: 17 (18, 19, 20) ins.

Tension: —As for Cardigan.

Abbreviations: —See page 20.

BACK AND FRONT ALIKE: As back of cardigan.

SLEEVES: As sleeves of cardigan.

YOKE: As Yoke of Cardigan.

MAKE UP: As Fair Isle Cardigan.

ARAN BAG, SCARF AND HAT

Simple Aran stitches used for the smart set

Materials: — 7 Fifty gram balls of Mahony's Blarney Bainin Wool for scarf; 6 balls for bag; 2 balls for hat; a pair each of Nos. 7 [6] and 9 [4] knitting needles; a cable needle; a crochet hook; 2 large press fasteners.

Measurements: — Scarf: 71 ins. approx.; Bag: 12½ by 16 ins.; Hat to fit average head.

Tension: — 5 sts. and 6½ rows to 1 inch.

Abbreviations: — See page 20.

SCARF

With No. 9 [4] needles, cast on 41 sts. and k. 1 row. Change to No. 7 [6] needles and patt. *1st row*: — K. 2, p. 1, k. 4, p. 1, * k. 1 t. b. l., p. 1, rep. from * 13 times, k. 4, p. 1, k. 2. *2nd and alt. rows*: — K. 3, p. 4, k. 27, p. 4, k. 3 *Note*: The centre 27 sts. are in Rice stitch and will now appear as RS. 27. *3rd row*: — K. 2, p. 1, C. 4 B., RS. 27, C. 4 F., p. 1, k. 2. *5th row*: — As 1st row. *7th row*: — K. 2, p. 1, C. 4 B., RS. 13, M. B., RS. 13, C. 4 F., p. 1, k. 2. *9th row*: — As 1st row. *11th row*: — K. 2, p. 1, C. 4 B., RS. 11, M. B., RS. 3, MB., RS. 11, C. 4 F., p. 1, k. 2. *13th row*: — As 1st. *15th row*: — K. 2, p. 1, C. 4 B, RS. 9, MB., RS. 7, M. B., RS. 9, C. 4 F., p. 1, k. 2. *17th row*: — As 1st row. *19th row*: — K. 2, p. 1, C. 4 B., R.S. 7, M.B., RS. 11, M.B., RS. 7, C. 4 F., p. 1, k. 2. *21st row*: — As 1st row. *23rd row*: — As 15th row. *25th row*: — As 1st row. *27th row*: — As 11th row. *29th row*: — As 1st row. *31st row*: — As 7th row. *32nd row*: — As 2nd row. These 32 rows form the patt. Cont. until 14 complete patts. have been worked. Now work 1st 5 rows of next patt. Change to No. 9 [4] needles and k. 1 row. Cast off. Press on wrong side and add fringe.

BAG

With No. 9 [4] needles cast on 65 sts. and k. 1 row. Change to No. 7 [6] needles and patt. *1st row*: — K. 2, p. 1, k. 4, p. 1, * k. 1 t. b. l., p. 1 rep. from * 25 times, k. 4, p. 1, k. 2. *2nd and alt. rows*: — K. 3, p. 4, k. 51, p. 4, k. 3. Cont. keeping 51 sts. in centre in RS. as now set. *3rd row*: — K. 2, p. 1, C. 4 B., RS. 51,

C. 4 F., p. 1, k. 2. *5th row*: — As 1st row. *7th row*: — K. 2, p. 1, C. 4 B., RS. 25, M.B., RS. 25, C. 4 F., p. 1, k. 2. *9th row*: — As 1st row. *11th row*: — K. 2, p. 1, C. 4 B., RS. 23, M.B., RS. 3, M.B., RS. 23, C. 4 F., p. 1, k. 2. Cont. in this way working the diamond of bobbles as given on scarf until 3 patts. have been completed. Work 5 rows of next patt. Change to No. 9 [4] needles and work 2½ ins. g. st. Cast off.

Work another piece to match for Back.

To make up

Press pieces on wrong side, Pin together with right sides outside and join with 1 row of double crochet, leaving garter stitch borders open. Fold borders to wrong side and catch down. Add press fasteners to top. Make a twisted cord for handle and trimming, 45 inches long and sew into place, leaving centre section free for shoulder strap.

HAT

With No. 9 [4] needles cast on 106 sts. and work 6 rows g. st. *Next row*: — K. 1, * p. 1, inc. in next st., p. 1, k. 23, rep. from * 3 times, k. 1. Change to No. 7 [6] needles and patt. *1st row*: — K. 1, * p. 1, (k. 1 t. b. l., p. 1) 11 times, k. 4, rep. from * 3 times, k. 1. *2nd and alt. rows*: — K. 1, * p. 4, k. 23, rep. from * 3 times, k. 1. Cont. to keep the 4 panels of 23 sts. in R.S. *3rd row*: — K. 1, * RS. 23, C. 4 B., RS. 23, C. 4 F., rep. from * once, k. 1. *5th row*: — As 1st row. *7th row*: — K. 1, * RS. 11, M.B., RS. 11, C. 4 B., RS. 11, M.B., RS. 11, C. 4 F., rep. from * once, k. 1. *9th row*: — As 1st row. *11th row*: — K. 1, * RS. 9, M.B., RS. 3, M.B., RS. 9, C. 4 B., RS. 9, M.B., RS. 3, M.B., RS. 9, C. 4 F., rep. from * once, k. 1. Cont. in this way, working diamond bobbles in each RS. panel until 17th row has been worked.

To Shape Top: — K. 1, * p. 4, k. 2 tog. t. b. l., k. 19, k. 2 tog., rep. from * 3 times more, k. 1. Work 3 rows in patt. with 21 sts. in RS. in each panel. *22nd row*: — K. 1. * p. 4, k. 2 tog. t. b. l., k. 17, k. 2 tog., rep. from * 3 times more, k. 1. Keeping bobble patt. correct, cont. to dec. in the same place on every wrong side row 5 times more. Cont. to work cables and RS. and cont. to dec. in same place on next 2 wrong side rows. *37th row*: — K. 1, p. 2

tog., k. 1 t. b. l., p. 2 tog. t. b. l., k. 4, rep. from * 3 times more, k. 1. *38th row*: —K. 1, * p. 4, sl. 1, k. 2 tog., p. s. s. o., rep. from * 3 times more, k. 1. *39th row*: —K. 1, * p. 1, (k. 2 tog.) twice, p. 1, (k. 2 tog. t. b. l.) twice, rep. from * once, k. 1. Break wool, thread into large eyed needle and draw up top of hat and fasten off securely. Join seam. Press seam.

ARAN CUSHION

The same stitches are used for the cushion. If it is your first attempt at Aran knitting, this is just a square, so you have no complicated shaping to work in with the pattern

HIS & HER ARAN SWEATERS

Materials: —17 (18, 20, 21) 2 ozs. balls of Mahony's Blarney Bainin Wool for roll-neck sweater; 1 oz. less on each size for crew-neck sweater; a pair each of Nos. 7 [6], 9 [4] and 10 [3] knitting needles; a cable needle.

Measurements: — Length: — 25½ (26, 27½, 28) ins.; Chest/Bust sizes: — 34 (36, 38, 40) ins. Sleeve: 18 (18, 19, 19½) ins.

Tension: —6 sts. and 6 rows to 1 inch over cross st. pattern.

Abbreviations: —See page 20.

BACK

With No. 10 [3] needles cast on 97 (103, 109, 115) sts. and work in rib as follows. *1st row*: — (Right side) K. 2, *p. 1, k. 1, rep. from * to last st., k. 1. *2nd row*: —K. 1, * p. 1, k. 1, rep. from * to end. Rep. these 2 rows 5 times more, then 1st row again. Work Inc. Row thus: K. 1, p. 2 (3, 4, 5), p. u. k., p. 2 (3, 4, 5), * k. 1, (p. 1, p. u. k.) twice, p. 1, p. u. k., p. u. k., k. 3, p. u. k., k. 3, p. 2, p. 2 tog., p. 1, k. 3, p. u. k., k. 3, p. u. k., p. u. k., (p. 1, p. u. k.) twice, p. 1, k. 1, * p. 7 (8, 9, 10) p. u. k., p. 7 (8, 9, 10), then rep. from * to * p. 2 (3, 4, 5), p. u. k., p. 2 (3, 4, 5), k. 1. 118 (124, 130, 136) sts. Change to No. 7 [6] needles and patt. *1st row*: —K. 1, CS. 3 (4, 5, 6) times, * p. 1, k. 7, p. 2, C 2 L., p. 6, C 2 R., C 2 L., p. 6, C 2 R., p. 2, k. 7, p. 1, * CS. 8

(9, 10, 11) times, rep. from * to *, CS. 3 (4, 5, 6) times, k. 1. *2nd row*: —K. 1, p. 6 (8, 10, 12), * k. 1, p. 7, k. 3, p. 2, k. 6, p. 2, k. 2, p. 2, k. 6, p. 2, k. 3, p. 7, k. 1, * p. 16 (18, 20, 22), rep. from * to *, p. 6 (8, 10, 12), k. 1. *3rd row*: —K. 2, CS. 2 (3, 4, 5) times, k. 1, * p. 1, CP. 7, p. 3, C 2 L., p. 4, C 2 R., p. 2, C 2 L., p. 4, C 2 R., p. 3, CP. 7, p. 1, * k. 1, CS. 7 (8, 9, 10) times, k. 1, rep. from * to * k. 1, CS. 2 (3, 4, 5) times, k. 2. *4th row*: —K. 1, p. 6 (8, 10, 12), * k. 1, p. 7, k. 4, (p. 2, k. 4) 4 times, p. 7, k. 1, * p. 16 (18, 20, 22), rep. from * to *, p. 6, (8, 10, 12) k. 1. These 4 rows give you the CS. over 7 (9, 11, 13) sts. at each end and 16 (18, 20, 22) sts. in centre panel. *5th row*: —CS. 7 (9, 11, 13), *p. 1, k. 7, p. 4, (C 2 L, p. 2, C 2 R, p. 4) twice, k. 7, p. 1, * CS. 16 (18, 20, 22), rep. from * to * CS. 7 (9, 11, 13). *6th row*: —K. 1, p. 6 (8, 10, 12), * k. 1, p. 7, k. 5, p. 2, k. 2, p. 2, k. 6, p. 2, k. 2, p. 2, k. 5, p. 7, k. 1, * p. 16 (18, 20, 22), rep. from * to *, p. 6 (8, 10, 12), k. 1. *7th row*: —CS. 7 (9, 11, 13), * p. 1, CP. 7, p. 5, C 2 L., C 2 R., p. 6, C 2 L., C 2 R., p. 5, CP. 7, p. 1, * CS. 16 (18, 20, 22), rep. from * to *, CS. 7 (9, 11, 13). *8th row*: —K. 1, p. 6 (8, 10, 12), * k. 1, p. 7, k.6, p. 4, k. 8, p. 4, k. 6, p. 7, k. 1, * p. 16 (18, 20, 22), rep. from * to *, p. 6, (8, 10, 12), k. 1. *9th row*: —CS. 7 (9, 11, 13), * p. 1, k. 7, p. 6, C 4 F., p. 8, C 4 F., p. 6, k. 7, p. 1, * CS. 16 (18, 20, 22), rep. from * to *, CS. 7 (9, 11, 13). *10th row*: —As 8th. *11th row*: —CS. 7 (9, 11, 13), * p. 1, CP. 7, p. 6, k. 4, p. 8, k. 4, p. 6, CP. 7, p. 1, * CS. 16 (18, 20, 22), rep. from * to * CS. 7 (9, 11, 13). *12th row*: —As 8th. *13th row*: —As 9 th. *14th row*: —As 8th. *15th row*: —CS. 7 (9, 11, 13), *p. 1, CP. 7, p. 5, C 2 R., C 2 L., p. 6, C 2 R., C 2 L., p. 5, CP. 7, p. 1, * CS. 16 (18, 20, 22), rep. from * to *, CS. 7 (9, 11, 13). *16th row*: —As 6th. *17th row*: —CS. 7 (9, 11, 13), * p. 1, k. 7, p. 4, (C 2 R, p. 2, C 2 L., p. 4) twice, k. 7, p. 1, * CS. 16 (18, 20, 22), rep. from * to * CS. 7 (9, 11, 13). *18th row*: —As 4th. *19th row*: —CS. 7 (9, 11, 13), * p. 1, CP. 7, p. 3, (C 2 R, p. 4, C 2 L., p. 2) twice, p. 1, CP. 7, p. 1, * CS. 16 (18, 20, 22), rep. from * to *, CS. 7 (9, 11, 13). *20th row*: —As 2nd. *21st row*: —CS. 7 (9, 11, 13), * p. 1, k. 7, p. 2, (C 2 R, p. 6, C 2 L.) twice, p. 2, k. 7, p. 1, * CS. 16 (18, 20, 22), rep. from * to * CS. 7 (9, 11, 13). *22nd row*: —K. 1, p. 6 (8, 10, 12),

* k. 1, p. 7, k. 2, p. 2, k. 8, p. 4, k. 8, p. 2, k. 2, p. 7, k. 1, * p. 16 (18, 20, 22), rep. from * to * p. 6 (8, 10, 12), k. 1. *23rd row*: —CS. 7 (9, 11, 13), * p. 1, CP. 7, p. 2, k. 2, p. 8, C 4 B., p. 8, k. 2, p. 2, CP. 7, p. 1, * CS. 16 (18, 20, 22), rep. from * to * CS. 7 (9, 11, 13). *24th row*: —As 22nd. *25th row*: —CS. 7 (9, 11, 13), * p. 1, k. 7, p. 2, k. 2, p. 8, k. 4, p. 8, k. 2, p. 2, k. 7, p. 1, * CS. 16 (18, 20, 22), rep. from * to * CS. 7 (9, 11, 13). *26th row*: —As 22nd. *27th row*: —As 23rd. *28th row*: —As 22nd. These 28 rows for one patt. Cont. in patt. until Back measures $17\frac{1}{2}$ ($17\frac{1}{2}$, $18\frac{1}{2}$, $18\frac{1}{2}$) ins. from beg., ending with a wrong-side row.

To Shape Armholes: —Cast off 7 (8, 7, 8) sts. at beg. of next 4 rows.
Note: The 2 smaller sizes will now have 1 st. at each end of claw patt. Keep this in g. st. to give a firm edge. For the 2 larger sizes. right side rows will beg. k. 2, and then the 2nd half of the claw and will end k. 2 after the first half of the claw. Wrong side rows will beg. k. 1, p. 4 and will end p. 4, k. 1.
Cont. in patt. until Back measures 25 ($25\frac{1}{2}$, 27, $27\frac{1}{2}$) ins. from beg., ending with a wrong-side row.
To Shape Neck and Shoulders: —Patt. 36 (37, 40, 41) and leave these sts. on a spare needle, cast off 18 (18, 22, 22) sts., patt. to end. Cont. on 36 (37, 40, 41) sts. now on needle for left side and work 1 row. **Next row*: —Cast off 4, patt. to end. *Next row*: —Cast off 7 (7, 8, 8) sts., patt. back to neck edge. Rep. last 2 rows once. *Next row*: —Cast off 3 (3, 4, 4) patt. to end. Cast off rem. sts. **
With wrong side of work facing, rejoin wool to inner edge of right back sts. Complete to match left back from ** to **.

FRONT
Work as given for Back until you have worked 8 rows less than on back to beg. of neck shaping, thus ending on a wrong-side row.
To Shape Neck and Shoulders: —Patt. 38 (39, 42, 43) sts., and leave then on a spare needle for left side. Cont. and cast off 14 (14, 18, 18) sts., patt. to end. Cont. the 38 (39, 42, 43) sts. now on needle and work 1 row. ***Cast off 3 (3, 4, 4) sts. at beg. of next

row, then dec. 1 st. at neck edge on next 8 rows. Cast off 7 (7, 8, 8) sts. at beg. of next row for shoulder, then dec. 1 st. at neck edge on foll. row. Rep. last 2 rows once. Cast off rem. sts. ***
Work from *** to *** to complete right side to match.

SLEEVES
With No. 10 [3] needles, cast on 47 (51, 55, 59) sts. and work in rib as for Back for 13 rows. *Inc. row*: —K. 1, p. 2 (3, 4, 5), p. u. k., p. 2 (3, 4, 5), rep. from * to * as on inc. row for Back, p. 2 (3, 4, 5), p. u. k., p. 2 (3, 4, 5), k. 1: 58 (62, 66, 70) sts. Change to No. 7 [6] needles and patt. *1st row*: —K. 1, CS. 3 (4, 5, 6) times, rep. from * to * in 1st patt. row of Back, CS. 3 (4, 5, 6) times, k. 1. Cont. in patt. as now set, but inc. 1 st. at each end of 5th, 11th, 16th, 22nd, and 28th rows of every patt. until there are 88 (94, 100, 106) sts. on needle, keeping extra sts. in CS. Cont. without further shaping until Sleeve measures 18 (18, 19, $19\frac{1}{2}$) ins. from beg. Place markers of contrasting wool at each end, then work 14 (16, 14, 16) rows straight. Cast off 6 (7, 7, 8) sts. at beg. of next 10 rows. Cast off rem. sts.

COLLAR
With No. 9 [4] needles, cast on 129 (129, 137, 137) sts. and work in rib for 5 rows. Change to No. 10 [3] needles and work 10 rows. Change to No. 9 [4] needles and work 5 rows. Cast off in rib.

ROLL COLLAR
With No. 9 [4] needles, cast on 133 (133, 141, 141) sts. and work in rib for 20 rows. Change to No. 10 [3] needles and work 13 rows. Cast off in rib.

To make up
Do not press. Join shoulder seams, matching pattern. Sew cast-off edges of sleeves to sides of armholes and straight edges of sleeves above markers, to armhole casting-off. Join side and sleeve seams. Press seams. For neckline, join ends of collar or band and set to neck edge.

FISHERMAN'S RIB SWEATER
Materials: —22 (23, 24) ozs. White; $\frac{1}{2}$ oz. each Green and Blue Lister Lavenda Double

Knitting Wool; a pair each of Nos. 10 [3] and 8 [5] knitting needles; a set of four double-pointed knitting needles No. 12 [1].

Measurements: — Chest: — 34 (36, 38) ins.; Length: — 24 ins.; Sleeve: — 17 ins.

Tension: — 5 sts. and 10 rows to 1 inch on No. 8 [5] needles.

Abbreviations : —See page 20.

BACK

With No. 10 [3] needles and White cast on 107 (109, 111) sts. and work in k. 1, p. 1 rib as foll. *1st row:* —P. 1 * k. 1, p. 1, rep. from * to end. *2nd row:* —K. 1, * p. 1, k. 1, rep. from * to end. Rep. these 2 rows for 2½ ins., ending with 1st row. Change to No. 8 [5] needles and patt. *1st row:* — (Right side) Sl. 1, k. to end. *2nd row:* —Sl. 1, * K. 1 below, p. 1, rep. from * to last 2 sts., k. 1 below, k. 1. These 2 rows form the patt. Cont. in patt. until Back measures 17 ins. from beg., ending with 2nd patt. row.

To Shape Raglan: —Cast off 6 (7, 7) sts. at beg. of next 2 rows. *Next row:* —Sl. 1, k. 3, sl. 1, k. 2 tog., p. s. s. o., k. to last 7 sts., k. 3 tog., k. 4. Patt. 5 rows straight. Rep. last 6 rows until 35 (35, 37) sts. rem. Work 5 rows straight. Cast off.

FRONT

Work as for Back until first 2 rows of armhole decrease have been worked and there are 95 (95, 97) sts. on needle.

To Divide for Neck: —*Next row:* —Sl. 1, k. 3, sl. 1, k. 2 tog., p. s. s. o., k. 40 (40, 41) sts., turn and work on this side first. ** Dec. 1 st. at neck edge on next and every foll. 5th (5th, 4th) row until 17 (17, 18) sts. in all have been decreased at neck edge. *At the same time,* dec. at armhole edge as before on every 6th row until all sts. have been worked off. Fasten off. ** Slip 1 st. at centre front on to a safety-pin. Rejoin White to next sts. and k. to last 7 sts., k. 3 tog., k. 4. Now work from ** to ** reversing all shapings.

SLEEVES

With No. 10 [3] needles and White, cast on 53 (55, 57) sts. and work in rib as for welt on back for 2½ ins., ending with 1st rib row. Change to No. 8 [5] needles and patt. Inc. 1 st. at each end of next and every foll. 10th

row until there are 79 (81, 81) sts. on needle. Work straight until sleeve measures 17 ins. from beg., ending with 2nd patt. row.

To Shape Top: —Cast off 6 (7, 7) sts., at beg. of next 2 rows. *Next row:* —Sl. 1, k. 3, sl. 1, k. 2 tog., p. s. s. o., k. to last 7 sts., k. 3 tog., k. 4. Work 5 rows straight. Rep. last 6 rows until 7 sts. rem., work 5 rows straight. Cast off.

NECKBAND

Join raglan seams. With right side of work facing and with set of No. 12 [1] double-pointed needles and White, pick up and k. 35 (35, 37) sts. from back of neck, 7 sts. from top of sleeve, 58 (60, 62) sts. down front, 1 st. from safety-pin, 58 (60, 62) sts. from centre front to shoulder and 7 sts. from top of second sleeve. Join into a circle and work in rounds keeping the centre front st. always as à k. st. and always decreasing 1 st. at each side of this centre st. on every round. *1st round:* —With Blue, K. *2nd, 3rd and 4th rounds:* —With Blue, k. 1, p. 1 rib to end. *5th round:* —With green, K. *6th, 7th and 8th rounds:* —With green, in k. 1, p. 1 rib. *9th Round:* —With Blue, k. *10th, 11th and 12th rounds:* —As 2nd, 3rd & 4th.

Now inc. 1 st. at each side of centre st. on every round and work in stripes as follows: — *1st, 2nd and 3rd rounds:* —With Blue, in k. 1, p. 1 rib. *4th round:* —With green, k. *5th, 6th and 7th rounds:* —With green, in k. 1, p. 1 rib. *8th round:* —With Blue, k. *9th, 10th, and 11th rounds:* —With Blue, in k. 1, p. 1 rib. *12th round:* —With Blue, cast off in rib.

To make up

Join side and sleeve seams. Turn neckband in half to wrong side and catch down neatly. Press seams.

SUMMER SWEATERS FOR MEN

Materials : —Short-sleeved Sweater: 16 (16, 18, 18, 20, 20) balls of Twilley's Bubbly in main colour and 1 ball of contrast ; zip-up Sweater : —20 (20, 22, 22, 24, 24) balls of main colour and 1 ball contrast ; an open-end zip 24 (24, 24, 24, 26, 26) ins. long ; For both garments a pair each of Nos. 8 [5] and 10 [3] knitting needles.

Measurements : —Chest : 36 (38, 40, 42, 44, 46) ins. ; Length 25 (25, 25, 25, 27, 27) ins. ; Short sleeve : 5 ins. ; Long sleeve : 19 ins.

Tension : —9 sts., and 12 rows to 2 ins. on No. 8 [5] needles.

Abbreviations : —See page 20.

SHORT-SLEEVED SWEATER
Using yarn double throughout,

BACK
With No. 10 [3] needles and M. cast on 88 (92, 98, 102, 108, 112) sts. and work 10 rows in k. 1, p. 1 rib. Change to No. 8 [5] needles and join in C. Work 2 rows st. st., beg. with a k. row. Break off C. * Cont., in st. st. in M. until Back measures 16 (16, 16, 16, 17, 17) ins. from beg.
To Shape Armholes : —Cast off 2 sts. at beg. of next 2 rows, then dec. 1 st. each end of next 10 rows. Cont. until work measures 23½ (23½, 23½, 23½, 25½, 25½) ins. from beg.
To Shape Shoulders : —Cast off 9 (10, 11, 12, 13, 14) sts. loosely at beg. of next 4 rows. Cast off rem. sts.

FRONT
As Back until work measures 23 (23, 23, 23, 25, 25) ins., ending with a p. row.
To Shape Neck : —*Next row :* —k. 20 (22, 24, 26, 28, 30) sts., k. 2 tog., turn. Work on these sts. only and dec. 1 st. at neck edge on next 3 rows.
To Shape Shoulder : —Cast off 9 (10, 11, 12, 13, 14) sts. at beg. of next and foll. alt. rows. Place centre 20 (20, 22, 22, 24, 24) sts. on to a stitch-holder. Complete other side of neck to match.

SLEEVES
With No. 10 [3] needles and M. cast on 60 (60, 60, 60, 66, 66) sts. Work as Back to *. Cont. in st. st. in M. Inc. 1 st. at each end of every 4th row until there are 68 (68, 68, 68, 74, 74) sts. Cont. without further shaping until sleeve measures 5 ins.
To Shape Top : —Cast off 2 sts. at beg. of next 2 rows, then dec. 1 st. each end of every alt. row until 26 sts. rem. Dec. 1 st. at each end of next 5 rows. Work 4 (4½, 5, 5½, 6, 6½) ins. on these 16 sts. for saddle shoulder, ending with a p. row.
To Shape Neck : —Cast off 8 sts., K. 8. Work 3¼ (3¼. 3½, 3½, 3¾, 3¾) ins. on these 8 sts., Cast off. Make another sleeve to match, casting off for saddle shoulder on a p. row.

NECKBAND
Sew straight saddle shoulder pieces of sleeves to front shoulder shapings. With No. 10 [3] needles and M. beg. at cast off edge of left sleeve and pick up and k. 34 (34, 36, 36, 38, 38) sts. around inner edge of neck, down left side of front neck, k. sts. from stitch-holder, pick up and k. 34 (34, 36, 36, 38, 38) sts. up right side of front neck and around neck edge to cast off edge of right sleeve. Join in C. and p. 1 row, k. 1 row. Break off C. With M. p. 1 row then work 10 rows k. 1, p. 1 rib. Cast off loosely in rib.

To make up
Press work lightly on wrong side with warm iron over a damp cloth, omitting ribbing. Join cast-off edges of sleeves and neckband seam, then sew straight saddle edge at neck of sleeves to back top, then set in remainder of sleeves. Join side and sleeve seams. Press seams.

ZIP-UP SWEATER

BACK
As short-sleeved Sweater.

LEFT FRONT
With No. 10 [3] needles and M. cast on 46 (48, 50, 54, 56, 58) sts. and work 10 rows k. 1, p. 1 rib. Change to No. 8 [5] needles and join C. K. 1 row C.

Next row: —With C. k. 2, p to end. Break off C. Cont. in M. and st. st., keeping 2 sts. in g. st. at Front edge until work measures 16 (16, 16, 16, 17, 17) ins. from beg., ending with a p. row.

To Shape Armhole: —Keeping 2 sts. in g. st. at Front edge, cast off 2 sts. at beg. of next row, then dec. 1 st. at armhole edge on next 10 rows. Cont. without further shaping but keeping g. st. border until work measures 23 (23, 23, 23, 25, 25) ins. from beg., ending with a k. row.

To Shape Neck: —*Next row:* —K. 2, p. 10 (10, 10, 12, 12, 12) sts. and place on a stitch-holder, p. to end. Now dec. 1 st. at neck edge on next 4 rows.

To Shape Shoulder: —Cast off 9 (10, 11, 12, 13, 14) sts. loosely at beg. of next and alt. row.

RIGHT FRONT
As Left Front, but reversing all shapings.

RIGHT SLEEVE
With No. 10 [3] needles and M. cast on 44 (44, 44, 44, 46, 46) sts. and work as Back of sweater to *. Cont. in st. st. in M. and inc. 1 st. at each end of every 8th (8th, 8th, 8th, 6th, 6th) row until there are 68 (68, 68, 68, 74, 74) sts. Cont. without further shaping until Sleeve measures 19 ins. from beg. Now complete as sleeve of sweater. Make another sleeve to match, reversing all shaping.

NECKBAND
Join cast-off edges of sleeves then sew straight back saddle edge of sleeves across Back of Jacket, placing cast-off edge seam at centre back. Sew front saddle shoulder edge to Front shoulder shapings. Place sts. at right front edge on to a No. 10 [3] needle and then with M. pick up and k. 64 (64, 70, 70, 72, 72) sts. evenly around neck edge, and k. sts. at left front edge. Join C. *1st row:* —With C., k. 2 sts., p. to last 2 sts., k. 2. *2nd row:* —With C., k. 2 sts., (k. 1, p. 1) to last 2 sts., k. 2. Break off C. With M. rep. 1st row, then rep. 2nd row in rib 10 times more. Cast off in rib.

To make up
Press pieces with a warm iron over a damp cloth, omitting ribbing. Set in remainder of sleeves. Join side and sleeve seams. Sew in zip. Press seams.

Knitting on 4 Needles

For socks and gloves or any knitting where no seam should show, four needles are used. The total number of stitches required for the item are divided equally between three needles and the fourth needle is used to knit. (See sketches Nos. 31 and 32) Take the first needle and cast on one third of the required number of stitches. Take the second needle and repeat this process, then again with the third needle. Take the fourth needle and starting at the beginning of the first needle, knit to end. Continue to knit across the stitches on second and third needles, using each empty needle in turn as it becomes free of stitches.

For stocking stitch, when knitting in rounds, all rounds will be knitted. For ribbed edges, each round will be the same. For instance, a knit 1, purl 1 edging will begin every round with knit 1, purl 1. The work is not turned as in knitting on two needles.

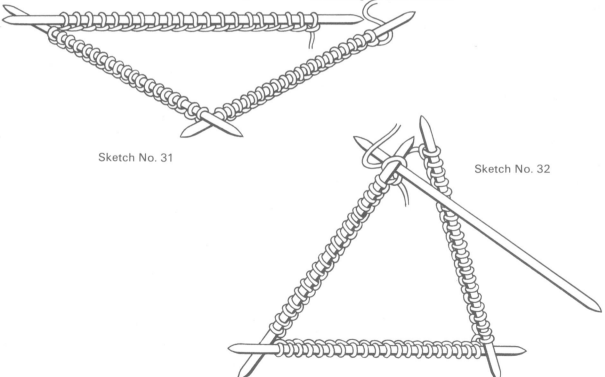

Sketch No. 31

Sketch No. 32

GREEN CABLE CARDIGAN

Materials : — 13 (14, 15) ozs. Lister Lavenda Double Knitting Wool ; a pair each of Nos. 9 [4] and 11 [2] knitting needles ; a cable needle ; 5 buttons.

Measurements : — Bust : 34 (36, 38) ins. ; Length : — 27 ins.

Tension : — 6 sts. and 8 rows to 1 inch on No. 9 [4] needles.

Abbreviations : — See page 20.

BACK

With No. 9 [4] needles, cast on 106 (112, 118) sts., and work in k. 1, p. 1 rib for 8 rows. Now work in patt. as folls. *1st row*: — K. 21 (22, 23), p. 2, k. 4, C 4 B., p. 2, k. 40 (44, 48), p. 2, k. 4, C 4 B., p. 2, k. 21 (22, 23). *2nd row*: — P. 21 (22, 23), k. 2, p. 8, k. 2, p. 40 (44, 48), k. 2, p. 8 k. 2, p. 21 (22, 23). *3rd row*: — K. 21 (22, 23), p. 2, k. 2, C 4 B., k. 2, p. 2, k. 40 (44, 48), p. 2, k. 2, C 4 B., k. 2, p. 2, k. 21 (22, 23). *4th row*: — As 2nd. *5th row*: — K. 21 (22, 23), p. 2, C 4 B., k. 4, p. 2, k. 40 (44, 48), p. 2, C 4 B., k. 4, p. 2, k. 21 (22, 23). *6th row*: — As 2nd. These 6 rows from the patt. Cont. in patt. until Back measures 19½ ins. from beg.
To Shape Armholes: — Keeping patt. correct and with right side facing, cast off 6 (7, 8) sts. at beg. of next 2 rows. Now dec. 1 st. at beg. of every row until 74 (78, 82) sts. rem. Cont. straight until Back measures 27 ins. from beg.
To Shape Shoulders: — Cast off 7 (8, 8) sts. at beg. of next 2 rows, then 7 (8, 9) sts. at beg. of next 2 rows, then 8 (8, 9) sts. at beg. of foll. 2 rows. Cast off rem. sts.

RIGHT FRONT

With No. 9 [4] needles, cast on 52 (56, 58) sts. and work in k. 1, p. 1 rib for 8 rows, increasing 1 st. at beg. of last row on 34 and 38 ins. sizes only.
Now work in patt.
1st row: — K. 20 (22, 24), p. 2, k. 4, C 4 B., p. 2, k. 21 (22, 23). *2nd row*: — P. 21 (22, 23), k. 2, p. 8, k. 2, p. 20 (22, 24). *3rd row*: — K. 20 (22, 24), p. 2, k. 2, C 4 B., k. 2, p. 2, k. 21 (22, 23). *4th row*: — As 2nd. *5th row*: — K. 20 (22, 24), p. 2, C 4 B., k. 4, p. 2, k. 21 (22, 23). *6th row*: — As 2nd. These 6 rows form the patt. Cont. until Front measures 18½ ins. from beg.
To Shape Neck: — Keeping patt. correct and with right side facing, *1st row*: — K. 1, s.k. p.o., patt. to end. *2nd row*: — Patt. *3rd row*: — Patt. *4th row*: — Patt. Rep. last 4 rows until Front measures 19½ ins. from beg., ending with 1 row more than back.
To Shape Armhole: — Cast off 6 (7, 8) sts., patt. to end. Still shaping at neck edge as before on every 4th row, now dec. 1 st. at armhole edge on next and every alt. row, until 30 (32, 34) sts. rem. Now, keeping armhole edge straight, cont. to shape neck edge as before until 22 (24, 26) sts. rem. Cont. straight until Front measures 27 ins. from beg.
To Shape Shoulder: — Beg. at armhole edge and cast off 7 (8, 8) sts. then cast off 7 (8, 9) sts. at beg. of foll. alt. row, Cast off rem. sts. Work left Front to match, reversing shapings.

ARMBANDS

Join shoulder seams. With right side of work facing, rejoin yarn and with No. 11 [2] needles, pick up and k. 90 sts. evenly round armhole. Work in k. 1, p. 1 rib for 4 rows. Cast off in rib.

FRONT BAND

With No. 11 [2] needles, cast on 8 sts. and work in k. 1, p. 1 rib for 4 ins. *Next row*: — — Rib 3, cast off 2, rib to end. *Next row*: — Rib 3, cast on 2, rib to end. Cont. in rib making buttonholes at 3½ inch intervals, measuring from base of previous buttonhole, until 5 have been made. Cont. in rib until band, slightly stretched, reaches up right front, round back of neck and down left front to lower edge. Cast off in rib.

To make up

Press pieces. Join side seams. Sew front band neatly into position. Add buttons. Press seams.

SHORT-SLEEVED LACE JUMPER WITH SLEEVELESS VERSION

Cool as a cucumber and knitted in cotton. Lacy jumper could be teamed with

summer skirts and trousers. A sleeveless version is given for those really hot summer days. It is a simple style to suit all ages and the instructions start at bust size **34 inches** and continue through six sizes to **44 inch** bust

Materials: —Short-sleeve jumper: 9 (10, 10, 11, 11, 12) ozs. Twilley's Lyscordet; the Sleeveless version: 8 (8, 9, 9, 10, 10) ozs. For both, a pair each of Nos. 12 [1] and 13 [0] knitting needles.

Measurements: —Bust: 34 (36, 38, 40, 42, 44) ins.; Length from shoulder: 21½ (21½, 22, 22, 22½, 22½) ins.; sleeve seam: 4 (4, 4½, 4½, 5, 5) ins.

Tension: —8 sts. and 10 rows to one inch on No. 12 [1] needles.

Abbreviations: —See page 20.

BACK AND FRONT (ALIKE)
With No. 13 [0] needles, cast on 134 (141, 149, 156, 164, 171) sts. and work 13 rows in k. 1, p. 1 rib.
Next row: Rib 6 (5, 9, 7, 11, 10), * inc. in next st., rib 9, rep. from * to last 8 (6, 10, 9, 13, 11) sts., inc. in next st., rib to end. 147 (155, 163, 171, 179, 187) sts. Change to No. 12 [1] needles and work in patt. thus:
1st row: K. 3, * k. 2 tog., y. fwd., k. 1, y. fwd., sl. 1, k. 1, p. s. s. o., k. 3, rep. from * to end.
2nd row: P.
3rd row: —K. 2, * k. 2 tog., y. fwd., k. 3, y. fwd., sl. 1, k. 1, p. s. s. o. k. 1, rep. from * to last st. k. 1
4th row: P.
5th row: —K. 1, k. 2 tog., * y. fwd., k. 5, y. fwd., sl. 1, k. 2 tog., p. s. s. o., rep. from * to last 8 sts., y. fwd., k. 5, y. fwd., sl. 1, k. 1, p. s. s. o., k. 1.
6th row: —P. 4, * p. 2 tog., y. r. n., p. 6, rep. from * to last 7 sts., p. 2 tog., y. r. n., p. 5.
7th row: —K. 2, * y. fwd., sl. 1, k. 1, p. s. s. o., k. 3, k. 2 tog., y. fwd., k. 1, rep. from * to last st., k. 1.
8th row: —P.
9th row: —K. 3, * y. fwd., sl. 1, k. 1, p. s. s. o., k. 1, k. 2 tog., y. fwd., k. 3, rep. from * to end.

10th row: —P.
11th row: —K. 4, * y. fwd., sl. 1, k. 2 tog., p. s. s. o., y. fwd., k. 5, rep. from * ending last repeat k. 4.
12th row: —K. 2 tog., y. r. n., * p. 6, p. 2 tog., y. r. n., rep. from * to last st., p. 1. These 12 rows form the patt. and are repeated throughout. Cont. in patt. until work measures 15½ ins., ending with wrong-side row.
To Shape Armholes: —Cast off 6 (8, 8, 10, 10, 12) sts. at beg. of next 2 rows, then dec. 1 st. at each end of next 8 rows and the foll. 2 (4, 4, 6, 6, 8) alt. rows. Cont. on rem. sts., until work measures 20 (20, 20½, 20½, 21, 21) ins., ending with a wrong-side row.
To Shape Neck: —*Next row:* —Patt. 46 (46, 48, 48, 50, 50) sts., turn and leave rem. sts. on a spare needle.
Now cast off 4 sts. at beg. of next row, then dec. 1 st. at neck edge on the foll. 8 rows. Cont. on rem. sts. until work measures 21½ (21½, 22, 22, 22½, 22½,) ins., ending at arm-hole edge.
To Shape Shoulder: —Cast off 8 (8, 9, 9, 9, 9,) sts. at beg. of next row and foll. 2 alt. rows. Work 1 row, then cast off rem. sts.
Return to sts. on spare needle and with right side of work facing, slip next 23 (23, 27, 27, 31, 31) sts. on to a stitch-holder, join on yarn and patt. to end. Work 1 row. Now complete to match first side.

SLEEVES
With No. 13 [0] needles cast on 83 (83, 91, 91, 99, 99) sts. and work 14 rows in k. 1, p. 1 rib. Change to No. 12 [1] needles and patt. as for Back.
Inc. 1 st. at each end of 7th and every foll. 4th (3rd., 4th., 3rd., 4th., 3rd.) row until there are 95 (99, 105, 109, 113, 117) sts., working extra sts. into patt.
Cont. without further shaping until sleeve measures 4 (4, 4½, 4½, 5, 5) ins., ending with a wrong-side row.
To Shape Top: —Cast off 6 (8, 8, 10, 10, 12) sts. at beg. of next 2 rows, then dec. 1 st. at each end of next row and every foll. alt. row until 49 sts. rem. Now dec. 1 st. at each end of next 7 rows, then cast off 3 sts. at beg. of foll. 6 rows. Cast off rem. sts.

NECK RIBBING
With right side of work facing, join yarn to

neck edge at shoulder and with a No. 13 [0] needle, pick up and k. 28 sts. along shaped edge of neck, k. sts. from stitch-holder, then pick up and k. 28 sts. along other side of neck. Work 8 rows k. 1, p. 1 rib. Cast off in rib.

To make up
Press pieces lightly on wrong side with a warm iron over a damp cloth, avoiding ribbing.
For short-sleeved jumper, join shoulder seams, set sleeves into armholes then join side and sleeve seams.
For sleeveless version, join shoulder seams. With No. 13 [0] needles, pick up and k. 122 (126, 130, 134, 138, 142) sts. round armhole edge. Work 8 rows k. 1, p. 1 rib. Cast off in rib. Work other armhole to match Join side seams, including armhole borders.

EVENING SHAWL
Knit a little bit of glamour for the evening. It's easy when you follow these instructions. Using No. 9 [4] needles and big needles of half inch diameter, you will make it faster than you might think. Every row gets shorter to make the shape, and the needles used in turn make the attractive lacy effect

Materials: —3 ozs. Twilley's Cortina in White and 6 ozs. Twilley's Goldfingering in gold; a pair of No. 9 [4] knitting needles; ½ inch Whizz-pins.

Measurements: —Length at widest edge: 65 ins.; depth at centre: 29 ins., excluding fringe.

Tension: —5 sts. and 6 rows to 1 inch.

Abbreviations: —See page 20.

TO MAKE
With No. 9 [4] needles and G. cast on 328 sts. K. 4 rows. Now work thus: —
1st row: With ½ inch pins and W., k. 2 tog., k. to last 2 sts., k. 2 tog.
2nd row: —With No. 9 [4] needles and W., p. 2 tog., p. to last 2 sts., p. 2 tog.
3rd row: —With No. 9 [4] needles and G., k. 2

tog., k. to last 2 sts., k. 2 tog. Rep. 3rd row 3 times more. Now rep. last 6 rows until 4 sts. rem. Cast off with No. 9 [4] needles and G. Press lightly. Cut 18 inch lengths of Gold and fringe along shaped edges.

SOCKS FOR MEN

Materials: —4 oz. of Patons Nylox Knitting 4-ply; a set of four No. 13 [0] double-pointed knitting needles.

Measurements: —Length of leg to base of heel: 13 ins. Foot length: 10½ ins. Both these measurements are adjustable.

Tension: —8½ sts. to 1 inch.

Abbreviations: —See page 20.

TO MAKE
Cast on 76 sts. (24 on 1st and 3rd needles and 28 on middle needle). Work in rounds of k. 1, p. 1 rib for 3½ ins. Now work in rounds of k. 2, p. 2 rib until leg measures 10½ ins. from cast-on edge. Adjust length here.
To Divide for heel and instep: —K. 34 sts. for heel, turn and place rem. sts. on 2 needles for instep.
Beg. with a p. row, work 35 rows st. st. on the 34 sts., ending with a p. row.
To Turn heel: —*Next row*: —Sl. 1, k. 19, k. 2 tog., turn. *Next row*: —Sl. 1, p. 6, p. 2 tog., turn. *Next row*: —Sl. 1, k. 7, k. 2 tog., turn. *Next row*: —Sl. 1, p. 8, p. 2 tog., turn. *Next row*: —Sl. 1, k. 9, k. 2 tog., turn. Cont. in this way, working 1 more st. before the dec. on every row until row worked, Sl. 1, p. 18, p. 2 tog. *Next row*: —K. these 20 sts., then with same needle, k. up 19 sts. from side of heel. This will now be the 1st needle. With another needle, rib the 42 sts. of instep. This will now be the 2nd needle. With 3rd needle, k. up 19 sts. from other side of heel, then k. 10 sts. from 1st needle. (100 sts.)
To Shape Instep: —*1st round*: —1st needle, k. to last 3 sts., k. 2 tog., k. 1, 2nd needle, Rib. 3rd needle, k. 1, s. k. p. o., k. to end. *2nd round*: —1st needle, k. 2nd needle, Rib. 3rd needle, K. *3rd round*: —As 2nd. Rep. last 3 rounds 7 times more. Cont. in st.st. and rib until foot measures 8 ins. from back of heel

Socks for a Man

for 10½ inch foot. Adjust length here.
To Shape Toe: —*Next round*: —1st needle, k. to last 3 sts., k. 2 tog., k. 1. 2nd needle, K. 1, s. k. p. o., k. to last 3 sts. k. 2 tog., k. 1. 3rd needle, k. 1, s. k. p. o., k. to end. *Next round*. K. Rep. last 2 rounds until 20 sts. rem. K. the sts. on 1st needle on to the 3rd needle. Graft stitches. Press sock. Make another sock to match.

KNEE-LENGTH STOCKINGS
Lace stockings made knee-length are better than nylon tights under slacks in the hot weather. Leg and foot lengths are adjustable for three sizes, so school-girl daughters will like them too

Materials: —5 balls of Coats Chain Mercer Crochet Cotton No. 20; a set of 4 double-pointed knitting needles No. 14 [00].

Measurements: —Length of foot: 9½ (10, 10½) ins. Length from base of heel: —18 ins.

Tension: —11 sts. and 15 rows to 1 inch over st. st.

Abbreviations: —See page 20.

TO MAKE
Cast on 100 sts. (35 on 1st needle. 35 on 2nd and 30 sts. on 3rd needle.) Work in k. 1 t. b. l., p. 1 rib for ¾ in. Change to pattern as follows:
1st round: —* K. 1 t. b. l., p. 1, y.o.n., sl. 1, k. 1, p. s. s. o., p. 1, rep. from * to end.
2nd round: —* K. 1 t. b. l., p. 1, k. 2, p. 1, rep. from * to end. *3rd round*: —As 2nd round.
4th round: —* K. 1 t. b. l., p. 1, k. 2 tog., y. r. n., p. 1, rep. from * to end.
5th and 6th rounds: —As 2nd round.
7th round: —As 1st round. These 7 rounds form the patt. Rep. them 12 times more. Now, keeping patt. correct, dec. 1 st. at each end of next and every foll. 5th round until 70 sts. rem. Cont. straight until 31 patts. have been worked.
To Divide for Heel: —K. 15, slip last 15 sts. of round on to other end of same needle. Divide remaining sts. on to 2 needles and leave for instep.
Heel: —*1st row*: —Sl. 1, p. to end.

2nd row: —Sl. 1, k. to end. Rep. these 2 rows 16 times more, then 1st row again.
Next row: —K. 20, sl. 1, k. 1, p. s. s. o., turn.
Next row: —P. 11, p. 2 tog., turn.
Next row: —K. 12, sl. 1, k. 1, p. s. s. o., turn.
Next row: —P. 13, p. 2 tog., turn.
Cont. in this way until all sts. are worked on to one needle. (20 sts.)
Next row: —K. 10.
Slip all instep sts. on to 1 needle. K. 10 from heel, pick up and k. 18 sts. along side of heel. With 3rd needle, patt. across instep sts., with 4th needle, pick up and k. 18 sts. along other side of heel, k. 10 heel sts. (96 sts.)
To Shape Instep: —1st needle, K. *2nd needle*: —Patt. *3rd needle*: —K.
2nd round: —K. to last 3 sts. on 1st needle, k. 2 tog., k. 1. *2nd needle*: Patt. *3rd needle*: —K. 1, k. 2 tog. t. b. l., k. to end. Rep. last 2 rows until 80 sts. rem. Cont. on these sts. until foot measures 6¾ (7¼, 7¾) ins. from side of heel.
Next round: —K.
To Shape Toe: —*1st round*: —K. to last 3 sts. of 1st needle, k. 2 tog., k. 1 *2nd needle*: —K. 1, k. 2 tog. t. b. l., k. to last 3 sts., k. 2 tog., k. 1. *3rd needle*: —K. 1, k. 2 tog. t. b. l., k. to end. *2nd round*: —K. Rep. these 2 rounds until 28 sts. rem. K. all sts. from 1st needle on to end of 3rd needle. Graft stitches, Press.

SUMMER DRESS AND SUMMER JUMPER WITH AND WITHOUT SLEEVES

Materials: —Sleeveless Dress: 9 (10, 10, 11, 11) ozs. white and 8 (8, 9, 9, 10) ozs. Contrast in Twilley's Bubbly; Jumper: 7 (7, 8, 8, 9) ozs. White and 6 (7, 7, 8, 8) ozs. Contrast; for both a pair each of Nos. 8 [5] and 9 [4] knitting needles; an 8 inch zip.

Measurements: —Bust: 32 (34, 36, 38, 40) ins. Dress Length: 33 (34, 34, 35, 35) ins.; Jumper Length: 21 (21½, 21½, 22, 22) ins.; Sleeve: 3 ins.

Tension: —9 sts. and 12 rows to 2 ins.

Abbreviations: —See page 20.

DRESS-BACK
Using Bubbly *double* throughout, with No. 8 [5] needles, cast on with one thread W. and

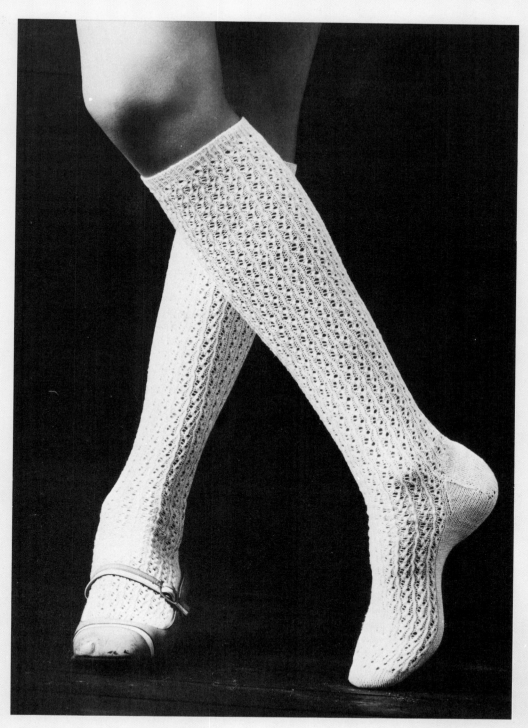

Knee-length stockings for a girl

one thread C. 90 (94, 98, 102, 106) sts. and k. 4 rows, Now work in st. st. and dec. 1 st. each end of every 20th row until there are 78 (82, 86, 90, 94) sts. on needle. Cont. straight until work measures 26 (26½, 26½, 27, 27) ins. from beg., ending with a p. row.

To Shape Armholes: — Cast off 4 sts. at beg. of next 2 rows, then dec. 1 st. at each end of next 8 rows. Cont. until armhole measures 7 (7½, 7½, 8, 8) ins. from beg. of armhole shaping.

To Shape Shoulders: — Cast off 6 (7, 8, 9, 10) sts. loosely at beg. of next 4 rows. Leave rem. sts. on a spare needle.

FRONT

As Back until work measures 23 (24, 24, 25, 25) ins. from beg., ending with a p. row.

** *To Divide for Front opening*: — K. 35 (37, 39, 41, 43) sts., turn. Leave rem. sts. on a spare needle. Work 17 (13, 13, 11, 11) rows more in st. st.

To Shape Armhole: — Cast off 4 sts. at beg. of next row and then dec. 1 st. at armhole edge on next 8 rows. Cont. until armhole measures 5 (5½, 5½, 6, 6) ins. from beg.

To Shape Neck: — Cast off 7 sts. at beg. of next row, then dec. 1 st. at neck edge on next 4 rows. Work 8 rows straight.

To Shape Shoulder: — Cast off 6 (7, 8, 9, 10) sts. at beg. of next and following alternate row. Return to rem. sts. on spare needle. Place centre 8 sts. on a safety-pin for front bands. Rejoin one strand each of W. and C. to rem. sts. and k. to end. Work 18 (14, 14, 12, 12) rows in st. st. beg. with a p. row. Beg. armhole shaping work to match other side, reversing shapings.

FRONT BANDS AND NECK BANDS

Join shoulder seams. With No. 9 [4] needles and 2 strands of W. return to 8 sts. on safety-pin and with right side facing, k. first 4 sts., turn. Work in g.st. on these 4 sts. for left front band until band is same length as front opening to beg. of neck shaping, ending at inner edge. Break yarn and place sts. on a safety-pin. Work on rem. 4 sts. for right front band to match, ending at outer edge. Do not break yarn. *Next row*: — K. 4 sts. pick up and k. 22 sts. evenly round right front neck edge, k. 30 sts. from back of neck, pick up and k.

22 sts. down left side of front neck, then 4 sts. from safety-pin. Knit 6 rows, cast off.

ARMBANDS

With 2 strands W. pick up and k. sts. round armhole. K. 2 rows. Cast off.

To make up

Press pieces. Set in sleeves. Join side and sleeve seams. Sew front bands to front edge. Insert zip.

JUMPER-BACK

With No. 9 [4] needles and one strand of W. and C. together, cast on 78 (82, 86, 90, 94) sts. k. 4 rows. Change to No. 8 [5] needles and cont. in st. st. until Back measures 14 ins. from beg., ending with a p. row. Now complete as for dress from Armhole Shaping.

FRONT

Work as for Back until Front measures 11 (11½, 11½, 12, 12) ins. from beg., ending with a p. row.

Now complete as for Dress from **

SLEEVES

With No. 9 [4] needles and one strand of W. and one of C. together, cast on 52 (56, 56, 60, 60) sts. K. 4 rows. Change to No. 8 [5] needles and work 18 rows in st. st., beg. with a k. row.

Inc. 1 st. at each end of 4th rows until there are 58 (62, 62, 66, 66) sts. on needle.

To Shape top: — Cast off 4 sts. at beg. of next 2 rows, then dec. 1 st. at each end of every alt. row until 34 sts. rem. Dec. 1 st. each end of next 8 rows. Cast off.

To make up

Join shoulder seams and finish as for dress.

PINK AND BROWN SUIT

Neat classic lines in smooth stocking stitch. The jacket and skirt make a timeless suit for all ages. To top dresses and trousers, the jacket makes a useful addition for daytime

Materials: — Jacket: 20 (21, 22) ozs. Sirdar Double Knitting Wool in Pink and 2 ozs. in Brown; Skirt: 11 (12, 13) ozs. Brown; a pair each of Nos. 8 [5] and 9 [4] knitting needles; 4 buttons; waist measurement of 1½ inch elastic.

Measurements: —Jacket: Bust: 36 (38, 40) ins.; Length: 26½ (27, 27½) ins.; Sleeve: 18 ins. Skirt: Hips: 38 (40, 42) ins.; Length: 25 ins.

Tension: —11½ stitches and 15½ rows to 2 ins. on No. 9 [4] needles.

Abbreviations: —See page 20.

SKIRT (BACK AND FRONT ALIKE)

Cast on 86 (92, 98) sts. on No. 9 [4] needles in Brown and work 14 rows in st. st. *Next Row*: K. 1, p. u. k., * k. 28 (30, 32), p. u. k., rep. from * 3 times, k. 1. Work 5 rows st. st.
Next row: K. 1, p. u. k., k. 29 (31, 33), p. u. k., k. 30 (32, 34), p. u. k., k. 29 (31, 33), p. u. k., k. 1. Work 5 rows in st. st.
Next row: —K. 1, p. u. k., k. 30 (32, 34), p. u. k., k. 32 (34, 36), p. u. k., k. 30 (32, 34), p. u. k., k. 1. Work 5 rows in st. st.
Next row: K. 1, p. u. k., k. 31 (33, 35), p. u. k., k. 34 (36, 38), p. u. k., k. 31 (33, 35), p. u. k., k. 1. Work 5 rows st. st.
Next row: K. 1, p. u. k., k. 32 (34, 36), p. u. k., k. 36 (38, 40), p. u. k., k. 32 (34, 36), p. u. k., k. 1 (106, 112, 118 sts. on needle). Now work in st. st. for 10 rows and then inc. both ends of next and every foll. 8th row until there are 126 (132, 138) sts. on needle. Then cont. to work without further increasing until piece measures 25 ins. from beg., ending with a right-side row. Adjust length here.
K. 1 row to mark hemline. Work 11 rows. Cast off.

JACKET-BACK

Cast on 106 (112, 118) sts. on No. 9 [4] needles in Pink and work 11 rows in st. st., ending with a k. row. K. next row to mark hemline. Beg. with a k. row, work in st. st. for 7 ins. from hemline. Now dec. 1 st. at both ends of next and every foll. 4th row until there are 96 (102, 108) sts. Work a further 3 ins., then inc. at both ends of next and every foll. 4th row until there are 106 (112, 118) sts. on needle. Cont. without further shaping until work measures 18½ ins. from hemline, ending with a p. row.

To Shape Armholes: Cast off 5 sts. at beg. of next 2 rows. Now dec. 1 st. at both ends of next and alt. rows until there are 82 (86, 90) sts. on needle. Work until armholes measure 8 (8½, 9) ins. from beg., ending with a p. row.
To Shape Shoulders: Cast off 9 (10, 11) sts. at beg. of next 2 rows and 9 (9, 10) at beg. of foll. 2 rows, then 8 sts. at beg. of next 2 rows. Cast off rem. sts.

LEFT FRONT

Cast on 59 (62, 65) sts. on No. 9 [4] needles in Pink and work 11 rows in st.st., ending with a k. row. K. next row to mark hemline. Beg. with a k. row work 7 rows in st. st. *Next row*: With wrong side facing, cast on 12 sts. for front edge facing, p. to end of row. *Next row*: K. to last 13 sts., sl. 1, k. 12.
Next row: P. Rep. these 2 rows until work measures 7 ins. from hemline. Continue in st.st. and slip the st. on every k. row as before, Dec. at side edge on next and every 4th row until there are 66 (69, 72) sts. on needle. Work a further 3 ins. without shaping, then inc. 1 st. at both ends at side edge on next and every foll. 4th row until there are 71 (74, 77) sts. on needle. Work until piece measures 18½ ins. from hemline, ending at side edge.
To Shape Armhole: Cast off 5 sts. at beg. of next row. Now dec. 1 st. at armhole edge on every foll. alt. row until there are 59 (61, 63) sts. Work without shaping until armhole measures 6 (6½, 7) ins., ending at front edge.
To Shape Neck: Cast off 25 (26, 26) sts. at beg. of next row and 2 sts. at beg. of next foll. 4 alt. rows. Work 4 rows, ending at armhole edge.
To Shape Shoulder: Cast off 9 (10, 11) sts. at beg. of next row and 9 (9, 10) sts. at beg. of next alt. row. Work 1 row. Cast off. Mark 4 button positions on this Front. The top one 1 in. from neck edge and the bottom one 6 ins. from lower edge, the other two evenly spaced between.

JACKET RIGHT FRONT

Work as for Left Front, reversing shapings and working four buttonholes thus, to match marked button positions.
On right side row. *1st buttonhole row*: K. 3, cast off 6 sts., k. 2, sl. 1, k. 3, cast off 6, k. to end.

2nd buttonhole row: P., cast on 6 sts. over cast off sts. in previous row.

SLEEVES

Cast on 52 (54, 56) sts. on No. 9 [4] needles in Pink and work as for Back to hemline. Work 2 ins., then inc. 1 st. at both ends of next and every 6th row until there are 82 (86, 90) sts. on needle. Cont. without further shaping until sleeve measure 18 ins. from hemline.

To Shape Top: — Cast off 5 sts. at beg. of next 2 rows. Now dec. 1 st. at both ends of every alt. row until 52 (54, 58) sts. rem. Cast off 2 sts. at beg. of next 6 (6, 8) rows and 3 sts. at beg. of foll. 8 rows. Cast off rem. sts.

COLLAR

Cast on 106 (110, 110) sts. on No. 9 [4] needles and Brown wool. *1st row*: (K. 2, p.2) to last 2 sts., k. 2.

2nd row: — (P. 2, k. 2) to last 2 sts., p. 2.

3rd row: — (K. 2 tog., then twist 2 thus: — without slipping sts. off needle, k. first st. on left hand needle, then slip both from needle together, P. 2) rep. to last 2 sts., twist 2.

Rep. 2nd and 3rd row until collar measures 5 ins. Cast off loosely.

To make up

Press all pieces except collar. Join all seams and set in sleeves. Turn all hems to wrong side and catch down. Turn under and hem down front facings and neaten all buttonholes. Add buttons. Sew cast off edge of collar to neck edge. Pin waist length of elastic to skirt and join ends. Attach to waist at wrong side with herringbone casing.

WHITE SWEATER
WITH STRIPED CUFFS

Materials: —20 (21, 22) balls of Robin Vogue Double Knitting Wool in White; 1 ball each in Black, Red and Oatmeal; a pair each of Nos. 8 [5] and 10 [3] knitting needles.

Measurements: —Bust: 34 (36, 38) ins.; Length: 27½ (28, 28½) ins.; Sleeve: —17 ins.

Tension: —6½ sts. and 8 rows to 1 inch over pattern on No. 8 [5] needles.

Abbreviations: —See page 20.

BACK

With No. 10 [3] needles and White, cast on 118 (124, 130) sts. *1st row*: —P. 1, * k. 2, p. 1, rep. from * to end. *2nd row*: —K. 1, * p. 2, k. 1, rep. from * to end. *3rd row*: —As 1st row. *4th row*: —K. These 4 rows form the patt., rep. them twice more. Change to No. 8 [5] needles and cont. in patt. until work measures 20 ins. from beg., ending with a wrong-side row.

To Shape Armholes: —Cast off 6 sts. at beg. of next 2 rows and 3 sts. at beg. of foll. 2 rows. Now dec. 1 st. at each end of every row until 88 (92, 96) sts. rem. Work without further shaping until armhole measures 7½ (8, 8½) ins., ending with a wrong-side row.

To Shape Shoulders: —Cast off 8 (9,.9) sts. at beg. of next 2 rows and 8 (8, 9) sts. at beg. of foll. 2 rows. Cast off.

FRONT

Work as for Back until armhole measures 1½ (1¾, 1¾) ins. less than Back to shoulder, ending with a wrong-side row.

To Shape Neck: —Patt. 33 (34, 35) sts. and leave these sts. on a spare needle. Cast off next 22 (24, 26) sts., patt. to end.

Work 1 row.

* Cast off 3 sts. at neck edge on next and foll. 2 alt. rows. Work to same length as Back to shoulder, ending at side edge.

To Shape Shoulder: —Cast off 8 (9, 9) sts. at beg. of next and foll. alt. row, work 1 row, cast off. Rejoin yarn to inner edge of sts. on spare needle and work from * to match.

SLEEVES

With No. 10 [3] needles and White, cast on 55 (58, 61) sts. and work 3 repeats of patt. Break white join Red and change to No. 8 [5] needles and k. 1 row. Beg. with a 2nd row, work 7 rows patt. Break Red and join Oatmeal, k. 1 row. Beg. with 2nd row, work 3 rows patt. Break oatmeal and join in Black, k. 1 row, then work 2nd patt. row. Break Black, join Oatmeal and k. 2 rows. Now work 1st and 2nd rows. Break Oatmeal join Red and k. 2 rows, then work patt. rows 1 to 4. Break Red, join White and k. 1 row.

Beg. with 2nd row cont. in patt. and inc. 1 st. at each end of next and every foll. 6th row until there are 75 (78, 81) sts. Then inc. 1 st. at each end of every 4th row until there are 87 (90, 93) sts. Work without further shaping until sleeve measures 17 ins. from beg., ending with a wrong-side row.

To Shape top: —Cast off 6 sts. at beg. of next 2 rows, then 3 sts. at beg. of foll. 4 (6, 6) rows. Now dec. 1 st. at each end of every right side row until 39 (40, 41) sts. rem. Cast off 3 sts. at beg. of next 6 rows. Cast off.

NECKBAND

Join right shoulder seam. With No. 10 [3] needles and white and with right side facing, K. pick up and k. 97 (100, 103) sts. evenly round neck edge. Beg. with 2nd row of patt. work 6 rows patt. Cast off loosely.

To make up

Press pieces. Join left shoulder seam, side and sleeve seams. Set in sleeves.

SHIRT-STYLE SWEATER IN 3 SIZES FOR MEN

Comfortable and casual, for a man at ease about the house

Materials: —20 (21, 22) ozs. Lee Target Motoravia Double Knitting Wool; a pair each of Nos. 9 [4] and 11 [2] knitting needles; 3 buttons.

Measurements: — Chest: —38 (40, 42) ins.; Length: —26 ins.; Sleeve: —8 ins.

Tension: —6 sts. and 8 rows to 1 inch on No. 9 [4] needles.

Abbreviations: —See page 20.

BACK

With No. 11 [2] needles, cast on 118 (124, 130) sts., and work in k. 1, p. 1 rib for 2½ ins. Change to No. 9 [4] needles and st. st. and work until Back measures 16 ins. from beg.

To Shape Armholes: —Cast off 5 sts. at beg. of next 2 rows, then dec. 1 st. at beg. of next 12 rows. * Cont. until Back measures 26 ins. from beg.

To Shape Shoulders: —Cast off 16 (17, 18) sts. at beg. of next 4 rows. Cast off rem. sts.

FRONT

Work as for Back as far as * Cont. on these sts. until Front measures 19 ins. from beg.

To Divide for neck opening: —With right side facing, k. 43 (46, 49) sts., turn and work back. Cont. on these sts. until work measures 24 ins from beg. Now dec. 1 st. at neck edge on every row until 32 (34, 36) sts. rem. Cont. straight until work measures 26 ins.

To Shape Shoulder: —Beg. at armhole edge, cast off 16 (17, 18) sts., at beg. of next and foll. alt. row. Return to remaining sts., rejoin yarn, cast off 10 sts., and work to match first side.

SLEEVES

With No. 11 [2] needles, cast on 54 (56, 58) sts., and work in k. 1, p. 1 rib for 3 ins. Change to No. 9 [4] needles and st.st. Inc. 1 st. at each end of 5th and every foll. 6th row until there are 90 (92, 94) sts. Cont. on these sts. until sleeve measures 18 ins. from beg.

To Shape Top: —Cast off 4 (4, 5) sts. at beg. of next 2 rows. Now dec. 1 st. at beg. of every row until 24 sts. rem. Cast off.

LEFT FRONT BAND

With No. 11 [2] needles, cast on 16 sts., and work in k. 1, p. 1 rib for 4 rows. *Next row*: — (Buttonhole row) Rib 7, cast off 2 sts., rib to end. *Next row*: —Rib 7, caxt on 2, rib to end. Cont. in rib making two more buttonholes at 2 inch intervals, measured from base of previous buttonhole.

Work 4 more rows. Cast off in rib. Right Front Band is worked in same way, omitting buttonholes.

COLLAR

With No. 11 [2] needles, cast on 146 (150, 154) sts., and work in k. 1, p. 1 rib for 3½ ins. Cast off loosely in rib.

To make up

Press pieces. Join shoulder, side and sleeve seams. Set in sleeves. Sew front bands into place and add buttons. Set collar to neck. Press seams.

BROWN AND WHITE CHECK DRESS

Warm winter dress in check stitch you will find simple to work. Firm double hems at cuff, neck and lower edge make the final effect neat and smart

Materials: —16 (16, 17) ozs. Lister Lavenda Crisp Crêpe 4-ply Wool in Light shade; 18 (19, 20) ozs. Dark; a pair each of Nos. 10 [3] and 12 [1] knitting needles; a set of 4 double-pointed knitting needles No. 12 [1]

Measurements: —Bust: 34 (36, 38) ins.; Length: 45 ins.; Sleeve: 17 ins.; Hips: 36 (38, 40) ins.

Tension: —9 sts. and 12 rows to 1 inch over pattern on No. 10 [3] needles.

Abbreviations: —See page 20.

BACK

With No. 12 [1] needles and D. Cast on 218 (226, 234) sts. and work 11 rows st. st., ending with a k. row. K. next row for hemline. Change to No. 10 [3] needles and work in patt. thus: *1st row:* —With D., k. 2 * with yarn at back of work, sl. 2, k. 2, rep. from * to end. *2nd row:* —With D., p. 2, * with yarn at front of work, sl. 2, p. 2, rep. from * to end. *3rd row:* —With D., k. 2, * sl. 1, k. 1, p. s. s. o., and k. into sl. st. before slipping it off needle, k. 2, rep. from * to end. *4th row:* —With D., p. *5th to 8th rows:* —As 1st to 4th rows, but with L. These 8 rows form the patt. Work straight for 2 ins. Now dec. 1 st. at each end of next and foll. 11th rows until 158 (166, 174) sts. rem. Work without further shaping until Back measures 38 (37¾, 37½) ins. from hemline.
To Shape Armholes: —Cast off 10 (11, 12) sts. at beg. of next 2 rows. Now dec. 1 st. at each end of next 12 (13, 14) rows. Work straight until armhole measures 7 (7¼, 7½) ins. from beg.
To Shape Shoulders: —Cast off 6 sts. at beg. of next 10 rows and 5 (6, 7) sts. at beg. of next 2 rows. Cast off rem. sts. for back of neck.

FRONT

Work as for Back until Front measures 1 inch less than Back to beg. of armhole shaping, ending with a wrong-side row.
To Divide for Neck: —*Next row:* —Patt. 79 (83, 87) sts. turn and work on this side first, leaving remaining sts. on a spare needle. **
Dec. 1 st. at neck edge on next and every foll. 4th row until 22 (23, 24) sts. have been decreased, *at the same time*, when Front is same length as Back to armhole, beg.
Armhole Shaping: —Cast off at side edge 10 (11, 12) sts. once, then dec 1 st. at this edge on next 12 (13, 14) rows. Keeping armhole edge straight, cont. neck shaping and work until armhole measures the same as Back to shoulder.
To Shape Shoulder: —Cast off 6 sts. at armhole edge on alt. rows 5 times and 5 (6, 7) sts. once. ** Rejoin yarn to inner edge of work and work other side to match, working from ** to **.

NECKBAND

Join shoulder seams. With right side of work facing, and with 4 double-pointed No. 12 [1] needles, with D. pick up and k. 70 (72, 74) sts. from centre front to shoulder, 32 (34, 36) sts. across back of neck and 70 (72, 74) sts. down front to centre front and 1 st. from centre front. Join sts. into a circle and work in rounds. Arrange sts. evenly on three needles and working in k. 1, p. 1 rib, dec. 1 st. at each side of centre front st. on every round. work for 1¼ ins. Now work a further 1¼ ins., increasing 1 st. at each side of centre front st. Cast off in rib.

SLEEVES

With D. and No. 12 [1] needles, cast on 66 (66, 70) sts. and work in st. st. for 11 rows, ending with a k. row. K. next row for hemline. Change to No. 10 [3] needles and work in patt. for 3 ins. Cont. in patt. and inc. 1 st. at each end of next and every foll. 6th row until there are 110 (114, 118) sts. on needle. Work until sleeve measures 17 ins. from hemline, ending with same row and colour as Back to Armhole.
To Shape Top: —Cast off 10 (11, 12) sts. at beg. of next 2 rows. Dec. 1 st. at both ends of next 10 rows, then dec. 1 st. at each end of every alt. row until 40 (42, 44) sts. rem. Cast off 2 sts. at beg. of next 6 rows. Then cast off 2 (3, 3) sts. at beg. of foll. 2 rows. Cast off rem. sts.

BELT

With No. 12 [1] needles and D. Cast on 19 sts. and work in k. 1, p. 1 rib for 56 ins. Cast off.

To make up

Press pieces on wrong side. Join side and sleeve seams. Set in sleeves. Turn hems to wrong side and catch down neatly. Fold neckband in half to wrong side and slip stitch to wrong side. Press seams.

PINK CLASSIC SWEATER

A raglan sweater you will find so useful. Team it with the jacket of the suit on page 98 for a twin set, or with the skirt for a two-piece

Materials : —10 (11, 12) ozs. Robin Vogue 4-ply ; a pair each of Nos. 10 [3] and 11 [2] knitting needles.

Measurements : —Bust : 30 (32, 34) ins. ; Length : 18½ (19½, 20½) ins. ; Sleeve : 15 (16½, 18) ins.

Tension : —7 sts. and 9 rows to 1 inch on No. 10 [3] needles.

Abbreviations : —See page 20.

FRONT

With No. 11 [2] needles cast on 106 (114, 120) sts. and work in k. 1, p. 1 rib for 2 ins. Change to No. 10 [3] needles and st.st. and work until Front measures 11 (11½, 12) ins. from beg., ending with a p. row.
To Shape Raglan : —Cast off 6 (7, 6) sts. at beg. of next 2 rows.
Next row : —K. 1, k. 2 tog., k. to last 3 sts., k. 2 tog., k. 1. *Next row :* —P. Rep. last 2 rows until 50 (52, 54) sts. rem.
To Shape Neck : —*Next row :* —K. 1, k. 2 tog., k. 14, turn. Work on this set of sts., leaving rem. sts. on a spare needle. Dec. 1 st. at armhole edge on every alt. row and *at the same time*, dec. 1 st. at neck edge on next and every alt. row until 5 sts. have been decreased at neck edge. Cont. to dec. at armhole edge as before until 1 st. remains. Fasten off.
With right side facing, slip centre 16 (18, 20) sts. on to a spare needle and rejoin yarn to rem. sts. and work to match first side, reversing shapings.

BACK

Work as for Front to beg. of raglan shaping.
To Shape Raglan : —Cast off 6 (7, 6) sts. at beg. of next 2 rows.

Next row : —K. 1, k. 2 tog., k. to last 3 sts. k. 2 tog., k. 1. Next row : —P. Rep. these 2 rows until 28 (30, 32) sts. rem. Cast off.

SLEEVES

With No. 11 [2] needles, cast on 50 (52, 54) sts. and work in k. 1, p. 1 rib for 2 ins. Change to No. 10 [3] needles and st. st. and inc. 1 st. at each end of every 7th row until there are 84 (90, 96) sts. on needle. Work straight until sleeve measures 15 (16½, 18) ins. from beg., ending with a p. row.
To Shape Raglan : —Cast off 6 (7, 6) sts. at beg. of next 2 rows. Then dec. 1 st. at each end of next and every alt. row until 4 (6, 8) sts. rem. Cast off.

NECKBAND

With No. 11 [2] needles, pick up and k. 106 (110, 114) sts. round neck. Work 18 rows k. 1, p. 1 rib. Cast off loosely in rib.

To make up

Press pieces, avoiding ribbing. Join raglan seams. Join side and sleeve seams. Press seams.

PRETTY PARTY DRESS

Simple stitches and a super yarn to make a dream of a dress for a little girl. Although it is warm enough for winter parties, it is as light as a feather and so dainty
Materials : —5 (6, 6, 7, 8, 8) balls of Twilley's Mohair ; a pair each of Nos 10 [3] and 11 [2] knitting needles ; 3 small buttons ; a medium size crochet hook.

Measurements : —Chest : 20 (22, 24, 26, 28, 30) ins. ; Length : 16 (18, 20, 22, 25, 28) ins. ; Sleeve : 8 (9½, 11, 12½, 14, 15½) ins.

Tension : 5 sts. and 9 rows to 1 inch on No. 10 [3] needles.

Abbreviations : —See page 20.

FRONT : YOKE

With No. 10 [3] needles and using yarn double, cast on 54 (58, 62, 70, 74, 78) sts. Cont. with single yarn and work 8 rows st.st. beg. with a k. row.

To Shape Armholes: — Cast off 2 sts. at beg. of next 2 rows, then dec. 1 st. at each end of next 3 rows ** Cont. in st. st. until work measures $3\frac{1}{2}$ (4, $4\frac{1}{2}$, 5, $5\frac{1}{2}$, 6) ins. from beg., ending with a p. row.

To Shape Neck: — *Next row:* K. 16 (17, 18, 21, 22, 23), k. 2 tog., turn. Work on these sts. only and dec. 1 st. at neck edge on next 5 rows. Cont. until work measures 5 ($5\frac{1}{2}$, 6, $6\frac{1}{2}$, 7, $7\frac{1}{2}$) ins. from beg., ending with a p. row.

To Shape Shoulder: — Cast off loosely, 6 (6, 7, 8, 9, 9) sts. at beg. of next row, work 1 row then cast off rem. sts. Place centre 8 (10, 12, 14, 16, 18) sts. on a stitch-holder. Complete other side of neck to match.

SKIRT

With No. 11 [2] needles and using yarn double, pick up and k. 54 (58, 62, 70, 74, 78) sts. along right side of lower edge of yoke, Cont. with single yarn. *Next row:* — (k. 1, p. 1, k. 1) all into 1st st., (k. 1, p. 1) into next st., to last st., (k. 1, p. 1, k. 1) all into last st.

Change to No. 10 [3] needles. *Next row:* — (Right side) K. 2, (p. 2, k. 2) to end. *Next row:* — P. 2, (k. 2, p. 2) to end. Rep. these last 2 rows for 3 ins., ending with a wrong-side row. *Next row:* — (k. 1, p. 1) into next st., k. 1 * p. 2, (k. 1, p. 1) into next st., k. 1., rep. from * to end. *Next row:* — (wrong side) P. 3, (k. 2, p. 3) to end. *Next row:* — K. 3, (p. 2, k. 3) to end. Rep. last 2 rows for 3 ins., ending with a wrong-side row. *Next row:* — K. 3, * (p. 1, k. 1) into next st., p. 1, k. 3, rep. from * to end. *Next row:* — (wrong side) P. 3, (k. 3, p. 3) to end. *Next row:* — K. 3, (p. 3, k. 3) to end. Rep. last 2 rows until skirt measures 11 ($12\frac{1}{2}$, 14, $15\frac{1}{2}$, 18, $20\frac{1}{2}$) ins. from beg., ending with a wrong-side row. Adjust length here. Using yarn double cast off very loosely in rib.

BACK: YOKE

As Front Yoke to ** Cont. in st. st., until work measures $2\frac{1}{2}$ (3, $3\frac{1}{2}$, 4, $4\frac{1}{2}$, 5) ins from beg., ending with a p. row.

To Divide for Back opening: — K. 24 (26, 28, 32, 34, 36) sts., turn. Work on these sts. only. *Next row:* — K. 4, p. to end. Cont. in st.st., keeping 4 sts. in g. st. for border at inner edge for 6 rows.

Buttonhole border: — K. to last 4 sts. cast off 2, k. 2. *Next row:* — K. 2, cast on 2, p. to end.

Cont. in st.st. with garter st. border making 2nd buttonhole $1\frac{1}{4}$ ins. above first, when work measures 5 ($5\frac{1}{2}$, 6, $6\frac{1}{2}$, 7, $7\frac{1}{2}$) ins. from beg., ending at armhole edge.

To Shape Shoulder: — Cast off very loosely, 6 (6, 7, 8, 9, 9) sts. at beg. of next row. Work 1 row then cast off 6 (7, 7, 9, 9, 10) sts. at beg. of next row. Work 1 row. Leave 12 (13, 14, 15, 16, 17) sts. on a spare needle. Return to right side of rem. sts., cast on 4, k. these 4 sts. then k. to end. Next row: — P. to last 4 sts. k. 4. Complete in this way to match other side of Back, omitting buttonholes and reversing shapings.

SKIRT: BACK

As for Front.

Next band: — Join shoulders. With No. 11 [2] needles, k. sts. from left side of back neck, pick up and k. 16 sts. down left side of front neck, k. sts. from centre front, pick up and k. 16 sts. up right side of front neck then k. sts. from right side of back of neck. *1st row:* — (wrong side) K. 4, (p. 2, k. 2) to last 2 sts. k. 2. *2nd row:* — k. 6, (p. 2, k. 2) to last 4 sts. k. 4. Rep. last 2 rows once then 1st row again. *6th row:* — As 2nd to last 4 sts., cast off 2, k. 2. *7th row:* — K. 2, cast on 2, work to end as 1st row. Rep. 2nd then 1st and 2nd rows again. Using yarn double, cast off very loosely.

SLEEVES

With No. 11 [2] needles and using yarn double, cast on 38 (42, 46, 50, 54, 58) sts. Cont. with single yarn and work 2 ins. k. 2, p. 2 rib. *Next row:* — (K. 1, p. 1) into each st. to end. Change to No. 10 [3] needles, cont. in st. st. beg. with a p. row until work measures 8 ($9\frac{1}{2}$, 11, $12\frac{1}{2}$, 14, $15\frac{1}{2}$) ins. from beg., ending with a p. row.

To Shape top of Sleeve: — Cast off 2 sts. at beg. of next 2 rows, then dec. 1 st each end of every row until 16 (18, 20, 22, 24, 26) sts. rem. Cast off very loosely.

To make up

Press pieces, omitting ribbed parts. Join side and sleeve seams, set in sleeves, easing the fullness into the shoulder seam. Sew down the cast on 4 sts. at lower edge of back opening. Press seams. Add buttons. Work 1 row double crochet round back opening.

BABY DRESS & JACKET

Materials : —4 ozs. Lister Baby Bel 4-ply Courtelle for the jacket and 3 buttons ; 4 ozs. and 2 buttons for the dress ; for both a pair each of Nos. 11 [2] and 12 [1] knitting needle.

Measurements : —Chest 18 ins. ; Jacket length : 10 ins. ; Sleeve : 5 ins. Dress length : 12 ins. Sleeve : 2 ins.

Tension : —7½ stitches and 10 rows to 1 inch on No. 11 [2] needles.

Abbreviations : —See page 20.

JACKET-BACK

With No. 11 [2] needles, cast on 109 sts. ** Knit 2 rows, then work in patt. thus : *1st row :* —K. 1, * m. 1, k. 1, (p. 3, k. 1) 4 times, m. 1, k. 1, rep. from * to end. *2nd row :* —P. 3, * k. 3, (p. 1, k. 3) 3 times, p. 5, rep. from * ending last rep. p. 3. *3rd row :* —K. 2, * m. 1, k. 1, (p. 3, k. 1) 4 times, m. 1, k. 3, rep. from * ending last rep. k. 2. *4th row :* —P. 4, * k. 3, (p. 1, k. 3) 3 times, p. 7, rep. from * ending last rep. p. 4. *5th row :* —K. 3, * m. 1, k. 1, (p. 3, k. 1) 4 times, m. 1, k. 5, rep. from * ending last rep. k. 3. *6th row :* —P. 5, * k. 3 (p. 1, k. 3) 3 times, p. 9, rep. from * ending last rep. p. 5. *7th row :* —K. 4, * m. 1, k. 1, (p. 2 tog., p. 1, k. 1) 4 times, m. 1, k. 7, rep. from * ending last rep. k. 4. *8th row :* —P. 6, * k. 2, (p. 1, k. 2) 3 times, p. 11, rep. from * ending last rep. p. 6. *9th row :* —K. 5, * m. 1, k. 1, (p. 2 tog., k. 1) 4 times, m. 1, k. 9, rep. from * ending last rep. k. 5. *10th row :* —P. 7, * k. 1, (p. 1, k. 1) 3 times p. 13, rep. from * ending last rep. p. 7. *11th row :* —K. 6, * m. 1, k. 1, p. 2 tog., k. 1, m. 1, k. 11, rep. from * ending last rep. k. 6. *12th row :* —P. 8, * k. 2, p. 1, k. 2, p. 15, rep. from * ending last rep. p. 8.

13th row : —K. 7, * m. 1, k. 1, p. 2 tog., k. 1, p. 2 tog., k. 1, m. 1, k. 13, rep. from * ending last rep. k. 7. *14th row :* —P. 9, * k. 1, p. 1, k. 1, p. 17, rep. from * ending last rep. p. 9. *15th row :* —K. 8, * m. 1, k. 1, k. 3 tog., k. 1, m. 1, k. 15, rep. from * ending last rep. k. 8. *16th row :* —P. *17th row :* —K. 9, * k. 3 tog., k. 17, rep. from * ending last rep. k. 9. *18th row :* —P. These 18 rows form the patt. Rep. them twice more. Knit one row. ***

Next row : —P. 1, * (p. 2 tog.) twice, p. 1, rep. from * to last 3 sts., p. 2 tog., p. 1. Now work 6 rows k. 1, p. 1 rib, then 2 rows st.st.

To Shape Armholes : —With right side facing, work in st.st. Cast off 3 sts. at beg. of next 2 rows. Then dec. 1 st. at each end of foll. 3 rows. Now work straight until Back measures 3½ ins. from beg. of armhole shaping.

To Shape Shoulders : —Cast off 9 sts. at beg. of next 4 rows. Cast off.

RIGHT FRONT

With No. 11 [2] needles, cast on 55 sts. and work from ** to *** as given for Back.

Next row : —P. 2 tog. twice, p. 1, rep. from * to end.

Next row : —K. 1, * p. 1, k. 1, rep. from * to end.

Next row : —P. 1, * k. 1, p. 1, rep. from * to end. Rep. last 2 rows twice more. Work 3 rows st. st.

To Shape Armhole : —With wrong side facing cast off 3 sts. at beg. of next row. Dec. 1 st. at armhole edge on next 3 rows. Work straight until armhole measures 2½ ins.

To Shape Neck : —With right side facing, cast off 3 sts. at beg. of next row, then dec. 1 st. at neck edge on every row until 18 sts. rem. Cont. straight until Front measures the same as back to shoulder shaping.

To Shape Shoulder : —With wrong side facing, cast off 9 sts. at beg. of next row, work 1 row and cast off.

LEFT FRONT

Work as for right front, reversing all shapings.

SLEEVES

With No. 11 [2] needles, cast on 37 sts. K. 2 rows. Work 18 rows of patt. as for Back. Now cont. in st. st. and inc. 1 st. at each end of next and every foll. 4th row until there are 49 sts.

on needle. Work straight until sleeve measures 5 ins.

To Shape Top: — Cast off 3 sts. at beg. of next 2 rows, then dec. 1 st. at each end of next and every alt. row until 23 sts. rem. Cast off 6 sts. at beg. of next 2 rows. Cast off.

COLLAR

With No. 11 [2] needles cast on 55 sts. K. 2 rows, then work 18 rows of patt. as for Back. Cast off.

With No. 12 [1] needles and with right side of collar facing, pick up and k. 18 sts. down side edge. Work 4 rows k. 1, p. 1 rib. Cast off. Finish other side to match.

RIGHT FRONT BAND

With No. 12 [1] needles and right side of work facing, pick up and k. 46 sts. to beg. of waist ribbing, 24 sts. to neck edge. Work 2 rows k. 1, p. 1 rib. *Next row:* — Rib 9, m. 1, p. 2 tog., rib 12, m. 1, p. 2 tog., rib to end. Work 2 rows rib, cast off.

Work Left front band to match, omitting buttonholes.

To make up

Press pieces. Join shoulder, side and sleeve seams. Set in sleeves. Join collar to cast off edge of neck. Add buttons.

DRESS - FRONT

** With No. 11 [2] needles cast on 91 sts. and k. 2 rows. Work 18 rows of patt. as for Back. *Next row:* — K. 18, patt. 55, k. 18. Keeping centre 3 patterns correct, and working edge sts. in st. st. dec. 1 st. at each end of next and every foll. 4th row until 9 decreases have been worked. Work 3 rows straight. This completes 2nd patt. on centre 3 patterns. Cont. to keep centre patt. correct and work edge sts. in st. st. dec. 1 st. at each end of next and foll. 4th row. Work straight until patt. is complete.

To Shape Armholes: — Keeping centre panel correct, cast off 3 sts. at beg. of next 2 rows. Then dec. 1 st. at each end of next 5 rows. Work straight until patt. is completed. ***

To Shape Neck: — *1st row:* — K. 21, slip 11 sts. on to a safety-pin for neckband and leave remaining sts. on a spare needle. Cont. on first set of 21 sts. Dec. 1 st. at neck edge on every row until 12 sts. rem. Cont. straight until work

measures 3⅓ ins. from beg. of armhole shaping. *To Shape Shoulders:* — Cast off 6 sts. at beg. of next row. P. 1 row. Cast off. Work other side to match, reversing shapings.

BACK

Work as for Front from ** to ***

To Divide for Back opening: — K. 24, cast off 5, k. to end. Working on last set of 24 sts. cont. without shaping until Back measures the same as Front to shoulder.

To Shape Shoulder: — Cast off 6 sts. at beg. of next row. Cast off. Return to remaining sts. and work to match first side, reversing shapings.

SLEEVES

With No. 11 [2] needles cast on 37 sts. and k. 2 rows. Work 18 rows of patt. as for Back of Jacket.

Next row: — * K. 2, k. 2IN, rep. from * to last st., k. 1. Work 3 rows st. st.

To Shape Top: — As for jacket sleeve.

RIGHT BACK OPENING BAND

With No. 12 [1] needles, pick up and k. 16 sts. down right side of opening. Work 2 rows k. 1, p. 1 rib. *Next row:* — Rib 8, m. 1, p. 2 tog., rib to end. Rib 2 rows. Cast off. Work left front band to match, omitting buttonholes.

NECKBAND

Join shoulder seams. With No. 12 [1] needles pick up and k. 74 sts. evenly round neck edge. Work 5 rows k. 1, p. 1 rib. Work buttonhole as for jacket, on 3rd row. Cast off.

To make up

Press pieces. Join side and sleeve seams. Set in sleeves. Sew lower edges of right and left back opening bands into position, placing right over left. Add buttons. Press seams.

SHORT WAISTCOAT FOR HIM
LONG-LINE CARDIGAN FOR HER

Materials : For waistcoat: 8 (8, 9, 10, 11, 12, 13, 14) balls of Twilley's Cortina; For cardigan: 11 (12, 13, 15, 16, 17, 18, 19) balls; a pair each of Nos. 8 [5] and 10 [3] knitting needles; 9 buttons.

Measurements : Bust/Chest : 32 (34, 36, 38, 40, 42, 44, 46) ins. ; Length : waistcoat : 20 (20, 21, 21, 22, 22, 23, 23) ins. ; cardigan : 30 (30, 31, 31, 32, 32, 33, 33) ins.

Tension : —6 sts. and 12 rows to 1 inch on No. 8 [5] needles.

Abbreviations : —See page 20.

LONG CARDIGAN

BACK

With No. 10 [3] needles, cast on 103 (109, 115, 121, 127, 133, 139, 145) sts. and work 11 rows in k. 1, p. 1 rib. Change to No. 8 [5] needles and patt. thus : —*1st row :* (wrong side) K. 1, (y. fwd., sl. 1, k. 1) to end. *2nd row :* —K. 1, (k. sl. st. and loop st. tog. t. b. l., k. 1) to end. These 2 rows form the patt. and are repeated throughout. Cont. until work measures 23 ins *

To Shape Armholes : — (Note: When casting off or decreasing, count sl. st. and loop st. as one st. on 1st patt. row.)

Cast off 6 (8, 8, 10, 10, 12, 12, 14) sts. at beg. of next 2 rows, then dec. 1 st. at each end of next 8 rows. Cont. in patt. until work measures 30 (30, 31, 31, 32, 32, 33, 33) ins. from beg., ending with 1st patt. row.

To Shape Shoulders : —Cast off 6 (6, 7, 7, 8, 8, 9, 9) sts. at beg. of next 6 rows. Change to No. 10 [3] needles and work 6 rows k. 1, p. 1 rib. Cast off in rib.

RIGHT FRONT

With No. 10 [3] needles cast on 51 (53, 57, 59, 63, 65, 69, 71) sts. and work as Back to * ending with 2nd patt. row.

To Shape Armhole and Front edge : Cast off 6 (8, 8, 10, 10, 12, 12, 14) sts. at beg. of next row. Dec. 1 st. at armhole edge on next 8 rows, and *at the same time* dec. 1 st. at front edge on next and foll. 4th row. Keeping armhole edge straight, dec. 1 st. at front edge on next and every foll. 4th row until 18 (18, 21, 21, 24, 24, 27, 27) sts. rem. Cont. without further shaping until work measures 30 (30, 31, 31, 32, 32, 33, 33) ins. from beg., ending at armhole edge.

To Shape Shoulder : — Cast off 6 (6, 7, 7, 8,

8, 9, 9) sts. at beg. of next and foll. 2 alt. rows.

LEFT FRONT

Work as for Right Front, reversing all shapings.

BUTTONHOLE BAND

With No. 10 [3] needles cast on 12 sts. and work 2 rows k. 1, p. 1 rib.

1st Buttonhole row : —Rib 5, cast off 2, rib 5.

Next row : —Rib 5, cast on 2, rib 5. Cont. in rib making 8 more buttonholes 2¾ ins. apart, measured from base of the previous buttonhole. When the 9th buttonhole has been completed, rib 4 more rows.

Next row : —Cast off 4 sts. in rib, then rib to end. Work a further 7 (7, 8, 8, 9, 9, 10, 10) ins. in rib on these 8 sts. Cast off in rib.

BUTTON BAND

Work as for buttonhole band, omitting buttonholes.

ARMBANDS

Join shoulders. With No. 10 [3] needles, pick up and k. 100 (104, 114, 118, 128, 132, 142, 146) sts. evenly round armhole edge. Work 5 rows k. 1, p. 1 rib. Cast off in rib.

To make up

Press pieces lightly on wrong side with a warm iron over a damp cloth, omitting the ribbing. Join side seams. Sew on frnt bands, sewing top of bands to the 6 rows of rib at back of neck. Press seams. Add buttons.

SHORT WAISTCOAT

BACK AND FRONTS

As for Cardigan, but begin armhole shaping when work measures 13 ins., instead of 23 ins. Begin shoulder shaping when work measures 20 (20, 21, 21, 22, 22, 23, 23) ins., instead of 30 (30, 31, 31, 32, 32, 33, 33) ins.

FRONT BANDS

As for Cardigan, but make buttonholes at 1½ in. intervals instead of 2¾ ins. and work 13 ins. for first part of band, instead of 23 ins.

ARMBANDS AND MAKING UP

As for Cardigan.

YELLOW BELTED JACKET

Materials: —15 (16, 17, 18) balls of Patons Piccadilly; a pair each of Nos. 10 [3], 9 [4], and 8 [5] knitting needles; 8 buttons.

Measurements: —Bust: 34 (36, 38, 40) ins.; Length: 23 (23½, 24, 24½) ins.; Sleeve: 16 ins.

Tension: —5¾ sts., and 7½ rows to 1 inch on No. 8 [5] needles over stocking stitch.

Abbreviations: —See page 20.

BACK
With No. 10 [3] needles, cast on 119 (128, 134, 140) sts. Work in rib thus: —

1st row: —(Right side) P. 2, * k. 1 t.b.l., p. 2, rep. from * to end of row.

2nd row: —K. 2, *p. 1 t.b.l., k. 2, rep. from * to end of row.

These 2 rows form the rib patt. Rep. them 4 times more. Change to No. 8 [5] needles and cont. in rib until Back measrues 14½ ins. from beg.

To Shape Raglan: —Cast off 3 sts. at beg. of next 2 rows, then dec. 1 st. at each end of next and every foll. 4th row until 107 (116, 120, 124) sts. rem. Work 3 rows straight. Now dec. at each end of next and every alt. row until 69 (74, 78, 82) sts. rem.

To Shape Shoulders: —Cast off 7 (7, 8, 8) sts. at beg. of next 2 rows, then 7 (8, 8, 9) sts. at beg. of foll. 2 rows. Work 1½ ins. straight. Cast off.

POCKET LININGS
With No. 8 [5] needles cast on 28 sts. and work 4 ins. in st. st., ending with a k. row. Inc. 7 sts. evenly across last row. (35 sts.) Leave on a spare needle. Make another one to match.

PANEL PATTERN (17 sts.).
1st row: —(Wrong side facing) K. 2, (k. 1, p. 1, k. 1, p. 1, k. 1) into next st., k. 2, (P. B. 1, k. 2) 3 times, (k. 1, p. 1, k. 1, p. 1, k. 1) into next st., k. 2.

2nd row: —P. 2, k. 5, p. 2, (K. B. 1, p. 2) 3 times, k. 5, p. 2.

3rd row: —K. 2, p. 5, k. 2, (P.B. 1, k. 2) 3 times, p. 5, k. 2.

4th row: —P. 2, sl. 1, k. 1, p. s. s. o., k. 1, k. 2 tog., p. 2, (K. B 1, p. 2) 3 times, sl. 1, k. 1, p. s. s. o., k. 1, k. 2 tog., p. 2.

5th row: —K. 2, p. 3, k. 2, (P. B. 1, k. 2) 3 times, p. 3, k. 2.

6th row: —P. 2, sl. 1, k. 2 tog., p. s. s. o., p. 2, (K. B. 1, p. 2) 3 times, sl. 1, k. 2 tog., p. s. s. o., p. 2.

7th row: —K. 2, P. B. 1, k. 2, (k. 1, p. 1, k. 1, p. 1, k. 1) into next st., k. 2, P. B. 1, k. 2, (k. 1, p. 1, k. 1, p. 1, k. 1) into next st., k. 2, P. B. 1, k. 2.

8th row: —P. 2, K. B. 1, p. 2, (k. 5, p. 2, K. B. 1, p. 2) twice.

9th row: —K. 2, P. B. 1, k. 2, (p. 5, k. 2, P. B. 1, k. 2) twice.

10th row: —P. 2, K. B. 1, p. 2, (sl. 1, k. 1, p. s. s. o., k. 1, k. 2 tog., p. 2, K. B. 1, p. 2) twice.

11th row: —K. 2, P. B. 1, k. 2, (p. 3, k. 2, P. B. 1, k. 2) twice.

12th row: —P. 2, K. B. 1, p. 2, (sl. 1, k. 2 tog., p. s. s. o., p. 2, K. B. 1, p. 2) twice.

13th row: —K. 2, (P. B. 1, k. 2) twice, (k. 1, p. 1, k. 1, p. 1, k. 1) into next st., (k. 2, P. B. 1) twice, k. 2.

14th row: —P. 2, (K. B. 1, p. 2) twice, k. 5, (p. 2, K. B. 1) twice, p. 2.

15th row: —K. 2, (P. B. 1, k. 2) twice, p. 5, (k. 2, P. B. 1) twice, k. 2.

16th row: —P. 2, (K. B. 1, p. 2) twice, sl. 1, k. 1, p. s. s. o., k. 1, k. 2 tog., (p. 2, K. B. 1) twice, p. 2.

17th row: —K. 2, (P. B. 1, k. 2) twice, p. 3, (k. 2, P. B. 1) twice, k. 2.

18th row: —P. 2, (K. B. 1, p. 2) twice, sl. 1, k. 2 tog., p. s. s. o., (p. 2, K. B. 1) twice, p. 2.

These 18 rows form Panel Patt.

LEFT FRONT
With No. 10 [3] needles, cast on 59 (62, 65, 68) sts. and work as for Back until piece measures 5½ ins., ending with right side facing.

Place pocket lining as folls.

Next row: —Patt. 12 (12, 15, 15) sts., slip next 35 sts. on to spare needle. In place of these, p. across sts. of one pocket lining, patt. 12 (15, 15, 18) sts. Work 2 rows straight.

Cont. in rib and panel patt. as folls.

1st row: —Rib patt. 21 (21, 24, 24) work 1st row of panel patt. across next 17 sts., rib patt. 21 (24, 24, 27).

2nd row: —Rib patt. 21 (24, 24, 27) work 2nd row of panel patt., rib patt. 21 (21, 24, 24).

Cont. in rib and panel patt. thus, until Front matches Back up to raglan shaping.

To Shape Raglan: —Cast off 3 sts. at beg. of next row. Work 1 row. Cont. to shape raglan and *at the same time*, shape front edge by decreasing 1 st. at each end of next and foll. 4th rows until 50 (53, 54, 55) sts. rem. Work 3 rows straight. Now dec. 1 st. at each end of next and every alt. row until 16 (19, 20, 21) sts. rem. Keeping front edge straight, cont. to dec. at raglan edge only until 14 (15, 16, 17) sts. rem., ending with right side facing.

To Shape Shoulder: —Cast off 7 (7, 8, 8) sts. at beg. of next row then 7 (8, 8, 9) sts. at beg. of foll. alt. row.

RIGHT FRONT

Work as for Left Front from * * to * *.

Place pocket lining as folls: —

Next row: —Patt. 12 (15, 15, 18) sts., slip next 35 sts. on to a spare needle, place pocket lining sts. and p. across these 35 sts., patt. 12 (12, 15, 15) sts. Work 2 rows straight.

Next row: —Rib patt. 21 (24, 24, 27), work 1st row of panel patt. across next 17 sts., rib patt. 21 (21, 24, 24).

Cont. to work to match Left Front, reversing all shapings.

SLEEVES

With No. 10 [3] needles, cast on 59 (59, 65, 65) sts. and work 9 rows in rib as for Back. Change to No. 8 [5] needles and cont. in rib and panel patt. thus: —

1st row: —Rib patt. 21 (21, 24, 24) sts., work 1st row of panel patt. across next 17 sts., rib patt. 21 (21, 24, 24).

2nd row: —Rib patt. 21 (21, 24, 24), work 2nd row of patt. panel, rib patt. 21 (21, 24, 24). Cont. in rib and panel patt. Inc. 1 st. at each end of 7th (6th, 7th, 6th), and every foll. 6th (5th, 6th, 5th) row until there are 89 (95, 95, 101) sts. on needle. Cont. straight until work measures 16 ins. from beg., ending with right side facing.

To Shape Raglan: —Cast off 3 sts. at beg. of next 2 rows, then dec. 1 st. at each end of every row until 59 (61, 69, 71) sts. rem. Then

dec. 1 st. at each end of next and every alt. row until 21 sts. rem. Cont. on rem. sts. for saddle shoulder until strip fits along shoulder edge on Front. Cast off.

FRONT BORDER

Join raglan seams, then sew saddle strip along shoulders on Back and Front and half of the cast off sts. to extra rows at top of back. With No. 10 [3] needles, cast on 13 sts.

1st row: —K. 2, * p. 1, k. 1, rep. from * to last st. k. 1.

2nd row: —K. 1, * p. 1, k. 1, rep. from * to end.

Rep. last 2 rows twice more.

Next 2 rows, make buttonholes. Rib 5, cast off 3, rib to end. Cast on 3 sts. over those cast off in previous row.

Cont. in rib and make 5 more buttonholes at 2½ inch intervals. Then work straight until strip fits up right front, round neck and down left front. Sew into position.

BELT

With No. 10 [3] needles, cast on 13 sts. and work as for Front band, omitting buttonholes, for 28 (30, 32, 34) ins. Now make a buttonhole on next 2 rows. Work a further 5 ins. straight and make another buttonhole on next 2 rows. Work 1 inch straight. Cast off.

To make up

Press pieces. Join side and sleeve seams.

Pocket Tops: With right side facing, and with No. 10 [3] needles, p. across 35 pocket sts. Inc. 4 sts. evenly across row. Work 7 rows k. 1, p. 1 rib. Cast off. Catch down sides of pocket tops and catch down linings on wrong side. Add buttons to Front band and belt.

SMALL GIRL'S ROUND NECKED SWEATER

Materials: —8 (9, 10) ozs. Lister Lavenda Double Crêpe; a pair each of Nos. 9 [4] and 11 [2] Knitting needles; a cable needle; 4. inch zip.

Measurements: —Chest: 24 (26, 28) ins.; Length: —13½ (15, 16½) ins.; Sleeve: —12 (13, 14) ins.

Tension: —6 sts. and 8 rows to 1 inch on No. 9 [4] needles.

Abbreviations: —See page 20.

BACK

With No. 11 [2] needles, cast on 72 (76, 80) sts. and work in k. 1, p. 1 rib for 12 rows. Change to No. 9 [4] needles and inc. on next row thus: —K. 10 (8, 6) * pick up and k. loop lying between last and next st., k. 10 (11, 12), rep from * to last 2 sts., k. 2. Cont. in st. st. beg. with a p. row and work until Back measures 8 (9, 10) ins. from beg.

To Shape Raglan: —*1st row:* —Cast off 3 sts., p. 1, (k. 1, pick up and k. loop before next st.) 3 times, p. 1, k. to last 9 sts., p. 1, (k. 1, pick up and k. loop before next st.) 3 times, p. 1, k. 4.

2nd row: —Cast off 3 sts., k. 1, p. 6, k. 3, p. to last 11 sts., k. 3, p. 6, k. 2. Now beg. cable patt.

3rd row: —K. 1, p. 1, k. 6, p. 1, k. 2, s. k. p. o., k. to last 13 sts., k. 2 tog., k. 2, p. 1, k. 6, p. 1, k. 1 *4th row:* —K. 2, p. 6, k. 3, p. to last 11 sts., k. 3, p. 6, k. 2.

5th row: —K. 1, p. 1, C 6 F, p. 1, k. 2, s. k. p. o., k. to last 13 sts., k. 2 tog., k. 2, p. 1, C 6 B, p. 1. k. 1. *6th row:* —As 4th row. Rep. 3rd and 4th rows twice more. ** Rep. last 8 rows until 34 sts. rem. Cast off.

FRONT

Work as for Back as far as ** Rep. last 8 rows until 46 sts. rem.

To Shape Neck: —With right side facing, *1st row:* —Patt. 11, s. k. p. o., k. 6, leave these 18 sts. on a spare needle, then cast off 8 sts., k. to last 13 sts., k. 2 tog., k. 2, p. 1, k. 6, p. 1, k. 1. Cont. on these 18 sts. as folls.

2nd row: —k. 2, p. 6, k. 3, p. to end.
3rd row: —Cast off 3, k. 1, k. 2 tog., patt. to end. *4th row:* —As 2nd.
5th row: —Cast off 3, patt. to end.
6th row: —K. 2, p. 6, k. 1, k. 2 tog.
7th row: —As 5th. *8th row:* —K. 2, p. 5.
9th row: —(K. 2 tog.) twice, k. 1, p. 1, k. 1.
10th row: —K. 2, p. 3 tog. Cast off. Rejoin yarn to neck edge of rem. sts. and work to match.

SLEEVES

With No. 11 [2] needles cast on 36 (40, 44) sts. and work in k. 1, p. 1 rib for 12 rows. Change to No. 9 [4] needles and st. st. Inc. 1 st. at each end of 5th and every foll. 6th row until there are 60 (64, 68) sts. on needle. Cont. straight until sleeve measures 12 (13, 14) ins.

To Shape Raglan: —Cast off 3 sts. at beg. of next 2 rows.

3rd row: —K. 3, s. k. p. o., k. to last 5 sts., k. 2 tog., k. 3. *4th row:* —K. 3, p. to last 3 sts., k. 3. Rep. last 2 rows until 10 sts. rem. Cast off.

COLLAR

With No. 11 [2] needles cast on 108 sts., work in k. 1, p. 1 rib for 24 rows. Cast off loosely in rib.

To make up

Press pieces. Join raglan seams, leaving left back seam open for 3 ins. from neck. Join side and sleeve seams. With right sides together, sew edge of neckband to neck edge. Fold in half and slip stitch to wrong side. Set zip into shoulder opening. Press seams.

All the Trimmings

Most garments have knitted welts in ribbing, to give a close fit at waist and wrist. Sometimes, however, a more decorative finish is called for.

Perhaps a hem would suit the style better than a ribbed welt and a hem can have a picot edge.

Knitted lace edgings in cotton can be starched for household linen and pretty frilled cuffs can be made by gathering knitted lace to sleeves. A plain baby shawl would be improved by a lace edging and fringes, tassels and pompons add that extra touch to many items.

HEMS

Determine first the depth of hem you require. Let us suppose it should be one inch. Knit the inch in stocking stitch, ending with a right-side row. Then, with the wrong side facing, knit the next row. This will mark the hemline. Continue in stocking stitch for a further inch, starting with a knit row. Fold the hem to the wrong side on hemline and knit together one stitch from the needle and one loop from cast-on edge all along the row. It is important not to miss any of the cast-on edge loops to make a perfect hem.

PICOT EDGING

This makes a double hem and in fine wool and a contrasting shade can make a dainty finish to finer work. For more husky garments, a deep hem with a picot finish can be a change from a ribbed welt. For a hem, cast on the stitches given in your pattern. Work to depth required for hem, then work a row of holes thus: —knit 1, make 1, knit 2 together, all along row. Continue for the depth of hem. Fold work on hemline and knit together 1 stitch from needle and one loop from cast-on edge. Then continue with pattern in usual way.

For a fine edge to add to the neck of a finer garment, with right-side facing, pick up and knit the stitches round neck and complete in same way. Casting off and fold to wrong side; slip stitch to finish.

(See sketches Nos. 28 and 29)

LACE EDGINGS

Knitted in cotton and lightly starched, these will make dainty but hard wearing decorations for household linen. Using wool and coarser needles, the edgings will be wider and

Sketch No. 28

Sketch No. 29

will make cuffs and collars for jumpers and dresses.

1. LEAF EDGING

Cast on 10 stitches and knit a row.

1st row: —Sl. 1, k. 1, (y. r. n., k. 2 tog.) twice, y. r. n. 4 times, k. 2 tog., y. r. n., p. 2 tog.

2nd row: —Y. r. n., p. 2 tog., k. 1, (k. 1, p. 1) twice into y. r. n. of previous row, (k. 1, p. 1) twice, k. 2.

3rd row: —Sl. 1, (k. 1, y. r. n., k. 2 tog.) twice, k. 4, y. r. n., p. 2 tog.

4th row: —Y. r. n., p. 2. tog., k. 5, (p. 1, k. 2) twice.

5th row: —Sl. 1, k. 1, y. r. n., k. 2 tog., k. 2, y. r. n., k. 2 tog., k. 3, y. r. n., p. 2 tog.

6th row: —Y. r. n., p. 2 tog., k. 4, p. 1, k. 3, p. 1, k. 2.

7th row: —Sl. 1, k. 1, y. r. n., k. 2 tog., k. 3, y. r. n., k. 2 tog., k. 2, y. r. n., p. 2 tog.

8th row: —Y. r. n., p. 2 tog., k. 3, p. 1, k. 4, p. 1, k. 2.

9th row: —Sl. 1, k. 1, y. r. n., k. 2 tog., k. 4, y. r. n., k. 2 tog., k. 1, y. r. n., p. 2 tog.

10th row: —Y. r. n., p. 2 tog., k. 2, p. 1, k. 5, p. 1, k. 2.

11th row: —Sl. 1, k. 1, y. r. n., k. 2 tog., k. 5, y. r. n., k. 2 tog., y. r. n., p. 2 tog.

12th row: —Cast off 3 sts., slip the st. from right-hand needle to left-hand needle, y. r. n., p. 2 tog., k. 5, p. 1, k. 2.

Repeat these 12 rows for length required.

2. FLOWER BORDER

Cast on 14 stitches and purl a row.

1st row: —(Right side) * Sl. 1, k. 2 tog., y. r. n., k. 1, y. r. n., sl. 1, k. 1, p. s. s. o., k. 1, *

y. r. n., k. 1, y. r. n., (k. 1, y. r. n., k. 1) all into next st., (y. r. n., k. 1) twice, y. r. n. twice, k. 2 tog., k. 1.

2nd row: —K. 3, p. 1, k. 1, p. 9, k. 1, p. 5, k. 1.

3rd row: —Rep. from * to * of 1st row, then (y. r. n., k. 3) 3 times, y. r. n., (k. 1, y. r. n. twice) twice, k. 2 tog., k. 1.

4th row: —K. 3, p. 1, k. 2, p. 1, k. 1, p. 5, p. 3 tog., (p. 5, k. 1) twice.

5th row: —Rep. from * to * of 1st row, then (y. r. n., sl. 1, k. 1, p. s. s. o., k. 1, k. 2 tog., y. r. n., k. 1) twice, (y. r. n. twice, k. 2 tog.) 3 times, k. 1.

6th row: —K. 3, p. 1, (k. 2, p. 1) twice, k. 1, p. 2 tog., p. 1, p. 2 tog. t. b. l., p. 1, p. 2 tog., p. 1, p. 2 tog. t. b. l., k. 1, p. 5, k. 1.

7th row: —Rep. from * to * of 1st row, then y. r. n., k. 3 tog. t. b. l., k. 1, k. 3 tog., y. r. n., k. 11.

8th row: —Cast off 7, k. 4, p. 3 tog., k. 2, p. 5, k. 1. Repeat 1st to 8th rows for length required.

DOUBLE EDGING

The orange lace edging shown in the colour picture on page 160 is a pretty one to use for cuffs. Make the length required to surround a neck or two pieces for cuffs. Lightly starch and press. Thread ribbon through the central line of holes and draw up to fit a neckline or to trim sleeves.

TO MAKE

Cast on 17 stitches and knit 1 row.

1st row: —Sl. 1, k. 1, y. r. n., k. 2 tog., y. r. n., k. 1, y. r. n., (k. 2 tog.) twice, (y. r. n.) twice, (k. 2 tog.) twice, y. r. n., k. 1, y. r. n., k. 3.

2nd row: —Sl. 1, k. 8, p. 1, k. 9.
3rd row: —Sl. 1, k. 1, y. r. n., k. 2 tog., y. r. n., k. 2, y. r. n., k. 2 tog., k. 4, k. 2 tog., y. r. n., k. 2, y. r. n., k. 3.
4th row: —Sl. 1, k. 20.
5th row: —Sl. 1, k. 1, y. r. n., k. 2 tog., y. r. n., k. 3, y. r. n., k. 2 tog., k. 4, k. 2 tog., (y. r. n., k. 3) twice.
6th row: —Sl. 1, k. 22.
7th row: —Sl. 1, k. 7, y. r. n., (k. 2 tog.) twice, (y. r. n.) twice, (k. 2 tog.) twice, y. r. n., k. 1. y. r. n., k. 2 tog., k. 1, y. r. n., k. 3. *8th row*: —Sl. 1, k. 11, p. 1, k. 11.
9th row: —Cast off 3, k. 4, y. r. n., k. 2 tog., k. 4, k. 2 tog., y. r. n., k. 2, y. r. n., k. 2 tog., k. 1, y. r. n., k. 3.
10th row: —Sl. 1, k. 21.
11th row: —Sl. 1, k. 1, y. r. n., k. 2 tog., y. r. n., k. 1, y. r. n., k. 2 tog., k. 4, k. 2 tog., y. r. n., k. 3, y. r. n., k. 2 tog., k. 1, y. r. n., k. 3. *12th row*: —Sl. 1, k. 23.
13th row: —Sl. 1, k. 1, y. r. n., k. 2 tog., y. r. n., k. 2, y. r. n., (k. 2 tog.) twice, (y. r. n.) twice, (k. 2 tog.) twice, y. r. n., k. 1, (y. r. n., k. 2 tog., k. 1) twice, y. r. n. k. 3. *14th row*: — Sl. 1, k. 14, p. 1, k. 10. *15th row*: —Sl. 1, k. 1, y. r. n., k. 2 tog., y. r. n., k. 3, y. r. n., k. 2 tog., k. 4, k. 2 tog., y. r. n., k. 2, (y. r. n., k. 2 tog., k. 1) twice, y. r. n., k. 3. *16th row*: —Sl. 1, k. 27.
17th row: —Sl. 1, k. 7, y. r. n., k. 2 tog., k. 4, k. 2 tog., y. r. n., k. 3, (y. r. n., k. 2 tog., k. 1) twice, y. r. n., k. 3. *18th row*: —Sl. 1, k. 28.
19th row: —Cast off 3 sts., k. 4, y. r. n., (k. 2 tog.) twice, (y. r. n.) twice, (k. 2 tog.) twice, y. r. n., k. 1, (y. r. n., k. 2 tog., k. 1) 3 times, y. r. n., k. 3.
20th row: —Sl. 1, k. 17, p. 1, k. 8.
21st row: —Sl. 1, k. 1, y. r. n., k. 2 tog., y. r. n., k. 1, y. r. n., k. 2 tog., k. 4, k. 2 tog., y. r. n., k. 2, (y. r. n., k. 2 tog., k. 1) 3 times. y. r. n., k. 3. *22nd row*: —Sl. 1, k. 28. *23rd row*: —Sl. 1, k. 1, y. r. n., k. 2 tog., y. r. n., k. 2, y. r. n., k. 2 tog., k. 4, k. 2 tog., y. r. n., k. 3, (y. r. n., k. 2 tog., k. 1) 3 times, y. r. n., k. 3.
24th row: —Sl. 1, k. 30.
25th row: —Sl. 1, k. 1, y. r. n., k. 2 tog., y. r. n., k. 3, y. r. n., (k. 2 tog.) twice, (y. r. n.) twice, (k. 2 tog.) twice, y. r. n., k. 1, (y. r. n., k. 2 tog., k. 1) 4 times, y. r. n., k. 3. *26th row*: —Sl. 1, k. 20, p. 1, k. 11.
27th row: —Sl. 1, k. 7, y. r. n., k. 2 tog., k. 4, k. 2 tog., y. r. n., k. 2, (y. r. n., k. 2 tog.,

k. 1) 4 times, y. r. n., k. 3.
28th row: —Sl. 1, k. 33.
29th row: —Cast off 3 sts., k. 4, y. r. n., k. 2 tog., k. 4, k. 2 tog., y. r. n., k. 18.
30th row: —Cast off 14 sts. loosely, k. 16.
Repeat 1st to 30th rows for length required.

CHECK COAT

Materials: —17 (18, 19) 50 gramme balls of Sirdar Pullman Wool in Light shade; 14 (15, 16) balls dark; a pair each of Nos. 4 [9] and 6 [7] knitting needles; 9 buttons.

Measurements: —Bust: 34 (36, 38) ins.; Length: 40 (40½, 41) ins.; Sleeve: 17 ins.

Tension: —4½ sts. and 4 rows to 1 inch on No. 4 [9] needles.

Abbreviations: —See page 20.

BACK
With No. 6 [7] needles and L. cast on 94 (97, 100) sts. Work in st.st. for 7 rows. K. next row to mark hemline. Change to No. 4 [9] needles and work in patt.
1st row: —* K. 1 t. b. l. L., k. 2 D., rep. from * to last st., k. 1 t. b. l. L.
2nd row: —* As 1st row in p.
3rd row: —* K. 1 t. b. l. D., k. 2 L., rep. from * to last st., k. 1 t. b. l. D.
4th row: —As 3rd row in p.
These 4 rows form the patt. and are repeated. Cont. in patt. until Back measures 6 ins. from hemline, ending on wrong side. Now dec. 1 st. at each end of next and foll. 12th rows 6 times in all. Work without further shaping until Back measures 32 ins. from hemline, ending on a wrong side row.
To Shape Armholes: —Cast off 3 sts. at beg. of next 2 rows and dec. 1 st. at each end of next 7 rows. Now work until armholes measure 8 (8½, 9) ins., ending on a wrong side row.
To Shape Shoulders: —Cast off 6 sts. at beg. of next 4 rows and 6 (8, 10) sts. at beg. of next 2 rows. Cast off rem. sts.

RIGHT FRONT
With No. 6 [7] needles and L. cast on 46 (49,

and change to No. 6 [7] needles. and work in k. 1, p. 1 rib for 6 rows. Cast off in rib.

To make up
Press pieces. Slip stitch hems to wrong side and press. Join shoulder seams, set in sleeves. Join side and sleeve seams. Add pockets to fronts. Sew borders to fronts and add buttons.

BEADED EVENING BAG

Materials : —3 balls of Coats Mercer Crochet Cotton No. 20 ; a pair of No. 14 [00] knitting needles ; approx. 2,100 beads ; $\frac{3}{8}$ yd. lining fabric ; $\frac{3}{8}$ yd. Vilene for inter-lining ; 2 press fasteners.
Tension : —8 sts. and 15 rows to 1 inch.
Note : The finished bag measures 10 by 3½ ins. The knitted piece measures 10 by 11 ins.

Abbreviations : —See page 20.

TO MAKE
Thread $\frac{1}{3}$ of the total beads on to first ball of cotton, using cotton double throughout.
Cast on 81 sts. *1st row :* —K. *2nd and every alt. row :* —P. *3rd row :* —** K. 2, * y. fwd., sl. a bead as close to work as possible, p. next st.,

52) sts. Work as for Back until Front measures 6 ins. from hemline, ending on a wrong-side row. Now dec. 1 st. at end of the next and foll. 12th rows, 6 times in all. Work without further shaping until Front measures 32 ins. from hemline, ending at armhole edge.
To Shape Armhole and Front edge : —Cast off 3 sts. work to end. *Next row :* —k. 2 tog. for front edge, work to last 2 sts. k. 2 tog. Cont. to dec. 1 st. at armhole edge on next 6 rows and dec. 1 st. at front edge on every foll, right side row 11 (14, 17) times more. Cont. until armhole measures the same as back, ending at armhole edge.
To Shape Shoulder : —Cast off 6 sts. at beg. of next 2 wrong-side rows and cast off rem. sts. on next wrong-side row.

LEFT FRONT
Work as for Right front, reversing shaping.

SLEEVES
With No. 6 [4] needles and L. cast on 40 (43, 46) sts. Work as for Back until hemline is complete. Change to No. 4 [9] needles and work in patt. for 6 rows. Now inc. 1 st. at each end of next and every foll. 6th row 6 times in all. Then inc. 1 st. at each end of every foll. 4th row 5 times in all. Now work without further shaping until sleeve measures 17 ins. from hemline.
To Shape Top : —Cast off 3 sts. at beg. of next 2 rows. Now dec. 1 st. at each end of next 5 rows. Now dec. 1 st. at each end of every foll. right-side row 10 times in all. Cast off 2 sts. at beg. of next 4 rows and 3 sts. at beg. of next 2 rows. Cast off rem. sts.

BORDER
With No. 6 [7] needles and L. cast on 8 sts. Work in k. 1, p. 1 rib for 4 rows. *1st Buttonhole row :* —Rib 2, cast off 4, rib 2. *2nd Buttonhole row :* —Rib 2, cast on 4, rib 2. Make a further 8 buttonholes in this way on foll. 19th and 20th rows. Then cont. until border is long enough to fit up right front, across back of neck, and down left front, measuring from marked hemline. Cast off.

POCKETS
Make 2. With No. 4 [9] needles, cast on 25 sts. with L. and work in patt. for 5 ins. Break off D.

123

Beaded Evening Bag.

now called bead 1 rep. from * to last 2 sts. k. 2.
5th row: —As 3rd row. *7th row:* —K. 2, bead
2, k. 73, bead 2, k. 2. *9th row:* —K. 2, bead 2,
k. 5, * bead 3, k. 3, rep. from * 9 times more,
bead 3, k. 5, bead 2, k. 2. *11th row:* —K. 2,
bead 2, k. 5, * bead 1, k. 1, bead 1, k. 3, rep.
from * 9 times more, bead 1, k. 1, bead 1, k. 5,
bead 2, k. 2. *13th row:* —K. 2, bead 2, k. 5, *
bead 1, k. 1, bead 1, k. 3, bead 3, k. 3, rep. from *
5 times more, bead 1, k. 1, bead 1, k. 5, bead 2,
k. 2. *15th row:* —K. 2, bead 2, k. 2, * bead 4,
k. 1, bead 4, k. 3, rep. from * 4 times more, bead
4, k. 1, bead 4, k. 2, bead 2, k. 2. *17th row:* —
K. 2, bead 2, k. 7, bead 1, k. 3, bead 1, rep.
from * 4 times more, k. 7, bead 1, k. 2, bead 2,
k. 2. *19th row:* —As 15th row. *21st row:* —
As 13th row. *23rd row:* —As 11th row. *25th
row:* —K. 2, bead 2, k. 5, * bead 3, k. 3, bead
1, k. 1, bead 1., k. 3, rep. from * 4 times more,
bead 3, k. 5, bead 2, k. 2. *27th row:* —K. 2,
bead 2, k. 2, bead 3, * k. 3, bead 4, k. 1, bead 4,
rep. from * 4 times more, k. 3, bead 3, k. 2,
bead 2, k. 2. *29th row:* —K. 2, bead 2, k. 2,
bead 1, k. 1, bead 1, * k. 3, bead 1, k. 7, bead 1,
rep. from * 4 times, k. 3, bead 1, k. 1, bead 1, k. 2,
bead 2, k. 2. *31st row:* —As 27th row. Now
work beaded rows in reverse on k. row as before, beg. with 25th, 23rd rows etc. to 3rd row
**. Work 5 rows st. st. Now rep. from ** to **
once more. Work 55 rows st.st. Cast off.
Damp and pin out and press carefully on
wrong side.

To make up
Cut 2 pieces of lining and 1 piece of inter-
lining, allowing ½ inch for hems. Place lining
right sides facing. Place inter-lining on wrong
side of one piece and stitch round, leaving an
opening for turning. Turn to right side, turn
in seams and stitch opening. Place lining cen-
trally on wrong side of knitting and slip stitch
into position. Turn back last 55 rows of st.st.
to form pocket and stitch. Sew press fasteners
under flap.

EMERALD SWEATER WITH LACY SLEEVES

Materials: —12 (13, 14) balls of Sirdar
Double Knitting wool in Emerald and 5 balls
in White; a pair each of Nos. 9 [4], 10 [3] and
0 [12] knitting needles; a buckle.

Measurements: —Bust: 34 (36, 38) ins.;
Length: 26 (27, 28) ins.; Sleeve: 18 ins.

Tension: —6 sts. to 1 inch on No. 9 [4]
needles.

Abbreviations: —See Page 20.

BACK
With No. 10 [3] needles and Emerald, cast on
114 (120, 126) sts. and work in k. 1, p. 1 rib
for 4 rows. Change to No. 9 [4] needles and
st. st. and cont. until Back measures 17½ (18,
18½) ins. from beg.
To Shape Armholes: —Cast off 2 (3, 4) sts.
at beg. of next 2 rows. Now dec. 1 st. at each
end of every row until 82 sts. rem. Work straight
until armhole measures 8½ (9, 9½) ins. from
beg.
To Shape Shoulders: —Cast off 10 sts. at beg.
of next 4 rows. Cast off.

FRONT
Work as for Back until Front measures 12 (13,
14) ins., ending with a p. row.
To Divide for Neck: —*Next row:* —K. 52 (55,
58) sts., cast off 10 sts., k. to end. *Next row:* —
P. 52 (55, 58) sts. Work on this set of sts. leaving rem. sts. on a spare needle for left side. **
Cont. until Front measures the same as Back
to armhole shaping, ending with a k. row.
To Shape Armhole: —Cast off 2 (3, 4) sts.,
p. to end. Now dec. 1 st. at armhole edge on
every row until 36 sts. rem. Cont. straight until
armhole measures 5 (5½, 6) ins. from beg. of
armhole shaping, ending with a p. row.
To Shape Neck: —Cast off 7 sts., k. to end.
Now dec. 1 st. at neck edge on every row until
20 sts. rem. Cont. straight until work measures
the same as Back to shoulder edge, ending
with a k. row.
To Shape Shoulder: —Cast off 10 sts. at beg.
of next and foll. alt. row. ** Return to sts. on
spare needle, rejoin yarn to neck edge and work
1 row p. Now work from ** to ** to match
first side, reversing shapings.

FRONT BANDS-LEFT SIDE
With right side of work facing and with No.
10 [3] needles and Emerald, beg. at neck end
and pick up and k. 80 sts. down front opening.
Work 4 rows k. 1, p. 1 rib. *Next row:* —Rib 5,
y. fwd., k. 2 tog., * rib 12, y. fwd., k. 2 tog., rep.

from * to last 3 sts., rib 3. Work 3 rows k. 1, p. 1 rib. Cast off in rib.

RIGHT SIDE

As left side, but beg. at lower end and work up to neck end. *Next Row:* —Rib 3 sts., y. fwd., k. 2 tog., * rib 12, y. fwd., k. 2 tog., rep. from * to last 5 sts., rib 5. Work 3 rows k. 1, p. 1 rib. Cast off in rib. Sew edges of front bands to 10 cast off sts. to meet at centre front.

BELT

With No. 9 [4] needles and Emerald, cast on 15 sts. *1st row:* —P. 1, * k. 1, p. 1, rep. from * to end. *2nd row:* —K. 1, * p. 1, k. 1, rep. from * to end. Work in rib thus until belt is required length.
To Shape Point: —Dec. 1 st. at each end of every row until 3 sts. rem. K. 3 tog. Fasten off.

SLEEVES

With No. 10 [3] needles and White, cast on 49 (51, 53) sts. and work in rib as for belt for 3 ins. Change to No. 0 [12] needles and work in patt. *1st row:* —P. *2nd row:* —K. 2, * y. fwd., k. 2 tog., rep. from * to last st. k. 1. Cont. in patt. until sleeve measures 18 ins. from beg. *To Shape Top:* —Cast off 4 sts. at beg. of next 8 rows. Cast off.

To make up
Press pieces. Join side and shoulder seams.

COLLAR

With right side facing, beg. at right front edge and with No. 9 [4] needles, and Emerald, pick up and k. 103 sts. round neck edge. Break Emerald and join in White and work 2 rows in rib as for belt for 4 ins. Cast off in rib. Set in sleeves and join seams. Sew buckle to belt. With 4 strands of White each 3½ yards long, make a twisted cord for front lacing. (See instructions on page 21) Thread cord through holes in front bands. Press seams.

Tips to Remember

UNEVEN KNITTING

This will spoil the appearance of any knitting and can be caused by using worn or bent needles. Since knitting needles are the tools with which you work, make sure they are the best and are kept clean and in good condition. Dirty needles will soil the work.

Remember to keep needles in pairs and marked with the correct size. This applies mostly to double-pointed needles, as good needles with knobs at the end are always marked clearly with the size.

When two sizes are to be used and they are close in size, it is easy to pick up one of each size and start your knitting. Uneven work will be the result.

FAIR ISLE KNITTING

When following a chart for Fair Isle knitting, each square represents one stitch in the row. Working on two needles in stocking stitch, starting with a knit row, the first and every odd-numbered row will be read from right to left across the chart. Purl rows and all even-numbered rows are read from left to right.

If the knitting is being worked on four needles or a circular needle, then the rounds are all knit rounds and are *all* read from right to left on each round.

Colours may be stranded and for this, you carry the yarn not in use across the back of the work, until it is required.

When working with two colours only, hold one colour in the right hand and the other in the left. It is best to hold the colour to be used most often in the row in the right hand. It becomes simple to take up a stitch or two of the second colour from the left hand, with the point of the right hand needle.

If too many stitches have to be worked in one colour, stranding becomes unsatisfactory. The work can be pulled and the final result be spoilt. In this case, weaving the yarns not in use is the best way. It can be done by weaving the colour not in use under that in use for one stitch and over the colour in use on the next stitch.

SIZES IN BRACKETS

Throughout this book, the first size given in the

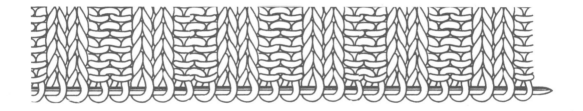

instructions appears outside brackets and extra sizes are inside the brackets. Some new knitters find this confusing when details of shaping are given. For example, if the instructions say, 'Cast off 4 (3, 2, 0) sts. at beg. of next row,' and the knitter is making the fourth size, she will wonder what she is to do. The answer is nothing. That particular row needs no further shaping at that point for the size being made.

TURNING TO LENGTHEN

When knitting trousers, it is necessary to make the back longer in the centre to make a comfortable and well fitting seat to the garment. This is done by turning rows. A few stitches are left at the centre seam edge on the first row, the work is turned and worked back. On the following row, a few more stitches are left and the work turned again. In this way, several rows can be worked for the seat, without making the rest of the garment too long. When the correct length has been made for the seat, a row is worked across all stitches and the piece continued in the usual way.

BRUSHING

Knitted fabric can be brushed to give a fluffy effect which can be attractive and cosy.
Loosely knitted work is easily damaged and brushing should be done only on fabric with a firm tension.
You will need a teazle brush, which is a fine wire brush with the wires well spaced. These are specially sold for the purpose.
Press the pieces and brush before making up. Avoid the ribbing and brush gently, taking care not to damage the threads. Brush from top to bottom, using a lifting and slight pull on the fabric.

FACING FRONT BANDS

Facing ribbon can be bought to finish the front bands of cardigans and jackets. Pin the facing ribbon to the wrong side of the front band and tack into place, taking care not to stretch the edge of the knitting. Slip stitch along each edge of the ribbon.
When ribbon has been sewn into position on a band with buttonholes, cut buttonholes in the ribbon to match, turn edges in and finish off neatly and firmly.

ZIP FASTENERS

Care is required in setting a zip fastener into a garment. If the fabric is stretched, the final appearance will be ugly and unsatisfactory.

Pin the zip fastener into position on the wrong side of work. Turn the end tapes in and tack the zip into position. On the right side, with matching silk or cotton, make a fine back-stitch seam inside the teeth of the zip. Then turn to the wrong side of work and slip stitch round the edges of the tape.

PREPARING WOOL FOR RE-KNITTING

Garments in good condition which have perhaps been out-grown, disliked or have a small stain or tear, can be unravelled and the wool used again.
The crinkles need to be removed and on a fairly new garment, steaming will do this. Older wool will need to be washed.
Unpick the seams and begin from the cast-off edges. As the knitting is pulled back, wind each ounce into a skein. Tie each skein with a piece of wool at each end and half way along side. In four places in all. This will prevent tangling while washing.
Using hand-hot water and a good soap powder as for washing woollens, hold the skein in shape and wash very carefully. Rinse thoroughly and remove all excess moisture. Hang each skein to dry. When absolutely dry, re-wind into balls ready for re-knitting.
Remember, you will have lost some of the damaged wool and some stretching may have taken place. Choose a pattern you are certain will not require more wool than you may have. Remember too, that new wool in stripes can help and if cuffs and welts can be made in new wool, or at least started in new wool, the garment will look like new again.

Short Waistcoat for him and long-line Cardigan for her (pattern, page 114)
Check Coat (pattern, page 122)
Emerald Sweater (pattern, page 125)
Holiday Jacket (pattern, page 142)

CARE OF KNITTED GARMENTS

WASHING KNITTED GARMENTS

It is always disappointing when a garment has been a favourite and then, at the first washing, it is spoilt.

Take care with washing and watch the following points.

Never wait until a garment is badly soiled. Use a good quality soap powder and make certain it is well dissolved in the water. Water should not be very hot, in fact just hot enough for your hands.

Do not leave woollens to soak. Gently squeeze the soiled garment in the water, always taking care to support the weight with your hands. If you lift a sweater by the shoulders and dunk it up and down in the basin, you will stretch it.

When all dirt has been removed, rinse thorroughly. No soap should be allowed to remain in the garment. When you are sure all soap has been removed and the water, which should still be hand-hot, is quite clear. Squeeze gently, until as much moisture has been removed. Do not twist or wring in the hands, as this will cause distortion in the shape too. Now wrap in a dry towel to remove more moisture and then dry flat, if possible. If a garment hangs and moisture runs to the bottom edge, this will also stretch. If you do have to hang a garment to dry, squeeze the lower ends from time to time, to remove moisture and to prevent it running to the bottom.

Dry away from direct heat and avoid drying in bright sunlight. This can spoil the colour. Finally, when dry, pin out and block and press, as you did when you first made the garment up. You should have a new looking fresh garment to wear with pride.

STORING KNITTED GARMENTS

Garments are best folded and kept on shelves and drawers. Never hang a coat, sweater, suit or dress. A coat hanger will mark the shoulders and press them out of shape. The garment may also stretch and become too long.

When you remove a knitted garment, shake it well, lay it down and pat into shape. A skirt may have seated, if you deal with it at once, you can avoid this remaining. Pull and pat sleeves into shape. When you are satisfied with the appearance, fold neatly and lay on a shelf or in a drawer.

If a sweater or garment is left to cool completely, before putting away, you will find woollens keep their shape, when stored in this way.

SHORTENING AND LENGTHENING GARMENTS

If a garment has stretched in wear and you wish to shorten it, this is a simple matter, if the stitch used was stocking stitch.

Decide the length you wish the finished work to be. Mark a line a few inches above the required length. Take one stitch in that row and pull gently. You will be able to pull the thread all the way along the row and break it off. This will remove the row and will leave a row of loops on the piece you wish to shorten. Pick the loop up on to the correct size needle.

Take the discarded piece of knitting and unravel it. Wash the wool, or steam it to remove crinkles. Winding the wool round a hot-water bottle will sometimes be enough to do this. Wind the wool into a ball and use it to add the welt, to make the garment the length you wish.

Lengthening can be done in the same way. If you are short of wool, add contrasting stripes, to give the extra length.

For patterns using plain and purl stitches, this can still be done, but removing the row in the first place takes just a little more time. Remove the stitches just above the welt to lengthen and add a longer welt. You will not be able to knit the pattern in reverse.

To shorten a garment in pattern, work in the same way as given for a plain garment.

BABY'S COAT AND LEGGINGS

Perfect for the pram parade on a nice day. Sweet for a girl but you could team the leggings with the plain coat which follows, to suit a baby boy

Materials: —9 ozs. Robin Vogue Double Knitting Wool; a pair each of Nos. 9 [4] and 8 [5] knitting needles; 1 small button; a waist length of elastic for leggings and 1 yd. baby ribbon for coat.

Measurements: —Coat: Chest: 18 ins; Length: 12 ins.; Sleeve: 5½ ins. Leggings: Front seam from waist to crutch: 8 ins.; Width all round at widest part: 24 ins.

Tension: —5¼ sts. and 7½ rows to 1 inch.

Abbreviations: —See Page 20.

COAT-BACK

With No. 8 [5] needles, cast on 58 sts. and work 4 rows in m. st. Change to patt.
1st row: —K. 1, p. to last st., p. 1.
2nd row: —K. 1, * (k. 1, p. 1, k. 1) all into next st., p. 3 tog., rep. from * to last st., k. 1.
3rd row: —As 1st row.
4th row: —k. 1, * p. 3 tog., (k. 1, p. 1, k. 1) all into next st., rep. from * to last st., k. 1. These 4 rows form the patt. Rep. them until work measures 7 ins. from beg., ending with a wrong-side row.
To Shape Raglan: —*1st row*: —K. 2, sl. 1, k. 1, p. s. s. o., k. to last 4 sts., k. 2 tog., k. 2.
2nd row: —K. 2, p. to last 2 sts., k. 2. Rep. last 2 rows until 18 sts. rem. Cast off.

RIGHT FRONT

With No. 8 [5] needles, cast on 32 sts. Work 4 rows m. st. Now work in patt. keeping m. st. border thus: —
1st row: —M. st. 3, p. to last st., k. 1.
2nd row: —K. 1, * (k. 1, p. 1, k. 1) all into next st., p. 3 tog., rep. from * to last 3 sts., m. st. 3. *3rd row*: —As 1st row.
4th row: —K. 1, * p. 3 tog., (k. 1, p. 1, k. 1) all into next st., rep. from * to last 3 sts., m. st. 3. Rep. last 4 rows until work measures 7 ins. from beg., ending at side edge.
Next row: —K. 2, p. to last 3 sts., m. st. 3.
**To Shape Raglan:* —*1st row*: —M. st. 3, sl. 1, k. 1, p. s. s. o., k. to last 4 sts., k. 2 tog., k. 2. *2nd row*: —K. 2, p. to last 3 sts., m. st. 3. Rep. last 2 rows until 8 sts. rem.
Next row: —M. st. 3, sl. 1, k. 2 tog., p. s. s. o., k. 2. *Next row*: —K. 2, p. 1, m. st. 3.
Next row: —M. st. 3, sl. 1, k. 1, p. s. s. o., k. 1. *Next row*: —K. 1, p. 1, m. st. 3.
Next row: —M. st. 2, k. 3 tog. Work 14 rows m. st. on these sts. for back neckband. Cast off.* *

LEFT FRONT

With No. 8 [5] needles cast on 32 sts., and work 4 rows in m.st. Now work in patt. thus:
1st row: —K. 1, p. to last 3 sts., m. st. 3.
2nd row: —M. st. 3, * (k. 1, p. 1, k. 1) all into next st., p. 3 tog., rep. from * to last st., k. 1. *3rd row*: —As 1st row.
4th row: —M. st. 3, * p. 3 tog., (k. 1, p. 1, k. 1) all into next st., rep. from * to last st., k. 1. Rep. last 4 rows until work measures 7 ins. from beg., ending at side edge.
Now shape raglan as for Right Front from * * to * *

SLEEVES

With No. 8 [5] needles, cast on 38 sts. and work 8 rows in m. st. Change to st. st. and work 5 rows. Now inc. 1 st. at each end of next and every foll. 8th row until there are 48 sts. Work straight until sleeve measures 5½ ins. from beg., ending with a p. row.
To Shape Raglan: —*1st row*: —K. 2, sl. 1, k. 1, p. s. s. o., k. to last 4 sts., k. 2 tog., k. 2.
2nd row: —K. 2, p. to last 2 sts., k. 2. Rep. these 2 rows until 8 sts. rem. Cast off.

LEGGINGS

With No. 9 [4] needles, cast on 66 sts. and work in k. 1, p. 1 rib for 10 rows. Change to No. 8 [5] needles and st. st. and work 2 rows. Now cont. as folls: —
1st row: —K. 8, turn and purl to end.
3rd row: —K. 16, turn and purl to end.
5th row: —K. 24, turn and purl to end.
7th row: —K. 32, turn and purl to end.
9th row: —K. 40, turn and purl to end.
Next row: —Knit across all sts. Cont. in st. st. and inc. 1 st. at each end of next and every 6th row until there are 72 sts. on needle. Work straight until piece measures 8 ins. from beg. measured along shortest edge.

Now dec. 1 st. at each end of next and every foll. 3rd row until there are 42 sts. on needle. Work 6 rows straight. Change to No. 9 [4] needles and work 12 rows k. 1, p. 1 rib. Cast off in rib.

Work another leg to match.

To make up

Press pieces. Join raglan seams of coat. Join side and sleeve seams. Join cast off ends of back neckband and join band to neck edge. Thread ribbon through last row of pattern at waist and sew ends neatly into position on wrong side. Sew button to left front and make a loop on right front.

Join centre back and front seams of leggings, long edges for back and shorter for front. Join leg seams. Pin elastic to wrong side of waist ribbing and case into position, by working in large cross stitch or herringbone stitch over the elastic. Join ends of elastic. Press seams.

BABY'S JACKET

Plain and simple for the small brothers. Worn with the leggings of the previous pattern, it will make a smart suit. The instructions are given in three sizes

Materials: —6 (7, 8) ozs. Robin Vogue Double Knitting Wool; a pair of No. 10 [3] knitting needles; 6 small buttons.

Measurements: —Chest: 22 (24, 26) ins.; Length: 10 (11, 12) ins.; Sleeve: 6 (6½, 7) ins.

Tension: —5 sts. and 5½ rows to 1 inch over pattern.

Abbreviations: —See page 20.

BACK

Cast on 56 (60, 64) sts. and work 6 rows g. st.

Now work in patt. thus: —

1st row: —(Right side) K.
2nd row: —P. 1, * y. b., sl. 1, y. fwd., p. 1 B, rep. from * to last st., p. 1.

3rd row: —K.
4th row: —P. 1, * p. 1 B, y. b., sl. 1, y. fwd., rep. from * to last st., p. 1.

These 4 rows form the patt. Cont. in patt. until Back measures 7 (7½, 8) ins. from beg.

To Shape Raglan: —Cast off 2 sts. at beg. of next 2 rows; then dec. 1 st. at each end of next and every 3rd row until 20 (22, 24) sts. rem.

Work 1 row. Cast off.

RIGHT FRONT

Cast on 24 (26, 28) sts. and work as for Back until Front measures the same as Back up to armhole shaping, ending with a right-side row.

To Shape Raglan: —Cast off 2 sts. at beg. of next wrong side row. Then dec. 1 st. at the same edge on the next alt. row.

Now cont. to dec. 1 st. at the same edge on every 3rd row until 8 sts. rem. Work 2 more rows. Cast off.

LEFT FRONT

Work as for Right Front, reversing all shapings.

FRONT BANDS

Cast on 8 sts. and work in g. st. until piece fits up front edge. Join to the appropriate side for boy or girl, for the button band.

Mark positions for 6 buttons, placing the first on 4th row from lower edge and the top button on the 4th row from top. Space the remaining 4 buttons evenly between.

Make a second band, working buttonholes to correspond with marked positions thus: —

Next row: —K. 3, y. r. n., k. 2 tog., k. 3.
Next row: —K. Cont. in g. st. to next buttonhole position. Finish to fit up front edge of jacket. Cast off and sew to right side for a girl and to left for a boy.

SLEEVES

Cast on 24 (26, 28) sts. and work as for Back but inc. at each end of 8th and every foll. 7th row until there are 38 (40, 42) sts. on needle. Cont. straight until sleeve measures 6 (6½, 7) ins. from beg.

To Shape Raglan: —Cast off 2 sts. at beg. of next 2 rows and then dec. as for Back until 2 sts. rem. Place these sts. on to a safety-pin and make another sleeve to match.

Join raglan sleeves to back and fronts. With right side of work facing, pick up and k. 8 sts. from right front band, 10 sts. up to raglan sleeve, 2 sts. from sleeve, 20 (22, 24) sts. from back of neck, 2 sts. from raglan sleeve, 10 sts. round front of neck and 8 from left front band. Work in g. st. for 16 rows and inc. 1 st. at each end of 4th and every alt. row. Cast off.

To make up

Press pieces. Join side and sleeve seams. Add buttons. Work 1 row double crochet round edge of collar. Press seams.

BABY'S BOOTEES

Materials: —2 ozs. of Patons Baby Quick-kerknit; a pair of No. 11 [2] knitting needles; 1 yard of baby ribbon.

Tension: —7 sts. to 1 in.

Measurements: —3½ ins. from top to sole; 4½ ins. from toe to heel.

Abbreviations: —See page 20.

TO WORK —(BOTH ALIKE)
Beg. with sole and cast on 53 sts. and shape as follows: —
1st row: —Inc. in first st., k. 24, inc. once in each of next 2 sts., k. to last 2 sts., inc. in next. st. k. 1.
2nd to 4th rows: —K.
5th row: —Inc. in first st., k. 26, inc. once in each of next 2 sts., k. to last 2 sts., inc. in next st., k. 1.
6th to 8th rows: —K.
9th row: —Inc. in first st., k. 28, inc. once in each of next 2 sts., k. to last 2 sts., inc. in next st., k. 1.
K. one row.
Work picot as follows: —
1st row: —K. 2nd row: —P. 3rd row: —K. 1, * y. fwd., k. 2 tog.; rep. from * to end.
4th row: —P. *5th and 6th rows:* —As 1st and 2nd rows.
7th row. — (on which picot is completed): —Fold work at row of holes and k. tog. one st. from needle and one st. from 1st row of picot all across the row.

K. 13 rows.
To Shape Foot: —1st row: —K. 36, k. 2 tog., turn.
2nd row: —K. 8, k. 2 tog., turn. Rep. last row 24 times more. Next row: —K. to end. *Next row:* —K. *Next row:* —(On which holes for ribbon are worked) —* K. 1, y. fwd., k. 2 tog.; rep. from * to last 2 sts., y. fwd., k. 2 tog.
Beg. with a p. row, work 18 rows in st. st.
Now work top as follows: —
1st row: —P. 3, * k. 3, p. 3; rep. from * to end. *2nd row:* —K. 3, * p. 3, k. 3; rep. from * to end. *3rd row:* —P. 3, keeping yarn at front sl. 1 knitwise, y. o. n., k. 2 tog., p. s. s. o., y. r. n., p. 3; rep. from * to end. *4th row:* —As 2nd row. Rep. these 4 rows twice more. K. 3 rows. Cast off.

To make up

Press lightly on wrong side. Using a flat seam, join seam. Press seam. Thread ribbon through holes at ankle. Turn over top.

RAGLAN BUTTON-UP CARDIGAN

Materials: —10 (11, 11, 12, 12, 13) ozs. Lister Lavenda Crisp Crêpe 4-ply Wool; a pair each of Nos. 10 [3] and 11 [2] knitting needles; 8 buttons.

Measurements: —Bust: 34 (36, 38, 40, 42, 44) ins.; Length: — 22 (22½, 23, 23½, 24, 24½) ins.; Sleeve seam: —18 ins.

Tension: —7 sts. and 9 rows to 1 inch on No. 10 [3] needles.

Abbreviations: —See page 20.

BACK
With No. 11 [2] needles, cast on 122 (130, 138, 146, 154, 162) sts. and work 1¼ ins. in k. 1, p. 1 rib. Inc. 1 st. at beg. of last row.
Change to No. 10 [3] needles and st. st. and work until Back measures 13 ins. from beg., ending with a right-side row.
To Shape Raglan: —Cast off 2 (3, 4, 5, 6, 7) sts. at beg. of next 2 rows.
Next row: —P. *Next row:* —K. *Next row:* —P. 2, p. 3 tog., p. to last 5 sts., p. 3 tog., p. 2.
Next row: —K. Rep. the last 4 rows and cont.

Raglan Button-up Cardigan

to dec. in this manner until 39 (41, 43, 45, 47, 49) sts. rem. Cast off.

RIGHT FRONT

With No. 11 [2] needles, cast on 60 (64, 68, 72, 76, 80) sts. and work 1½ ins. in k. 1, p. 1 rib. Inc. 1 st. at end of last row. Change to No. 10 [3] needles and st. st. and work until Front measures 13 ins. from beg., ending with a right-side row.

To Shape Raglan: —Cast off 2 (3, 4, 5, 6, 7) sts. at beg. of next row. *Next row*: —K. Next row: —P.

Next row: —K. to last 5 sts., sl. 1, k. 2 tog., p. s. s. o., k. 2. *Next row*: —P. Rep. the last 4 rows until 13 (13, 14, 14, 15, 15) decreasings in all have been worked at armhole edge, ending at armhole edge. Work 1 (3, 1, 3, 1, 3) rows straight, ending at front edge. Cont. to dec. at armhole edge on every 4th row and *at the same time*.

Shape Neck: —Cast off 7 sts. at beg. of neck edge row, then dec. 1 st. at neck edge on next and every alt. row until 11 (12, 13, 14, 15, 16) decreasings have been worked at neck edge. Work 3 rows.

Next row: —Sl. 1, k. 2 tog., p. s. s. o. Fasten off.

LEFT FRONT

Work as for Right Front, reversing all shapings.

SLEEVES

With No. 11 [2] needles, cast on 60 (62, 64, 66, 68, 70) sts. and work 2 ins. in k. 1, p. 1 rib. Change to No. 10 [3] needles and st.st. Inc. 1 st. at each end of 3rd and every foll. 8th (7th, 7th, 6th, 6th, 5th) row until there are 92 (98, 104, 110, 116, 122) sts. on needle. Work straight until sleeve measures 18 ins. from beg.

To Shape Raglan: —Work as for Back until 8 sts. rem. Work 1 row. Cast off.

RIGHT FRONT BAND

With No. 11 [2] needles, cast on 11 sts.

Next row: —K. 2, * p. 1, k. 1, rep. from * to last st., k. 1.

Next row: —*k. 1, p. 1, rep. from * to last st., k. 1. Rep. these 2 rows 1 (2, 3, 4, 5, 6) times more.

1st buttonhole row: —Rib 4, cast off 3, rib to end.

2nd buttonhole row: —Rib 4, cast on 3, rib to end. Cont. in rib and work buttonholes at intervals of 3 ins., measured from base of previous buttonhole, until 7 in all have been worked. Work a further 3 ins. Slip these sts. on to a safety-pin.

LEFT FRONT BAND

Work to match right front band, omitting buttonholes.

Join Raglan seams.

NECKBAND

With No. 11 [2] needles and with right side facing, pick up and k. 11 sts. from right front band, 120 (130, 136, 140, 146, 152) sts. round neck and 11 sts. from left front band. Work 8 rows in k. 1, p. 1 rib, making a buttonhole on 2nd and 3rd rows. Cast off in rib.

To make up

Press pieces, avoiding ribbing. Join side and sleeve seams. Add buttons to match buttonholes. Press seams.

RED, WHITE & BLUE JACKET

Materials: —12 (13, 14) balls of Sirdar Double knitting Wool in Blue; 3 balls Red; and 1 ball of White; a pair each of Nos. 9 [4] and 10 [3] knitting needles; 5 buttons and a buckle.

Measurements: —Bust: 34 (36, 38) ins.; Length: 25½ (27, 28½) ins.; Sleeve: 6½ ins.

Tension: —6 sts., and 8 rows to 1 inch on No. 9 [4] needles.

Abbreviations: See page 20.

Blue belted sweater
The instructions for this sweater start on page 38 and it is shown in colour on page 51.
Good use is made of double hems at lower edge and sleeve, as well as at neckline, to make a classic shape into a fashion garment

BACK

With No. 10 [3] needles and Red, cast on 110 (115, 122) sts. and work 4 rows k. 1, p. 1 rib. Change to No. 9 [4] needles and st. st. Work 4 rows Blue, *1 row White, 6 rows Red, 1 row White, 2 rows Blue. Rep. from * 5 times more, then work 1 row White. Cont. with Blue only and work until Back measures 16 (17, 18) ins. from beg., ending with a p. row.

To Shape Armholes: —** Cast off 2 (3, 4) sts. at beg. of next 2 rows, then dec. 1 st. at each end of next and every alt. row ** until 36 sts. rem. Cast off.

LEFT FRONT

Cast on 54 (57, 60) sts. with No. 10 [3] needles and work as for Back from beg. to armhole shaping, ending with a p. row.

To Shape Armhole and Neck edge: Next row: —Cast off 2 (3, 4) sts., k. to last 2 sts., k. 2 tog.

Next row: —P. Now dec. 1 st. at beg. of next and every k. row (armhole edge) and *at the same time* dec. 1 st. at neck edge on every 3rd row until 12 (13, 14) sts. rem. Then dec. on every k. row until 2 sts. rem. Fasten off.

RIGHT FRONT

Work as for Left Front, reversing all shapings.

SLEEVES

With No. 10 [3] needles and Red, cast on 64 (70, 76) sts. and work in k. 1, p. 1 rib for 4 rows. Change to No. 9 [4] needles and st. st. and work 4 rows Blue. Now inc. 1 st. at beg. of every row and rep. striped patt. as for Back from * twice. Then work 1 row White. Cont. in Blue only until sleeve measures 6½ ins. from beg., ending with a p. row.

To Shape top: Work as for Back from ** to ** until 11 sts. rem. Cast off.

To make up

Press pieces. Join side and sleeve seams. Set in sleeves.

FRONT RIB BAND

With No. 10 [3] needles and Blue cast on 11 sts.

1st row: —P. 1, *k. 1, p. 1, rep. from * to end.

2nd row: —K. 1, * p. 1, k. 1, rep. from * to end. Work for 9½ (10, 11) ins.

Next row: —Rib 5, y. fwd., k. 2 tog., rib to end. Work another 1½ ins. then make another buttonhole. Cont. in this way until 5 buttonholes have been made and until band is long enough to fit all round front edges. Cast off. Sew ribbed band to edge, stretching slightly. Add buttons. Cast on 15 sts. for belt and work in rib as for band until length required. Cast off. Attach buckle to one end of belt. Press seams.

CHILD'S PINAFORE DRESS

Although very light, this little dress is as warm as toast. Worn over a pretty blouse, it will make a dainty outfit for special occasions. Six sizes are given in the instructions

Materials: —3 (3, 4, 5, 5, 6) balls of Twilley's Mohair, a pair each of Nos. 10 [3] and 11 [2] knitting needles; a No. 300 crochet hook.

Measurements: —Chest: 20 (22, 24, 26, 28, 30) ins.; Length: 16 (18, 20, 22, 25, 28) ins.

Tension: —7 sts. and 10 rows to 1 inch on No. 11 [2] needles measured over rib.

Abbreviations: —See page 20.

BACK AND FRONT ALIKE

The dress is worked from the shoulder downwards.

* With No. 11 [2] needles, and using yarn double, cast on 10 sts. Now cont. but use single yarn.

1st row: —(Right side) K. 2, (p. 2, k. 2) rep. sts. in brackets to end of row.

2nd row: —P. 2, (k. 2, p. 2) rep. sts. in brackets to end of row.

Rep. these 2 rows 5 times more. * Cont. in rib and inc. 1 st. at beg. of next row and at the same edge on foll. 9 (11, 13, 15, 17, 19) rows. Leave these 20 (22, 24, 26, 28, 30) sts. on a spare needle.

Make another piece to match, working from * to *

Cont. in rib and inc. 1 st. at end of next and foll. 9 (11, 13, 15, 17, 19) rows at the same edge.

Next row: —Rib to end. Join in a second ball of yarn and with yarn double, cast on 10 (14, 18, 22, 26, 30) sts. Break off one strand of yarn and cont. with single yarn. Rib across the sts. on spare needle. 50 (58, 66, 74, 82, 90) sts. Work straight on these sts. until piece measures 2½ (3, 3½, 4, 4½, 5) ins. from beg., ending with a wrong-side row.

Now inc. 1 st. at each end of next 8 rows.

To Shape Armholes: —Cast on 4 sts. at beg. of next 2 rows for armhole. 74 (82, 90, 98, 106, 114) sts. Work 4 rows in rib.

Next row: —Inc. for skirt. K. 1, m. 1 by picking up the loop before the next st. and knitting into the back of it, k. 1, (p. 2, k. 1, m. 1, k. 1), rep. sts. in brackets to end of row.

Next row: —P. 3, (k. 2, p. 3), rep. sts. in brackets to end of row.

Next row: —K. 3, (p. 2, k. 3) rep. sts. in brackets to end of row.

Change to No. 10 [3] needles and rep. the last 2 rows until the piece measures 6 (7, 8, 9, 10, 11) ins. from beg., ending with a wrong-side row.

Next row: —K. 2, m. 1, k. 1, (p. 2, k. 2, m. 1, k. 1), rep. sts. in brackets to end of row.

Next row: —P. 4, (k. 2, p. 4), rep. sts. in brackets to end of row.

Next row: —K. 4, (p. 2, k. 4), rep. sts. in brackets to end of row.

Rep. these last 2 rows until work measures 9 (10½, 12, 13½, 15, 16½) ins. from beg., ending with a wrong-side row.

Next row: —K. 2, m. 1, k. 2, (p. 2, k. 2, m. 1, k. 2), rep. sts. in brackets to end of row.

Next row: —P. 5, (k. 2, p. 5), rep. sts. in brackets to end of row.

Next row: —K. 5, (p. 2, k. 5), rep. sts. in brackets to end of row.

Rep. these last 2 rows until work measures 12 (14, 16, 18, 20, 22) ins. from beg., ending with a wrong-side row.

Next row: —K. 3, m. 1, k. 2, (p. 2, k. 3, m. 1, k. 2), rep. sts. in brackets to end of row.

Next row: —P. 6, (k. 2, p. 6), rep. sts. in brackets to end of row.

Next row: —K. 6, (p. 2, k. 6), rep. sts. in brackets to end of row.

Rep. these last 2 rows until work measures 16 (18, 20, 22, 25, 28) ins. from beg. Length can be adjusted here.

Using yarn double, cast off very loosely in rib.

To make up
Press skirt out very lightly. Join shoulder and side seams. With double yarn and the crochet hook, work in double crochet round neck.

Next round: —1 double crochet into first loop, (5 chain, slip stitch to 3rd of 5 chain to make a picot, 2 chain, miss 1 double crochet and work 1 double crochet into each of next 2 double crochet) rep. sts. in brackets all round neck. Slip stitch to first double crochet and fasten off. Work armholes to match. Press seams and border lightly.

LACE TABLE MAT

Materials: —1 ball of Coats Chain Mercer Crochet Cotton No. 20; a set of 4 double-pointed knitting needles No. 12 [1]; a No. 1.5 m. m. steel crochet hook.

Measurements: —12 ins. diameter.

Tension: —14 sts. to 1 inch over st. st.

Abbreviations: —See page 20.

To make
Cast on 9 sts., (3 sts. on each of 3 needles). Work in rounds as folls. *1st round*: —K. *2nd round*: —* Y. fwd., k. 1, rep. from * to end. *3rd and 4th rounds*: —As 1st and 2nd. *5th round*: —* K. 3, y. r. n. twice, k. 1, y. r. n. twice, rep. from * to end. *6th to 12th rounds*: —Work 1 st. only into each 2 y. r. n. of 5th and foll. rounds, * k. 3, y. r. n. twice, sl. 1, k. 2 tog., p. s. s. o., y. r. n. twice, rep. from * to end. *13th round*: —* Sl. 1, k. 2 tog., p. s. s. o., y. r. n. twice, k. 3, y. r. n. twice, rep. from * to end. *14th round*: —* K. 1 t. b. 1., y. r. n. twice, k. 5, y. r. n. twice, rep. from * to end. *15th round*: —* K. 4, y. r. n. twice, k. 1 t. b. 1., y. r. n. twice, k. 3, rep. from * to end. *16th round*: —* K. 5, y. r. n. twice, k. 1 t. b. 1., y. r. n. twice, k. 4, rep. from * to end. *17th round*: —* K. 6, y. r. n. twice, k. 1 t. b. 1., y. r. n. twice, k. 5, rep. from * to end. *18th to 25th rounds*: —* K. 5, k. 2 tog., y. r. n. twice, k. 5, rep. from * to end. *18th*

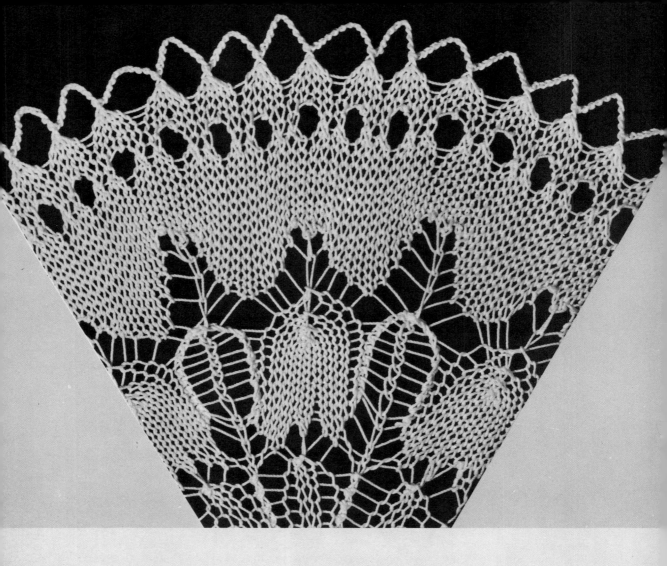

Detail of stitch

Here shown in use, the crisp cotton table mat
will be a proud possession for many years

to 25th rounds: —* K. 5, k. 2 tog., y. r. n. twice, k. 1 t. b. 1., y. r. n. twice, sl. 1, k. 1, p. s. s. o., k. 4, rep. from * to end. *26th round:* —Before beg. round, sl. 1 st. from right-hand needle on to left-hand needle. * Sl. 1, k. 2 tog., p. s. s. o., k. 3, y. r. n. twice, k. 2 tog., k. 1 t. b. l., sl. 1, k. 1, p. s. s. o., y. r. n. twice, k. 3, rep. from * to end. *27th round:* —Slip 1 st. from right-hand needle on to left-hand needle. * Sl. 1, k. 2 tog., p. s. s. o., k. 2, y. r. n. twice, k. 1, y. r. n. twice, sl. 1, k. 2 tog., p. s. s. o., y. r. n. twice, k. 1, y. r. n. twice, k. 2, rep. from * to end. *28th round:* —Slip 1 st. from right-hand needle on to left-hand needle. * Sl. 1, k. 2 tog., p. s. s. o., k. 1, y. r. n. twice, k. 3, y. r. n. twice, k. 1 t. b. l., y. r. n. twice, k. 3, y. r. n. twice, k. 1, rep from * to end. *29th round:* —K. 2 sts. from left-hand needle on to right-hand needle. * Y. r. n. twice, k. 5, y. r. n. twice, k. 1 t. b. l., y. r. n. twice, k. 5, y. r. n. twice, sl. 1, k. 2 tog., p. s. s. o., rep. from * to end. *30th round:* —* Y. r. n. twice, k. 7, y. r. n. twice, k. 1 t. b. l., rep. from * to end. *31st round:* —* Y. r. n. twice, k. 9, y. r. n. twice, k. 1 t. b. l., rep. from * to end. *32nd round:* —* Work 2 sts. thus (k. 1, p. 1) into the 2 y. r. n. of previous round, k. 9, (k. 1, p. 1) into 2 y. r. n. of previous round, k. 1, rep. from * to end. *33rd to 41st round:* —K. *42nd round:* —* Y. r. n. twice, (sl. 1, k. 1, p. s. s. o.) twice, rep. from * to end. *43rd round:* —* Work 2 sts. thus (k. 1, p. 1) into 2 y. r. n. of previous round, k. 2, rep. from * to end. *44th to 47th rounds:* —K. sl. 1 st. from right-hand needle on to left-hand needle, at end of last round. With crochet hook, work 1 double crochet into first 4 sts., * 10 chain, 1 double crochet into next 4 sts., rep from * to end. 10 chain, 1 slip stitch into first double crochet. Fasten off. Damp and pin out carefully, pinning each point out evenly. Press with warm iron.

LACE TABLE MAT
Knitted from the centre on four needles, fine lace in cotton makes a dainty tray cloth or table mat. It would make a beautiful gift for a young bride and a piece of work you could show with pride

Materials : —3 balls of Coats Mercer Crochet Cotton No. 20 ; a set of 4 double-pointed No. 12 [1] knitting needles ; a circular knitting needle No. 12 [1], 30 ins. long ; a No. 1.5 m. m. steel crochet hook.

Measurements : —20 ins. square.

Tension : —8 sts. and 9 rows to 1 inch.

Abbreviations : —See page 20.

To make
Cast on 12 sts. (3 sts. on each of 2 needles and 6 sts. on the 3rd needle.) *1st and 2nd rounds :* —K. *3rd round:* —* K. 1 t. b. l., y. fwd., k. 2 t. b. l., rep. from * to end. (16 sts.) *4th round:* —* K. 1 t. b. l., k. 1, k. 2 t. b. l., rep. from * to end. *5th round:* —* Y. fwd., k. 1 t. b. l., rep. from * to end. (32 sts.) *6th round:* —* K. 1, (k. 1 t. b. l., p. 1) twice, k. 1 t. b. l., k. 1, k. 1 t. b. l., rep. from * to end. *7th round:* —* (Y. fwd., k. 1 t. b. l.) twice, p. 1, y. o. n., k. 1 t. b. l., y. r. n., p. 1, k. 1 t. b. l., (y. fwd., k. 1 t. b. l.) twice, rep. from * to end. (56 sts.) *8th and foll. alt. round:* —Work sts. as set. *9th round:* —* Y. fwd., k. 1 t. b. l., y. fwd., k. 2 tog., y. fwd., k. 1 t. b. l., p. 2, y. o. n., k. 1 t. b. l., y. r. n., p. 2, k. 1 t. b. l., y. fwd., sl. 1, k. 1, p. s. s. o., (y. fwd., k. 1 t. b. l.) twice, rep. from * to end. (80 sts.) *11th round:* —* Y. fwd., k. 2 tog., y. r. n. twice, sl. 1, k. 2 tog., p. s. s. o., y. fwd., k. 1 t. b. l., p. 2, y. o. n., sl. 1, k. 2 tog., p. s. s. o., y. r. n., p. 2, k. 1 t. b. l., y. fwd., sl. 1, k. 2 tog., p. s. s. o., y. r. n. twice, sl. 1, k. 1, p. s. s. o., y. fwd., k. 1 t. b. l., rep. from * to end. (88 sts.) *12th and foll. alt. rounds:* —As 8th round, working k. 1, p. 1 into each (y. r. n. twice). *13th round:* —* Y. fwd., k. 1 t. b. l., y. fwd., k. 2 tog., y. r. n. twice, sl. 1, k. 2 tog., p. s. s. o., y. fwd., k. 1 t. b. l., p. 2, y. o. n., sl. 1, k. 2 tog., p. s. s. o., y. r. n., p. 2, k. 1 t. b. l., y. fwd., sl. 1, k. 2 tog., p. s. s. o., y. r. n. twice, sl. 1, k. 1, p. s. s. o., (y. fwd., k. 1 t. b. l.) twice, rep. from * to end. (104) sts. *15th round:* —* Y. fwd., k. 2 tog., (y. r. n. twice, sl. 1, k. 2 tog., p. s. s. o.) twice, y. fwd., k. 1 t. b. l., p. 2, y. o. n., sl. 1, k. 2 tog., p. s. s. o., y. r. n., p. 2, k. 1 t. b. l., y. fwd., (sl. 1, k. 2 tog., p. s. s. o., y. r. n. twice) twice, sl. 1, k. 1, p. s. s. o., y. fwd., k. 1 t. b. l., rep. from * to end. (112 sts.) *17th round:* —* Y. fwd., k. 1 t. b. l., y. fwd., k. 2 tog., (y. r. n. twice, sl. 1, k. 2 tog., p. s. s. o.) twice, y. fwd., k. 1 t. b. l., p. 2, y. o. n., sl. 1, k. 2 tog., p. s. s. o., y. r. n., p. 2, k. 1 t. b. l., y. fwd., (sl. 1, k. 2 tog., p. s. s. o., y. r. n., twice) twice, sl. 1, k. 1, p. s. s. o., (y. fwd., k. 1 t. b. l.)

Detail of the stitch used for the square table
mat

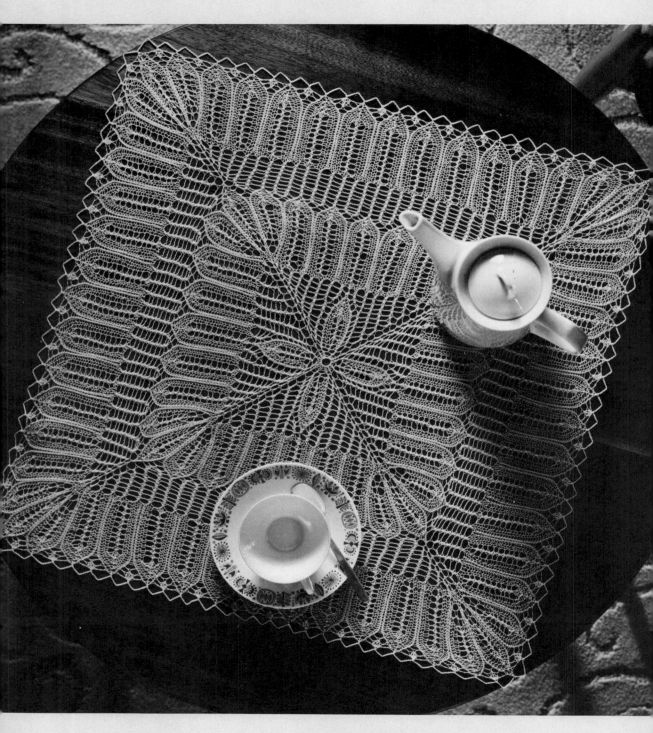

Square Table mat in fine cotton lace

twice, rep. from * to end. (128 sts.) *19th round:* — * Y. fwd., k. 2 tog., (y. r. n. twice, sl. 1, k. 2 tog., p. s. s. o.) 3 times, y. fwd., k. 1 t. b. l., p. 2, k. 3, p. 2, k. 1 t. b. l., y. fwd., (sl. 1, k. 2 tog., p. s. s. o., y. r. n. twice) 3 times, sl. 1, k. 1, p. s. s. o., y. fwd., k. 1 t. b. l., rep. from * to end. (136 sts.) *21st round:* — * Y. fwd., k. 1 t. b. l., y. fwd., k. 2 tog., (y. r. n. twice, sl. 1, k. 2 tog., p. s. s. o.) 3 times, y. fwd., k. 1 t. b. l., p. 2, sl. 1, k. 2 tog., p. s. s. o., p. 2, k. 1 t. b. l., y. fwd., (sl. 1, k. 2 tog., p. s. s. o., y. r. n. twice) 3 times, sl. 1, k. 1, p. s. s. o., (y. fwd., k. 1 t. b. l.) twice, rep. from * to end. (144 sts.) *23rd round:* — * Y. fwd., k. 2 tog., (y. r. n. twice, sl. 1, k. 2 tog., p. s. s. o.) 3 times, y. r. n. twice, sl. 1, k. 1, p. s. s. o., (y. fwd., k. 1 t. b. l.) twice, p. 1, p. 3 tog., p. 1, (k. 1 t. b. l., y. fwd.) twice, k. 2 tog., y. r. n. twice, (sl. 1, k. 2 tog., p. s. s. o., y. r. n. twice) 3 times, sl. 1, k. 1, p. s. s. o., y. fwd., k. 1 t. b. l., rep. from * to end. (160 sts.) *25th round:* — * Y. fwd., k. 1 t. b. l., y. fwd., k. 2 tog., (y. r. n. twice, sl. 1, k. 2 tog., p. s. s. o.) 4 times, y. r. n. twice, sl. 1, k. 1, p. s. s. o., y. fwd., k. 1 t. b. l., p. 3 tog., k. 1 t. b. l., y. fwd., k. 2 tog., y. r. n. twice, (sl. 1, k. 2 tog., p. s. s. o., y. r. n. twice) 4 times, sl. 1, k. 1, p. s. s. o., (y. fwd., k. 1 t. b. l.) twice, rep. from * to end. (176 sts.) *27th round:* — * Y. fwd., k. 2 tog., (y. r. n. twice, sl. 1, k. 2 tog., p. s. s. o.) 6 times, y. fwd., sl. 1, k. 2 tog., p. s. s. o., y. fwd., (sl. 1, k. 2 tog., p. s. s. o., y. r. n. twice) 6 times, sl. 1, k. 1, p. s. s. o., y. fwd., k. 1 t. b. l., rep. from * to end. (176 sts.) *29th round:* — * Y. fwd., k. 1 t. b. l., y. fwd., k. 2 tog., (y. r. n. twice, sl. 1, k. 2 tog., p. s. s. o.) 6 times, y. fwd., k. 1 t. b. l., y. fwd., (sl. 1, k. 2 tog., p. s. s. o., y. r. n. twice) 6 times, sl. 1, k. 1, p. s. s. o., (y. fwd., k. 1 t. b. l.) twice, rep. from * to end. (192 sts.). *31st and 32nd rounds:* — K. (192 sts.) *33rd round:* — Before beg. round, k. 1 st. from left-hand needle over to right-hand needle. * (k. 1 t. b. l., p. 2, y. o. n., sl. 1, k. 2 tog., p. s. s. o., y. r. n., p. 2, k. 1 t. b. l.) 5 times, (work k. 1, k. 1 t. b. l. into next st.) 3 times, rep. from * to end. (204 sts.) *34th & foll. alt. rounds:* — As 8th. *35th round:* — * (K. 1 t. b. l., p. 2, y. o. n., sl. 1, k. 2 tog., p. s. s. o., y. r. n., p. 2, k. 1 t. b. l.) 5 times, (k. 1 t. b. l., y. fwd., k. 1 t. b. l.) 3 times, rep. from * to end. (216 sts.) *37th round:* — * (K. 1 t. b. l., p. 2, y. o. n., sl. 1, k. 2 tog., p. s. s. o., y. r. n., p. 2, k. 1 t. b. l.) 5 times, (k. 1 t. b. l., y. fwd., k. 1, y. fwd., k. 1 t. b. l.) 3 times, rep. from * to end. (240 sts.) *39th round:* — * (K. 1 t. b. l., p. 2, y. o. n., sl. 1, k. 2 tog.,

p. s. s. o., y. r. n., p. 2, k. 1 t. b. l.) 5 times, (k. 1 t. b. l., p. 1, y. o. n., k. 1 t. b. l., y. r. n., p. 1, k. 1 t. b. l.) 3 times, rep. from * to end. (264 sts.) *41st round:* — * (K. 1 t. b. l., p. 2, y. o. n., sl. 1, k. 2 tog., p. s. s. o., y. r. n., p. 2, k. 1 t. b. l.) 5 times, (k. 1 t. b. l., p. 2, y. o. n., k. 1 t. b. l., y. r. n., p. 2, k. 1 t. b. l.) 3 times, rep. from * to end. (288 sts.) *43rd round:* — * K. 1 t. b. l., p. 2, y. o. n., sl. 1, k. 2 tog., p. s. s. o., y. r. n., p. 2, k. 1 t. b. l., rep. from * to end. (288 sts.) *45th, 47th, 49th, & 51st round:* — As 43rd. Now change to circular needle and mark beg. of a round with a coloured thread. *53rd round:* — * K. 1 t. b. l., p. 2, k. 3, p. 2, k. 1 t. b. l., rep. from * to end. (288 sts.) *55th round:* — * Y. fwd., k. 1 t. b. l., p. 2, sl. 1, k. 2 tog., p. s. s. o., p. 2, k. 1 t. b. l., rep. from * to end. (256 sts.) *57th round:* — * Y. fwd., work k. 1, k. 1 t. b. l., into next st., y. fwd., k. 1 t. b. l., p. 1, p. 3 tog., p. 1, k. 1 t. b. l., rep. from * to end. (288 sts.) *59th round:* — * Y. fwd., k. 2 tog., y. r. n. twice, sl. 1, k. 1, p. s. s. o., y. fwd., k. 1 t. b. l., p. 3 tog., p. 1, k. 1 t. b. l., rep. from * to end. (288 sts.) *61st round:* — * Y. r. n. twice, sl. 1, k. 2 tog., p. s. s. o., rep. from * to end. (288 sts.) *63rd round:* — Before beg. round, k. 1 st. from left-hand needle over to right-hand needle. * (Y. r. n. twice, sl. 1, k. 2 tog., p. s. s. o.) 20 times, y. r. n. twice, k. 1 t. b. l., (y. fwd, k. 1 t. b. l.) twice, (y. r. n. twice, sl. 1, k. 2 tog., p. s. s. o.) 3 times, rep. from * to end. (304) sts. *65th round:* — Before beg. round, k. 1 st. from left-hand needle over to right-hand needle. * (Y. r. n. twice, sl. 1, k. 2 tog., p. s. s. o.) 20 times, y. r. n. twice, sl. 1. k. 1, p. s. s. o., (y. fwd., k. 1 t. b. l.) 3 times, y. fwd., k. 2 tog., (y. r. n. twice sl. 1, k. 2 tog., p. s. s. o.) 3 times, rep. from * to end. (320 sts.) *67th round:* — Before beg. round, k. 1 st. over to right-hand needle as last round, now called k. 1 to right. * (Y. r. n., twice, sl. 1, k. 2 tog., p. s. s. o.) 21 times, y. r. n. twice, sl. 1, k. 1, p. s. s. o., y. fwd., k. 1 t. b. l., y. fwd., k. 2 tog., (y. r. n. twice, sl. 1, k. 2 tog., p. s. s. o.) 4 times, rep. from * to end. (328 sts.) *69th round:* — K. 1 to right. * (Y. r. n. twice, sl. 1, k. 2 tog., p. s. s. o.) 21 times, y. r. n. twice, sl. 1, k. 1, p. s. s. o., (y. fwd., k. 1 t. b. l.) 3 times, y. fwd., k. 2 tog., (y. r. n. twice, sl. 1, k. 2 tog., p. s. s. o.) 4 times. rep. from * to end. (344 sts.) *71st round:* — K. 1 to right. * (Y. r. n. twice, sl. 1, k. 2 tog., p. s. s. o.) 22 times, y. r. n. twice, sl. 1, k. 1, p. s. s. o., y. fwd., k. 1 t. b. l., y. fwd., k. 2

tog., (y. r. n. twice, sl. 1, k. 2 tog., p. s. s. o.) 5 times, rep. from * to end. (352 sts.) *73rd round:* —K. 1 to right. * (Y. r. n. twice, sl. 1, k. 2 tog., p. s. s. o.) 22 times, y. r. n. twice, sl. 1, k. 1, p. s. s. o., (y. fwd., k. 1 t. b. l.) 3 times, y. fwd., k. 2 tog., (y. r. n. twice, sl. 1, k. 2 tog., p. s. s. o.) 5 times, rep. from * to end. (368 sts.) *75th round:* —K. 1 to right. * (Y. r. n. twice, sl. 1, k. 2 tog., p. s. s. o.) 23 times, y. r. n. twice, sl. 1, k. 1, p. s. s. o., y. fwd., k. 1 t. b. l., y. fwd., k. 2 tog., (y. r. n. twice, sl. 1, k. 2 tog., p. s. s. o.) 6 times, rep. from * to end. (376 sts.) *77th round:* —K. *78th round:* —K. and mark the beg. of round here with contrast thread. *79th round:* —* (K. 1 t. b. l., p. 2, y. o. n., k. 1 t. b. l., y. r. n., p. 2, k. 1 t. b. l.) twice, (k. 1 t. b. l., p. 2, y. o. n., sl. 1, k. 2 tog., p. s. s. o., y. r. n., p. 2, k. 1 t. b. l.) 7 times, (k. 1 t. b. l., p. 2, y. o. n., k. 1 t. b. l., y. r. n., p. 2, k. 1 t. b. l.) twice, (work k. 1, k. 1

t. b. l. into next st.) 3 times, rep. from * to end. (420 sts.) *80th and every foll. alt. round:* —As 8th. *81st, 83rd, 85th, and 87th rounds:* —Rep. the sts. between first brackets in 35th round 11 times. (432 sts.); 37th round (456 sts.); 39th round (480 sts.) 41st round (504 sts.) *89th to 101st rounds:* —As 43rd to 55th. (448 sts.) *103rd round:* —* (Y. fwd., k. 1 t. b. l.) twice, p. 1, p. 3 tog., p. 1, k. 1 t. b. l., rep. from * to end. (448 sts.) *105th round:* —* Y. fwd., k. 3, y. fwd., k. 1 t. b. l., p. 3 tog., k. 1 t. b. l., rep. from * to end. (448 sts.) *106th round:* —K.

Edging: —With crochet hook, * 1 double crochet into back of next 5 sts., and slip off, 10 chain, 1 double crochet into back of next 3 sts., and slip off, 10 chain, rep. from * ending with 1 slip stitch into first double crochet. Fasten off.

Damp and pin out carefully. Press.

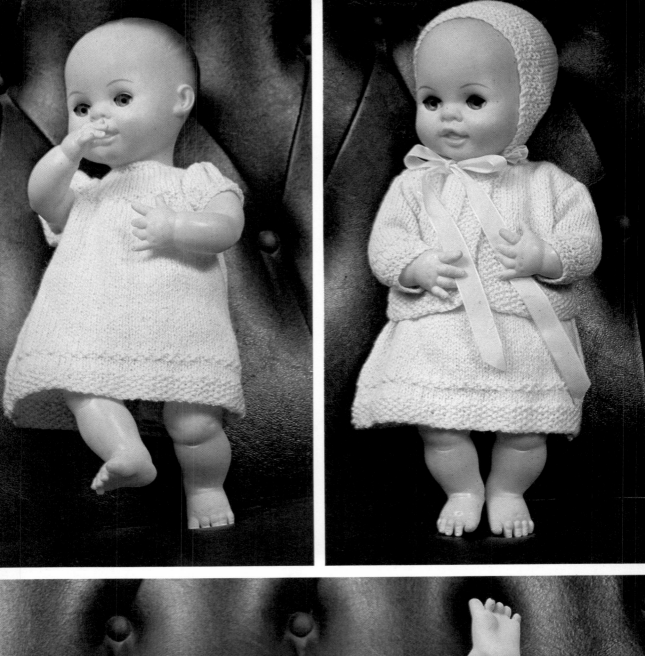
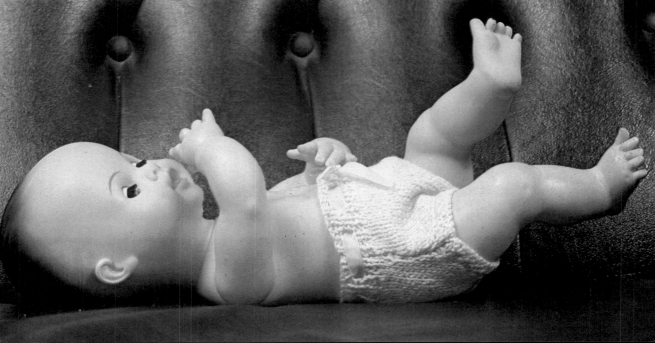

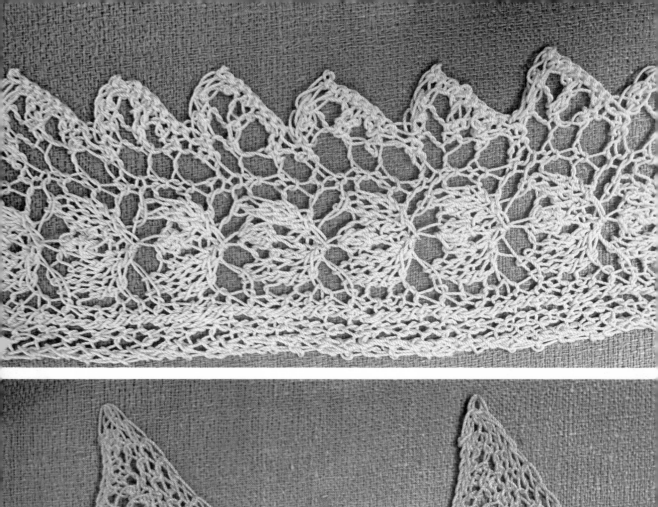

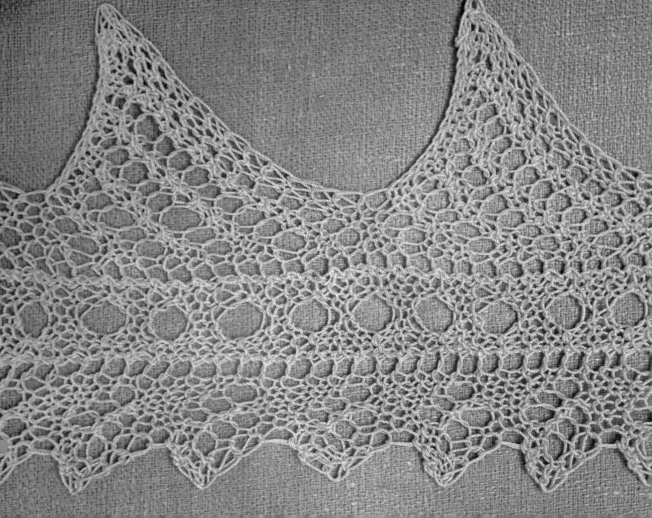

Toys and Gifts

There are so many occasions during the year when gifts are required. Not only Christmas and birthdays, but the Bazaar and garden fêtes to which one is asked to contribute.

Most of these small items take very little outlay in money, as many of them require small amounts of different colours.

Toys can be made so easily. Each piece is small and takes a very short time to complete. Keep a bag, marked with the name of the item you are making. When you have a short time available, make a piece and keep it, until all the parts are ready. You can then sew, stuff with kapok and join together. Kept in a box, you will soon have a small store of toys and gifts for those unexpected occasions.

When stuffing the parts of a toy, make certain each piece is stuffed very firmly. Unless you do, the finished toy will be floppy and quickly destoroyed by a child.

Avoid using buttons or sharp objects for baby toys. These can be pulled off and swallowed. It is best to embroider eyes and mouths and any details of that nature.

If you enjoy fine knitting you will like the cotton table mats on page 145 and page 148. They would certainly be most appreciated as gifts.

Knitted cotton lace edgings are also useful to add to household items and make acceptable gifts for brides. A simple linen tray cloth with a hand knitted lace edging will last a life time.

All knitted lace should be pinned out very carefully. Use as many pins as required and pin out all points. This does take time, but it is time well spent, as you can see in the pictures of the lace mats.

For cotton lace use a warm iron and a well damped cloth. Pins should be good steel, to avoid any rust marks appearing on the finished work. Leave pinned out until quite dry. Mats and edgings in cotton are greatly improved by starching.

Socks, caps, mitts, baby bootees, all make welcome gifts too. You will find patterns for all of these in this book.

KNITTED BALL

Materials: —One oz. of Patons Double Knitting in brown and one oz. in yellow; a pair of No. 12 [1] knitting needles; Kapok for stuffing.

Measurements: —Approximately 14 in. all round, when stuffed.

Tension: —$6\frac{1}{2}$ sts. and 12 rows to 1 in.

Abbreviations: —See page 20.

N.B. Ball is worked in one piece.

To work
With Brown cast on 36 sts.
1st row: —K.
** *2nd row:* —Sl. 1, k. to last st., turn.
3rd and 4th rows: —Sl. 1, k. to last 2 sts., turn. *5th and 6th rows:* —Sl. 1, k. to last 3 sts., turn.
Cont. in this way, working 1 st. less at end of every row, until 8 sts. rem. unworked at each end.
Next row: —Sl. 1, k. to last 9 sts., turn.
Next row: —Sl. 1, k. across all sts., picking up horizontal loop and knitting it tog. with next st. at each turning point. **
Join on yellow. *Next row:* —K. with yellow. Rep. from ** to ** in yellow. Cont. in this way, working 18 rows brown, 18 rows yellow, until 8 sections in all (4 each brown, and yellow) have been worked.
Cast off in yellow picking up horizontal loops as before.
Join seam, leaving opening for stuffing. Stuff firmly and sew up opening.

COMPLETE OUTFIT FOR A 14 INCH DOLL

Baby doll's are never out of fashion and so often arrive without a thing to wear. Here is a set of four garments. A dress and jacket with a little bonnet and for underneath, a tiny pair of pants.
These can all be made from left-over balls of 4-ply yarn and take very little time to make. Any small girl would be delighted to have them for her baby doll.
Turn to page 153 to see all of these little garments in colour

Materials: —4 ozs. Emu Super Crêpe to knit to 4-ply weight for the set; a pair of No. 11 [2] knitting needles; 3 small buttons for the dress and 1 for the jacket; 1 yd. baby ribbon.

Measurements: —To fit a 14-inch doll.

Tension: —$7\frac{1}{2}$ sts. and $9\frac{1}{2}$ rows to 1 inch over stocking stitch.

Abbreviations: —See page 20.

THE DRESS-BACK
With No. 11 [2] needles, cast on 60 sts. and work 8 rows in m.st. Then work 4 rows in st.st. and 2 rows m.st. Change to st.st. and work 38 rows.
To Shape Armholes: —K. 3 tog., k. 25, turn. Slip the remaining sts. on to a spare needle and leave for left back shoulder.
Next row: —Cast on 4 sts. for button band, m. st. these 4 sts. and p. to end.
Next row: —K. 2 tog., k. to last 4 sts., m. st. 4.
Next row: —M. st. 4, p. to last 2 sts., p. 2 tog.
Yoke: —*Next row:* —* K. 2 tog., rep. from * 12 times in all, m. st. 4. Now work 2 rows in m. st. and then 11 rows st. st., keeping the 4 sts. for button band in m. st. Cast off.
Rejoin yarn to remaining sts. for left back shoulder and complete to match, reversing shaping.

FRONT
Work as for Back until armhole shaping is reached, ending on a wrong-side row.
To Shape Armholes: —K. 3 tog., work to last 3 sts., k. 3 tog. Work 1 row, then dec. 1 st. at each end of next 2 rows.
The Yoke: —K. 2, *k. 2 tog., rep. from * 24 times in all, k. 2.
Now work 2 rows in m. st. and 9 rows st. st.
To Shape Neck: —K. 5, turn and work 5 rows in st. st. on these sts., then cast off.
Cast off centre sts., leaving 5 on needle. Work 5 rows st. st. on these sts. Cast off.

SLEEVES
Cast on 26 sts. and work 3 rows m. st.
Next row: —K. 4, k. twice into next 18 sts., k. 4. Work 3 rows st. st., beg. with a p. row.
To Shape Top: —Dec. 1 st. at each end of

next 4 right-side rows. Next row: —P. 2 tog. to end of row. Cast off.

NECKBAND
Join shoulder seams. With right side facing, pick up and knit 58 sts. round neck and work in m. st. for 4 rows. Cast off.

To make up
Press pieces. Join side and sleeve seams and set in sleeves. Catch down the buttonhole band. Work 3 small loops for buttons on edge of band. Sew buttons to opposite side of back neck to correspond with button loops.

THE JACKET-BACK
Cast on 42 sts. and work in m. st. for 8 rows. Then work 4 rows st. st. and 2 rows in m. st. Change to st. st. and work straight for 14 rows.
To Shape Armholes: —Dec. 1 st. at each end of next and foll. 3 right-side rows. Work 7 more rows straight in st. st. and cast off.

LEFT FRONT
Cast on 26 sts. and work 8 rows m. st.
9th row: —K. to last 5 sts., m. st. 5.
10th row: —M. st. 5, p. to end. Rep. last 2 rows once more. Work 2 rows in m. st. then rep. the 9th and 10th rows 7 times.
To Shape Armholes: —Dec. 1 st. at beg. of next and foll. 3 right-side rows. Work 6 rows straight, keeping border in m. st.
To Shape Neck: —Cast off 8 sts. at neck edge, work to end. Now dec. 1 st. at neck edge on next 3 rows.
Cast off rem. sts.

RIGHT FRONT
Work as for Left Front, reversing all shapings.

SLEEVES
Cast on 20 sts. and work in m. st. for 4 rows. Inc. 8 sts. evenly along next row. Work 3 rows in st. st. Then work 2 rows m. st. and 16 rows st. st.
To Shape Top: —Dec. 1 st. at each end of next and foll. 3 right-side rows.
Cast off.

NECKBAND
Join shoulder seams. With right side facing, pick up and k. 43 sts. round neck.

Next row: —* K. 1, y. r. n., k. 2 tog., rep. from * to end. K. 1 row. Cast off.

To make up
Press pieces. Join side and sleeve seams. Set in sleeves. Sew button to neckband.

BONNET
Cast on 56 sts. and work 8 rows in m. st. Keeping 3 sts. in m. st. at each end and the rest in st. st. Work 20 rows.
To Shape Crown: —*1st row:* —Cast off 3 sts., work to end.
2nd row: —Cast off 3 sts., work to end.
3rd row: —K. 1, * k. 3, k. 2 tog., rep. from * to last 4 sts., k. 4.
4th to 6th rows: —K.
7th row: —K. 3, * k. 2 tog., k. 2, rep. from * to last 2 sts., k. 2.
8th row: —K.
9th row: —K. 2, * k. 2 tog., k. 1 rep. from * to end.
10th row: —K.
11th row: —*k. 2 tog., rep. from * to end.
Break yarn, leaving a length of 12 ins. Thread into a large eyed needle and thread through the remaining sts. Draw up and secure firmly. Join back seam for 1½ ins. Join ribbon ties to each end of front border.

THE PANTS
Cast on 34 sts. for back waist edge. Work 2 rows in k. 1, p. 1 rib.
Next row: —* K. 1, p. 1, y. r. n., p. 2 tog., rep. from * to last 2 sts., k. 1, p. 1. Work 3 rows k. 1, p. 1 rib.
To Shape Back: —*1st row:* —K. *2nd row:* —P. Rep. these 2 rows 4 times.
Now inc. 1 st. at each end of next row, then at each end of foll. 4th and 8th rows. P. 1 row.
To Shape Legs: —Dec. 1 st. at each end of next 15 rows. P. 1 row. Now inc. 1 st. at each end of next 15 rows. P. 1 row and k. 1 row. Now dec. 1 st. at each end of next row, then at each end of 4th and 8th rows. Work 4 rows straight. Now work 3 rows in k. 1, p. 1 rib. Work row of holes as worked at beg. of waist edge. Work 2 rows k. 1, p. 1 rib. Cast off in rib.

LEG BANDS
With right side facing, pick up and k. 40 sts.

round one leg. Work 3 rows in m. st. Cast off. Work other leg band to match.

To make up
Press pieces. Join side seams. Thread ribbon through holes at waist and tie in a bow at front. Press seams.

TOY SOLDIER
Scraps of yarn from your odd ounce bag will make this soft toy for a tiny tot. All the pieces are quickly made, but put together, they make a smart guardsman in his scarlet tunic and busby. He is knitted in cotton, so use washable stuffing and he need never be a disgrace to the regiment

Materials: —2 ozs. of Twilley's Lyscordet in Black and Red, 1 oz. each of white, gold and pink; a pair of No. 12 [1] knitting needles; kapok for stuffing; scraps of felt for features; a gilt buckle and 5 small buttons.

Measurements: —Height: 18 ins.

Tension: —7½ sts. and 10 rows to 1 inch.

Abbreviations: —See page 20.

Note: Use Lyscordet double throughout.

JACKET-SKIRT
With 2 strands of Lyscordet in R. cast on 35 sts. and k. 5 rows. *Next row*: K. 3, p. 29, k. 3. Rep. the last 2 rows 7 times more. *Next row*: —K. 5, *k. 2 tog., k. 4, rep. from * 5 times. *Next row*: —K. 3, p. 24, k. 3. Break yarn and leave sts. on a spare needle. Work another piece to match.

BODY
With B. cast on 10 sts. for left foot. Work 2 rows st. st., beg. with a k. row.
Next row: —K. 2, * inc. in next st., k. 1, rep. from * 4 times. Work 3 rows st. st.
Next row: —K. 2, * inc. in next st., k. 2, rep. from * 4 times. Work 3 rows st. st.
Next row: —K. 2, * inc. in next st., k. 3, rep. from * 4 times. Work 3 rows st. st.
Next row: —Inc. into 1st st., * k. 2, inc. in next st. rep. from * 7 times. (30 sts.)
Next row: —P. *Next 2 rows*: —With 2 strands

of G. k. 2 rows. Break G. and cont. in st. st. in B. beg. with a k. row for 7 ins., ending with a p. row. Leave these sts. on a spare needle. Make another piece to match. Return to first set of 30 sts. in R. Place first 15 on spare needle and remaining 15 on No. 12 [1] needle. Now place first 15 B. sts. of right leg on spare needle and place remaining 15 on No. 12 [1] needle and place behind 15 R. sts. With 2 strands of R. and a 3rd No. 12 [1] needle k. the two sets of sts. tog. Place matching red and black sts. on separate needles and k. tog. in same way.
Work on these 30 sts. for 1¼ ins. st.st. for Back, beg. with a p. row. Cast off 2 sts. at beg. of next 2 rows for armholes. Work 1¾ ins. more in st. st., ending with a p. row. Cast off 4 sts. at beg. of next 2 rows for shoulders.
Next row: —K. 3, * inc. into next st., k. 2, rep. from * 5 times. (23 sts.) P. 1 row. Break off R. and join 2 strands of Pink Work 17 rows st. st. Break off Pink and join in B. Work a p. row. *Next row*: —k. 1, * inc. into next st., k. 1, rep. from * 11 times. Work 2 ins. st. st.
Now dec. 1 st. at each end of next and every alt. row until 24 sts. rem. Now dec. 1 st. at each end of next 6 rows. Cast off.
Return to remaining sts. for Front. Fold the 2 sets of B. sts. so that they form a ring with Back and with right side facing, place all 30 sts. on a No. 12 [1] needle. Fold R. sts. in same way and place them on No. 12 [1] needle in front of B. sts. K. these sts. tog. in same way as for Back. Complete Front as for Back.

ARMS
With 2 strands of W. cast on 11 sts. and work 2 rows st. st., beg. with a k. row. *Next row*: — K. 1, *inc. into next st., k. 1, rep. from * 5 times. Work 3 rows st. st. *Next row*: — K. 1, * inc. into next st., k. 3, rep. from * 5 times. Work 3 rows. *Next row*: —K. 1, * inc. in next st., k. 3, rep. from * 5 times: (26 sts.). P. 1 row. Break off W. and join 2 strands of G. and k. 2 rows. Break off G., join 2 strands R. and cont. in st. st., beg. k. row until work measures 5½ ins.
To Shape Top: —Cast off 3 sts. at beg. of next 6 rows. Cast off rem. sts.

BELT
With 2 strands W. cast on 13 sts. and work 10 ins. k. 1, p. 1 rib. Cast off.

EPAULETTES AND CHIN STRAP

With 2 strands G. cast on 4 sts. for chin strap and work 5 ins. g. st. With 2 strands G. cast on 10 sts. for each epaulatte and work 8 rows g. st., Cast off.

To make up

Join back and front seams of B. legs for 2 ins., then fold remainder to form legs and feet and join seams. Join head and shoulder seams. Set in top of arms to armholes, joining ½ in. of sides of arms to cast off 2 sts. of armhole shapings. Join arm and side seams. Sew on epaulettes and chin strap. Sew buckle to belt and fasten round waist. Add buttons, and make features with felt scraps.

GOLLIWOG

Cheery chap to make a companion for a child. Soft toys are always welcome to children and make a useful contribution to fêtes and Bring-and-Buy stalls. Turn to page 158 to see him in colour
Materials: —2 ozs. of Patons Double Knitting in red and 2 ozs. in royal blue and a small ball in yellow, white and black (less than½ -oz. in each of these colours); also 1 oz. of Patons Purple Heather 4-ply in black; scraps of red and white for the features; a pair of Nos. 11 [2] and 12 [1] knitting needles; Kapok for stuffing; ½ -yard of ribbon for bow tie.

Measurements: —Height, about 16 in.

Tension: 11½ sts. to 2 ins. over garter stitch on No. 11 [2] needles.

Abbreviations: —See page 20.

BODY AND LEGS

Begin with legs. With No. 11 [2] needles and Royal cast on 17 sts. Work 6 rows in g. st. for first leg. Break off yarn. On to same needle, cast on 17 sts. and work 64 rows in g. st. for 2nd leg.
Next row: —K. across both sets of sts.
Next row: —K. 2 tog., k. to last 2 sts., k. 2 tog.
G. st. 3 rows.
Rep. last 4 rows twice more. Break off Royal. Join in Red and g. st. 30 rows. Cast off 3 sts.

at beg. of next 4 rows for shoulders. Cast off rem. sts.
Make another piece in the same way. Join halves tog., leaving neck open for stuffing. Stuff firmly.

HEAD

With No. 11 [2] needles and Black cast on 19 sts. Work in st. st. as foll.: —
Next row: —K. *Next row:* —P., increasing. 1 st. at each end.
Rep. last 2 rows twice more. Work 6 rows straight. *Next row:* —Inc. in 1st st., then k. until 1 st. remains, inc.
Work 17 rows straight.
Next row: —K. 2 tog., k. to last 2 sts., k. 2 tog.
Work 3 rows straight.
Next row: —K. 2 tog., k. to last 2 sts., k. 2 tog.
Cast off.
Make another piece the same. Join halves tog., leaving cast-off edges open for stuffing. Stuff firmly.

NECK

With No. 11 [2] needles and White cast on 34 sts. G. st. 8 rows. Cast off. Join short ends. Join cast-off edge of neck round neck opening on body. Stuff neck firmly, then sew neck opening on head round top edge of neck, adding extra stuffing if required.

Hair

With No. 11 [2] needles and Black 4-ply cast on 39 sts. *Next row:* —K. 1, * insert needle knitways into next st., place fore-finger at back of st., then wind yarn anti-clockwise round needle and finger twice, draw through 3 loops; rep. from * to last st., k. 1.
Next row: —K. 1, * k. 3 tog. through back of loops, then give loops a slight pull to tighten, rep. from * to last st., k. 1.
Rep. last 2 rows 9 times more. Cast off. Gather up cast-off edge, then fold in half to fit round face and over back of head. Stuff lightly adding extra to top of head to make a good shape. Sew in position.

FEATURES

Using 4-ply. Indicate eyes in white buttonhole st. and black satin-st. *Nose:* — 2 small

Work 100 rows in g. st. Cast off.
Sew to body at waistline.
Tie ribbon bow round neck, to form bow tie.

Tassel Golliwog

A quick toy to make for a child. The instructions are given in the section on cords and tassels on page 21 and are so simple that a child could make this toy

KNITTED SQUARES

So many people use their odd balls of yarn for squares and then are doubtful about the best method to join them up into a useful article. Here are helpful instructions on making, blocking, pressing and making up into useful articles.

We made a shawl and a blanket for the Kitten's basket which you can see in colour on the appropriate pages. They have made colourful items which already have happy owners

Many people make squares for blankets and send them to the various charity organisations. The squares are usually made in plain stitches, for speed, but are very much more interesting if pretty stitches are used.

It seems such a good idea to combine the most important starting point for perfect knitting, the tension square, with this operation. The squares used for the rainbow shawl, shown in colour on page four, were all made in double knitting yarn. They were made at a tension of six stitches to one inch on number ten [three] knitting needles. Each square measured six inches and the finished shawl was thirty six inches by thirty inches, when finished, without the fringe.

From a collection of squares, made over a period of time, the rainbow shades were chosen. First, six in shades of yellow, starting with the palest colour and working up to scarlet. Then six in green, blue, mauve tints and lastly, from pink through to a dark wine colour.

The squares were joined with a flat seam, but first, each was pinned out to the correct size and pressed.

At this stage the right size of six inches square could be ensured. We had cast on 36 stitches

straight sts. in Red. *Mouth*: —Straight sts. in Red 3 long sts. for top lip, 3 long sts. caught down with a vertical straight st. for lower lip; a long white straight st. across middle of mouth for teeth.

FEET

With No. 11 [2] needles and yellow cast on 9 sts. *Next row*: —K. *Next 2 rows*: —Inc. in 1st st., k. to last st., inc.
G. st. 19 rows.
Next 2 rows: —K. 2 tog., k. to last 2 sts., k. 2 tog. Cast off.
Make 3 more pieces the same.
Sew each pair tog., leaving opening for stuffing. Stuff firmly and sew up opening. Sew feet to legs.

ARMS AND HANDS

With No. 12 [1] needles and Black 4-ply cast on 24 sts. Work in st. st. as foll.
Next row: —K. *Next row*: —P. *Next row*: —Inc. in 1st st., k. 10, inc. into each of the next 2 sts., k. 10, inc. into last st.
Work 9 rows straight.
Next row: —K. 2 tog., k. 10, (k. 2 tog.) twice, k. 10, k. 2 tog.
Next row: —P. Break off 4-ply. Change to No. 11 [2] needles and white. G.st. 8 rows. Change to Red and G. st. 36 rows. *Next row*: —Inc. into 1st st., k. to last st., inc. G.st. 5 rows. Cast off.
Make another piece the same.
Fold each piece in half lengthwise and join leaving top open for stuffing. Stuff firmly and sew up opening. Sew arms to body.

REVERS

With Red cast on 5 sts. G.st. 3 rows. *Next row*: —Inc. into 1st st., k. to last st., inc. Rep. last 4 rows once more. G.st. 8 rows straight. *Next row*: Inc. into 1st st., k. to last st., inc.
Rep. the last 9 rows twice more. G.st. 2 rows. Cast off.
Fold in half lengthwise. Sew to body as shown in the photograph on page 158.

BELT

With No. 11 [2] needles and yellow cast on 4 sts.

166

whenever it was possible, but some patterns demanded a slightly different number, in order to obtain an even number of pattern repeats, when we were testing tension.

After each square was pressed, they were first joined in strips of each colour. Then the strips were sewn together, starting with the paler shades at the same end. Corners were carefully matched and finally, the shawl was put together.

The fringing was then added all round and the rainbow effect maintained in this way. For each square, the main colour used was that of the square itself. Mixed with this was the colour of the squares on either side. For the method of adding a fringe, see page 21.

The blanket in the kitten basket was made in the same way, but left without a fringe. It used twelve squares each of which measured six inches square.

As a matter of fact, the basket really belongs to Henry, the spaniel. Being a dog of good sense, a little time was taken, investigating the new blanket. The kitten had no doubts at all and took immediate possession. We had to make another and Henry took no time to decide it was a good thing, so both are now happy.

There are so many items one can make from simple squares and patchwork has been used since the old days of the pioneers. Every scrap of material had to be used and nothing wasted. Goods took too long to reach their destination then. A bedspread of knitted squares must have kept many beds warm for our pioneer ancestors.

Whatever you decide to make with your squares, remember it is better to use the same weight of yarn for an item. Perhaps all squares of double knitting yarn for a bedspread, all chunky yarn for a garden cushion. Grandma might like a shawl in pale pastel shades, and it would perhaps be nice in three or four-ply yarn.

The quickest way to join the squares is to sew them with a flat seam. For a more decorative effect, each square can have a row of double crochet all round. If this is done in one colour throughout, it will finally make a uniform background for the bright squares. A flat seam can still be used to join up, keeping to the colour worked for the crochet.

Squares can be blanket-stitched all round and then joined with a flat seam. If you choose to join with a seam, and if you have used plain stitches for the squares, a pretty touch can be added by working in feather stitch over the seams in a contrasting colour.

Certainly it sounds like a lot of work, but it is a job which can be done bit by bit, in odd moments and when you feel like it. The end product is well worth the odd moments you will use.

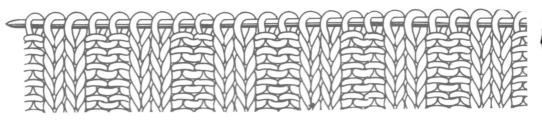

Comparative Wool and Yarn Chart

All patterns in this book have been made in specific yarns. It is always best to use the yarn stated whenever possible. This will ensure the best results and give the most satisfaction.

When a specific yarn is not easily obtainable in any country, the following chart may be used as a guide to a second choice.

If it is essential to use a different yarn from that stated in the pattern, it is most important to make a tension check. Even yarns of the same thickness can vary in the number of yards there may be in a ball and more or less yarn may be required for the work.

UNITED KINGDOM	AUSTRALIA	CANADA	S. AFRICA	U.S.A.
COATS — Yarns are available in U.K., Australia, Canada and S. Africa. equivalent is given for U.S.A.				
Mercer Cotton No. 20				J. & P Coats 6/c crochet cotton No. 20
Templeton's H. O (Scotland) Ltd.				
Templeton's H. O. Shetland Fleece	Standard 4-ply Shetland	Standard 4-ply Shetland	Standard 4-ply Shetland	Standard 4-ply Shetland
TWILLEY — Yarns should be available in all above countries.				
WENDY 4-ply Nylonised	Standard 4-ply	Standard 4-ply	Standard 4-ply	Standard 4-ply

	UNITED KINGDOM	AUSTRALIA	CANADA	S. AFRICA	U.S.A.
EMU					
	Super Crêpe	Standard	Standard	Standard	Standard
	To Knit to 4-ply	4-ply	4-ply	4-ply	4-ply
	weight				

LEE TARGET — Wools are generally available in all countries above. In case of difficulty use:

	UNITED KINGDOM	AUSTRALIA	CANADA	S. AFRICA	U.S.A.
	Leemont Double				
	Crêpe.	Standard D.K.	Standard D.K.	Standard D.K.	Standard D.K.
	Motoravia D.K.	Standard D.K.	Standard D.K.	Standard D.K.	Standard D.K.

LISTER — Yarns should be readily available in all countries above. In case of difficulty use:

	UNITED KINGDOM	AUSTRALIA	CANADA	S. AFRICA	U.S.A.
	Lavenda D.K.	Standard D.K.	Standard D.K.	Standard D.K.	Standard D.K.
	Lavenda Double Crêpe	Standard D.K.	Standard D.K.	Standard D.K.	Standard D.K.
	Lavenda Crisp	Standard	Standard	Standard	Standard
	Crêpe 4-ply	4-ply	4-ply	4-ply	4-ply
	Baby Bell 4-ply	Standard	Standard	Standard	Standard
	Courtelle	4-ply	4-ply	4-ply	4-ply

MAHONY — Wools should be readily available in all countries. In case of difficulty.

	UNITED KINGDOM	AUSTRALIA	CANADA	S. AFRICA	U.S.A.
	Blarney Bainin	As U.K.	As U.K.	As U.K.	Bernat Blarney Spun

PATONS

	UNITED KINGDOM	AUSTRALIA	CANADA	S. AFRICA	U.S.A.
	Piccadilly	Swifta-knit Bri-Nylon	Beehive Astra	Fiona	Standard 4-ply

PATONS — Generally available but in case of difficulty see below

	UNITED KINGDOM	AUSTRALIA	CANADA	S. AFRICA	U.S.A.
	Nylox Knitting	Standard	Standard	Standard	Standard
	4-ply	4-ply	4-ply	4-ply	4-ply
	Double Knitting				
	Limelight				
	Double Crêpe	Standard D.K.	Standard D.K.	Standard D.K.	Standard D.K.
	Baby QuickerKnit	Baby D.K.	Baby D.K.	Baby D.K.	Baby D.K.

UNITED KINGDOM	AUSTRALIA	CANADA	S. AFRICA	U.S.A.

ROBIN — Wools are generally available in all countries above. In case of difficulty use:

UNITED KINGDOM	AUSTRALIA	CANADA	S. AFRICA	U.S.A.
			Vogue D.K.	
Vogue D.K.	Standard D.K.	Standard D.K.	Standard D.K.	Standard D.K.
Vogue	Standard	Standard	Standard	Standard
4-ply	4-ply	4-ply	4-ply	4-ply

SIRDAR — Available generally, in case of difficulty use:

UNITED KINGDOM	AUSTRALIA	CANADA	S. AFRICA	U.S.A.
Double Knitting	Standard D.K.	Standard D.K.	Standard D.K.	Standard D.K.
Double Crêpe	Standard D.K.	Standard D.K.	Standard D.K.	Standard D.K.
Talisman	Standard	Standard	Standard	Standard
4-ply	4-ply	4-ply	4-ply	4-ply
		Standard		Standard
Pullman	As U.K.	Double D.K.	As U.K.	Double D.K.

The author would like to thank the above spinners for their kind co-operation.

List of Patterns
in this Book

Index

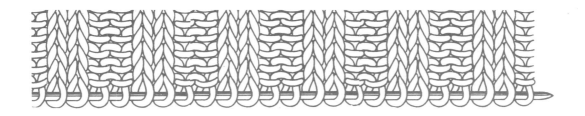

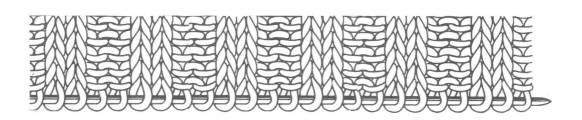